GUNS OF THE NRA
NATIONAL SPORTING ARMS MUSEUM

SPRINGFIELD, MO

JIM SUPICA | DOUG WICKLUND | PHILIP SCHREIER

PHOTOGRAPHY BY
JASON CONNEL | MICHAEL IVES | STONEY ROBERTS

Inspiring | Educating | Creating | Entertaining

Brimming with creative inspiration, how-to projects, and useful information to enrich your everyday life, Quarto Knows is a favorite destination for those pursuing their interests and passions. Visit our site and dig deeper with our books into your area of interest: Quarto Creates, Quarto Cooks, Quarto Homes, Quarto Lives, Quarto Drives, Quarto Explores, Quarto Gifts, or Quarto Kids.

This edition published in 2017 by Chartwell Books
an imprint of The Quarto Group,
142 West 36th Street, 4th Floor,
New York, NY 10018, USA
T (212) 779-4972 F (212) 779-6058
www.QuartoKnows.com

Published with permission from:
Blue Book Publications, Inc.
8009 34th Ave. S. Suite 250
Minneapolis, MN, 55425 U.S.A.
bluebookofgunvalues.com

You can join the NRA by contacting them at:
The National Rifle Association of America
11250 Waples Mill Road Fairfax, VA 22030
or by visiting their website, www.nra.org/museumoffer
You can view the collection of the NRA Museums at www.NRAMuseums.com

The NRA National Sporting Arms Museum at Bass Pro Shops in Springfield, MO, is open every day of the year except Christmas. Admission is free.

ISBN-13: 978-0-7858-3532-5

Printed in China.

10 9 8 7 6 5 4 3 2

CONTENTS

INTRODUCTION

Guns are central to the grand heritage of hunting, conservation, and freedom in America. These three subjects are the theme of the NRA National Sporting Arms Museum at Bass Pro Shops in Springfield, MO.

The firearms featured in this book are the guns that were on exhibit there in its first year of operation. They include some of the most historically significant firearms in the world along with true masterpieces of firearms engraving. There are guns used by champion shooters, presidents, European royalty, colorful figures of the Old West, Medal of Honor recipients, and in blockbuster movies.

Like the Museum, this book begins with a timeline of American sporting arms. Here the reader will find a chronological parade of hunting firearms, from guns used by the earliest settlers and Native Americans for subsistence hunting through today's most popular guns used for modern recreational hunting.

The personal firearms of Theodore Roosevelt help explain the founding of the conservation movement, foreshadowing the vital role that hunters play today in preservation, while other exhibits showcase the arms carried by America's troops in protecting our freedom.

In addition to the guns of hunting, conservation, and freedom, a special section features remarkable prototype and milestone guns from the factory collection of the country's oldest continuous gun-maker, Remington Arms Co.

Other groupings in this book include historic guns, competition firearms, elegant arms, and Hollywood guns.

HUNTING

"In the school of woods there is no graduation day."
-Horace Kephart, *Camping and Woodcraft*, 1916

CONSERVATION

"In a civilized and cultivated country, wild animals only continue to exist at all when preserved by sportsmen."
-Theodore Roosevelt

FREEDOM

"The price of freedom is eternal vigilance."
-Thomas Jefferson

Facing page: entry to the NRA National Sporting Arms Museum at Bass Pro Shops.

ACKNOWLEDGEMENTS

ADDITIONAL TEXT BY:

STONEY ROBERTS
ERIN SABATINI
LOGAN METESH
TAMMY SAPP
JOHN ZENT
EDWARD J. WOOD
DAN MCADOO
CAROLINE SIMMS
LARS DALSEIDE
JEREMY GREENE
MATT SHARPE
TERESA BUFFENBARGER

PHOTOGRAPHY BY:

JASON CONNEL
MICHAEL IVES
STONEY ROBERTS

ADDITIONAL PHOTOGRAPHY BY:

MIKE LODER
LOGAN METESH
ERIN SABATINI
AND THE AUTHORS

This book is dedicated to Johnny Morris, whose vision and generosity made the NRA National Sporting Arms Museum at Bass Pro Shops a reality.

The NRA Museums Division staff includes Jim Supica, Director; Philip Schreier and Doug Wicklund, Senior Curators; Logan Metesh, Firearms Specialist; Erin Sabatini, Registrar; Megan Ekhaml, Special Projects Coordinator; Ernie Lyles, Special Projects Coordinator; Katherine Hoppe, Administrative Assistant; Sylvia Schneider, former Administrative Assistant; and Bill Trible and Jerry Keathley, Curatorial Assistants.

Special thanks to members of the Bass Pro Shops team including Stoney Roberts who supervised the day-to-day operation of the Museum for its first three years; Mike Loder, who oversaw the installation; Laura Derrick, Bob Sopchick, and Chuck Treon for creative efforts in the design and construction; and Mickey Black, Bob Ziehmer, and Pete Duchrow who provided key leadership.

At right:

The case flanking the doors to the Museum represents three centuries of American sporting arms, from early muzzleloaders to today's sophisticated arms.

The flintlock is an exquisite contemporary American long rifle hand crafted by W. Buchele for presentation to Gen. Joe Foss from the NRA in 1978.

Joseph Jacob "Joe" Foss (1915-2003) was awarded the Congressional Medal of Honor in 1943 as the top Marine pilot ace in World War II. He later served as the Governor of South Dakota, first Commissioner of the American Football League, and President of the National Rifle Association of America.

The Armalite AR-10 chambered for the .308 Winchester illustrates the advances in technology available to the modern hunter.

Facing page:
A Milestone Presentation to the NRA.
This Savage Model 99, .300 Savage, ca. 1960, s/n 1,000,000 was a special presentation to the NRA from the Savage Arms Company to celebrate the one millionth Model 99 manufactured.

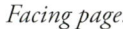

INTRODUCTION

Today the NRA Museums house the largest and finest collection of firearms and related material on exhibit in the United States.

The mission of the NRA Museums Division is to educate the public about firearms history, technology, and artistry in an accurate, accessible, responsible, and entertaining manner, with special focus on the role of firearms in American history and culture.

Central to this mission is the operation of three museums:

- **NRA National Firearms Museum** located at NRA Headquarters in Fairfax, VA.
- **NRA National Sporting Arms Museum** at Bass Pro Shops in Springfield, MO.
- **Frank Brownell Museum of the Southwest** at the NRA Whittington Center near Raton, NM.

Each has free admission. Combined, they attract over 400,000 visitors annually.

The Museum also operates the seasonal NRA Museum of the Old West at the Single Action Shooters Society Founders Ranch in New Mexico, and has developed firearms exhibits for other museums; including the Evergreen Aviation and Space Museum in McMinnville, OR, and the National Scouting Museum in Irving, TX. NRA Museums exhibits can regularly be seen at gun shows and shooting events across the country.

The NRA Museums reach outside the brick-and-mortar walls with a strong media presence. Internet users can find great firearms material at:

- **NRAmuseums.com** website, with over 10,000 zoomable photos of guns from the NRA Firearms Collection.
- **NRA Museums Facebook page**, featuring "Gun-of-the-Day" postings.
- **NFMCurator YouTube channel**, home to hundreds of videos featuring the guns of the NRA firearms collection.

The NRA Museums have been featured regularly on television programs such as NRA Gun Gurus, American Rifleman Television, NRA News with Cam & Co, and many other shows.

Extensively illustrated books of guns from the NRA Collection have proven very popular, including *Illustrated History of Firearms* featuring the collection of the NRA National Firearms Museum and *Treasures of the NRA National Firearms Museum* featuring exceptional photos of historic arms and masterpieces of engraving from the Robert E. Petersen Gallery. Photos and articles on the Museums' guns appear in numerous magazines, including a centerfold of a special treasure gun each month in *America's First Freedom* magazine.

THE NRA MUSEUMS

WHERE DID THESE GUNS COME FROM?

The first gun came to the NRA's collection in 1876, shortly after the founding of the organization in 1871. The first NRA Museum opened in 1935. The earliest guns displayed were primarily samples and gifts to the early NRA publications.

In this book, the reader will notice numerous lenders and donors listed with the various guns. The vast majority of the 8,500 guns that the NRA Museums conserve have been donated by generous individuals over more than eight decades. These are people who understand the importance of preserving America's firearms heritage and communicating the story of our guns to this and future generations.

The NRA Foundation is a 501(c)(3) educational nonprofit organization, and qualifying donations are usually tax deductible. It can receive gifts or bequests of guns for the NRA Museums. Guns or collections with historical significance may be directed to the Museum Curator's attention by emailing nfmstaff@nrahq.org

In addition, through the NRA Firearms for Freedom program individuals can donate their firearms to benefit the Foundation or other NRA programs. These can be current gifts, or estate gifts from far-sighted individuals who would like to see their guns provide firearms education, support the shooting sports, or protect Second Amendment rights. All donated guns are reviewed for possible display in the NRA Museums. Interested parties may call (877) NRA-GIVE, or email nrafff@nrahq.org.

While the vast majority of guns in the NRA Collection have been donated, some exhibits in the NRA National Sporting Arms Museum shown in this book feature large collections on loan, several of which would be worthy of a dedicated museum on their own.

These include:

- The Remington Factory Collection of firearms and artwork on loan from the Remington Arms Company.
- The Pachmayr Collection of exceptional custom arms on loan from the Frank and Nanita Pachmayr Foundation.
- U.S. Martial Pistols exhibit on loan from Frederick Starbuck.
- Exceptional engraved and historic Colt revolvers on loan from Kurt House.
- Hollywood guns on loan from Al Frisch and Chris Hearn.
- Savage pistols on loan from Bailey and Taz Brower.
- Early St. Louis-made long arms on loan from Cletus Klein.
- Remarkable guns from the Doc Thurston, III, collection.

The Second Amendment Gallery at the NRA National Firearms Museum at Bass Pro Shops.

At the end of the Civil War, a group of Union generals gathered to discuss their concerns about the new recruits who had come to war with no familiarity with firearms and the carnage that had resulted. In response, they formed the National Rifle Association of America in 1871 to promote civilian marksmanship.

Today, the NRA has more than five million members. Together, they unite to further the American traditions of shooting and firearms ownership; to promote hunting and conservation; to provide firearms education and safety training; and to protect our constitutionally guaranteed right to keep and bear arms.

Today, the NRA is the world's leader in firearm education, safety, and training. Early on in the organization's history, the NRA turned its interest to promoting the shooting sports, especially among our nation's youth. Those fundamental ideas of education and training sustain many of the programs the NRA offers to the public today. NRA training courses develop safe and responsible shooters through a network of certified instructors, training more people annually than any other organization.

Whether you're a new or experienced gun owner or hunter, NRA's instructors and training materials have you covered. The NRA also engages gun owners in programs that promote all aspects of the outdoor lifestyle. Gun owners know that it only takes one exposure to the shooting sports to be hooked for life, and the NRA makes sure gun owners have opportunities to hunt, safe ranges to shoot on, and places to enjoy the outdoor traditions.

Some of the programs and services of NRA include:

EDUCATION & TRAINING

The NRA is the world's leader in firearm training as more than 100,000 NRA Certified Instructors pass on the lessons of safe and efficient use of firearms to nearly 1,000,000 students a year.

SAFETY

NRA's safety programs focus on the individuals and institutions. The Eddie Eagle Gunsafe program teaches pre-K through third graders four important steps to take if they find a gun; School Shield provides resources for schools to evaluate and improve their security procedures; and Refuse to be a Victim outlines an overall personal safety strategy to avoid any unnecessary risks.

NRA'S INSTITUTE FOR LEGISLATIVE ACTION

The Institute for Legislative Action (ILA) is the lobbying arm of the NRA. Established in 1975, ILA is committed to preserving the right of all law-abiding individuals to purchase, possess and use firearms for legitimate purposes as guaranteed by the Second Amendment to the U.S. Constitution.

COMPETITIONS & MATCHES

NRA's Competitive Shooting Division sanctions more than 11,000 matches every year. With disciplines ranging from Action Pistol to Long Range High Power Rifle to Air Guns and Muzzle Loading, there's an event for everyone. The National Rifle & Pistol Championships, NRA's premier competition, has been held at the Ohio National Guard base at Camp Perry since 1907.

RECREATIONAL SHOOTING

NRA's Recreational Shooting Department creates programs that focus on the latest trends in the world of shooting sports. With events such as NRA 3-Gun and the Action Rifle Challenge, shooters of every skill level have the opportunity to experience an action-packed adventure in the realm of rifles, pistols, and shotguns.

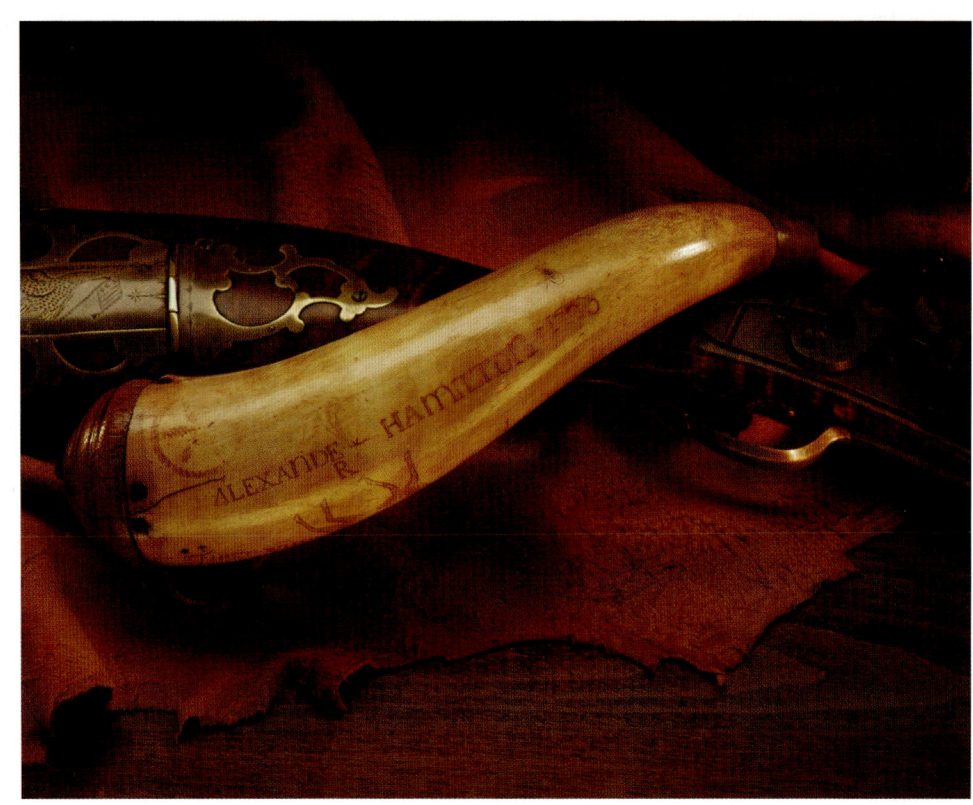

Powder Horn attributed to Alexander Hamilton
Hamilton is considered one of the most influential of America's founding fathers. This powder horn is inscribed with his name. Analysts believe the iconography reflects his political philosophy, episodes from his life, and his future goals. It has been displayed in the Museum's entry area. Loaned by Delta Star Associates

NRA PUBLICATIONS

NRA Publications produces the NRA's official journals *American Rifleman*, *American Hunter*, and *America's 1st Freedom*, as well as *Shooting Illustrated*, *NRA Family InSights*, and *Shooting Sports USA*. *American Rifleman*, the association's flagship magazine, is ranked amongst the top 25 consumer titles by circulation.

LAW ENFORCEMENT SERVICES

NRA's Law Enforcement Division provides firearm instructor training for those who wake each day to protect and serve. Teaching local, state, federal, and military instructors around the globe, their work is tested every day on patrol and through a number of competitions, including the National Police Shooting Championships.

NRA DAYS

NRA Days are an opportunity for ranges and clubs to welcome the neighborhood. Whether a Youth SportsFest, Basic Shooting, Safety & Education, or Hunter's themed day, clubs can customize their event to ensure that their visitors learn, share, and develop an appreciation for the shooting sports.

WOMEN'S WILDERNESS ESCAPE

The NRA Women's Wilderness Escape is an eight-day adventure getaway under the New Mexico skies. Created for novice and seasoned outdoor enthusiasts alike, ladies can expect to walk out of the wilderness with a new set of skills including proficiency in all three firearm disciplines, survival training, game calling, and more.

FIELD OPERATIONS

NRA Field Operations oversees the Friends of NRA banquets - an evening of auctions, games, and feasts with those passionate and concerned about the Second Amendment in the local community. Created in 1992, more than 16,000 events have reached almost 3 million attendees and raised nearly $250 million.

BUSINESS ALLIANCE & CLUBS

The NRA Clubs & Associations Department furnishes services, discounts, and assistance through an ever growing network of more than 15,000 NRA-affiliated clubs, associations, and businesses. Non-firearm related operations are encouraged to join.

HUNTER SERVICES

The National Rifle Association's Hunter Services Department is dedicated to strengthening America's rich hunting traditions. Training tomorrow's outdoorsmen through the Youth Hunter Education Challenge and providing personalized hunting and fishing guides with NRA Outdoors are just a few programs that keep America's hunting heritage alive.

GUNSMITHING

NRA gunsmithing schools offer courses on general gunsmithing, bluing, stockmaking, checkering, engraving, and parkerizing along with specialized courses focused on accurizing the AR-15 rifle, fine tuning single-action revolvers and long guns, English Gunsmithing, and more.

RANGE SERVICES

With more than 125 years experience in shooting range design, construction, maintenance and operations, no one has more field expertise than the NRA. The NRA Range Technical Team, a nationwide network of volunteers specializing in all operations of a range, can be called for assistance at any time. The NRA has a state of the art range open to the public at the NRA Headquarters building in Fairfax, VA.

JOIN THE NRA

To join the millions of Americans who belong to the National Rifle Association call 877-672-2000 or join online at nra.org/museumoffer.

The NRA Museum's First Gun

This Remington Rolling Block rifle in .50-70 caliber was won by D. Barclay of the NRA in an 1876 International Match at Creedmoor, New York. It was the first gun in the NRA collection. Engraving attributed to L. D. Nimschke.

Trophy Rifle

This Swineburn Peabody Martini rifle in .577-450 caliber was presented to NRA Secretary (later President) George Wingate by Arthur B. Leech in recognition of the American win over Ireland at the first Creedmoor match in 1874.

The NRA National Sporting Arms Museum at Bass Pro Shops

THE NRA NATIONAL SPORTING ARMS MUSEUM AT BASS PRO SHOPS

One look at the 200 muzzleloaders flanking the staircase that leads to the NRA National Sporting Arms Museum, and it's clear this will be an experience to remember. The museum, which opened its doors in August 2013, houses one of the most historic, and valuable collections of firearms and other artifacts ever assembled. The museum is located in one of the most visible, high traffic areas in the country's heartland — the Bass Pro Shops flagship superstore in Springfield, MO. This facility is the number one tourist attraction in Missouri, with nearly 4 million visitors streaming through the doors each year.

In the museum's first year alone, over 375,000 visitors flocked to see the treasures within the 7,500-square-foot museum. In total, the museum features more than a thousand sporting arms from the 1600s to modern day, and lifelike dioramas that trace the history of hunting, conservation, and freedom.

Visitors can see this one-of-a-kind collection by visiting the NRA National Sporting Arms Museum, located at 1935 S. Campbell in Springfield, MO. The Museum is open every day from 10 a.m. to 7 p.m. and admission is free.

The NRA National Sporting Arms Museum is a perfect example of a concept Johnny Morris believes in wholeheartedly — that for great things to happen in conservation, it takes team work. When people from all walks of the outdoor industry — companies such as Bass Pro Shops, organizations like NRA, state and federal agencies, and more — reach out to each other, they can figure out ways to align their resources and accomplish big things.

The Museum had its beginnings with two good friends who are also avid sportsmen and conservation visionaries — Bass Pro Shops Founder Johnny Morris and Richard Childress, owner of Richard Childress Racing. Together, Childress, a member of NRA's Board of Directors and Chairman of the NRA Hunting and Wildlife Conservation Committee, and Johnny visited the NRA National Firearms Museum in Fairfax, VA. Awed by the collection, Johnny envisioned bringing the artistry and history of sporting arms to the heartland of America where millions more people could see it. He proposed building a sporting arms museum at the mecca for the outdoors – the granddaddy of all outdoor stores, the Bass Pro Shops Outdoor World in Springfield, Missouri.

Childress shared the idea of making sporting arms history accessible to a wider audience with NRA's Executive Vice President Wayne LaPierre. Combining NRA's expertise and Bass Pro Shops offer of

Entry to the Timeline of American Sporting Arms at the NRA National Sporting Arms Museum at Bass Pro Shops.
In less than three and a half years of operation, the Museum has welcomed over one million visitors.

its space and design resources was the key to making the museum a reality. Nearly ten years in the making, the 7,500-square-foot space donated by Bass Pro Shops features the company's trademark high-quality, customized design. With its walnut and glass cabinetry, heart pine and walnut flooring, and design details such as hardened steel inlays of NRA's logo in the stairway leading to the museum, the gallery provides a striking backdrop to its treasure trove of sporting arms. NRA's role was no less critical. The firearms collections, text and storylines for the exhibits were headed by Jim Supica, NRA's director of museums. His knowledge and leadership were invaluable for telling the story about the evolution

of hunting arms in America from precolonial times to the present.

Today, the visiting public is invited to wander throughout the museum. On any given day, you'll see a family pausing at a diorama to wonder what it must have been

like for Lewis and Clark to explore the west with a .46 caliber, 20-shot Girardoni air rifle. Or to marvel at the Remington Arms Factory Collection or reminisce at the recreation of a 1950s hunting cabin. While everyone has a different favorite display, one

thing is guaranteed — the visual banquet presented at the NRA National Sporting Arms Museum is a fascinating history lesson that visitors won't soon forget.

BY TAMMY SAPP, BASS PRO SHOPS

Bass Pro Shops paid tribute to the NRA National Sporting Arms Museum with a special paint scheme for the NASCAR Sprint Cup Series Coke Zero 400. The Richard Childress Racing's No. 3 Chevrolet SS, sponsored by Bass Pro Shops, was driven by Austin Dillon at Daytona International Speedway in 2014. Left to right: Wayne LaPierre, Executive Vice President of the NRA; Johnny Morris, founder and CEO of Bass Pro Shops; Austin Dillon, two-time NASCAR champion; and Richard Childress, founder and CEO of Richard Childress Racing.

JOHNNY MORRIS

When you first walk into the NRA National Sporting Arms Museum, there's a display case immediately to the left. It houses a 16 gauge Browning Automatic 5. A very special one. At first glance, though, this A5 looks like it has seen better days. Cracks in the stock are visible between layers of black electrical tape that wind around the wood. The butt pad is crumbling and there's a gouge on the forearm. And at the end of the barrel is a wad of white medical tape, a homespun sighting device in use long before red dots were all the rage.

The owner of that old, beat up 16 gauge is Johnny Morris, founder of Bass Pro Shops. Johnny received it on his 21st birthday as a gift from his father, John A. Morris. The A5, considered the first mass-produced semi-automatic shotgun, is so much more than that. John A. loved to quail hunt in the Ozarks, shouldering that beloved 16 gauge and covering up a bird with the medical tape before downing it.

That same A5, on display at the NRA National Sporting Arms Museum, stands as a symbol of the times John A. and young Johnny spent together in the field. It conjures up images of faithful bird dogs, covey rises, and a handful of feathers that made for perfect days afield. It speaks to a larger American tradition - fathers and sons, mothers and daughters sharing their hunting experiences, connecting with nature, and building their own storehouse of memories.

The times that John A. mentored Johnny in the field and while fishing their favorite Ozark lakes and streams, ignited a passion in Johnny for enjoying the outdoors as well as conserving it. This was a love he was destined to share with millions of others with the founding of Bass Pro Shops, Tracker Marine Group, Big Cedar Lodge, Top of the Rock, Wonders of Wildlife and more. It all began in 1971, when Johnny, frustrated by the lack of tackle in local stores, rented a U-Haul® trailer and took off across the country filling it with all the newest premium fishing tackle he could find. When he returned home to Springfield, MO, he set up shop in his dad's liquor store, which was located on the way to Table Rock Lake. With this simple idea, Bass Pro Shops® was born.

From its humble beginnings, Bass Pro Shops has become America's leading outdoor retailer. Every Bass Pro Shops store offers an incredible array of fishing and boating equipment as well as being the premier shopping destination for hunting, camping, and outdoor cooking gear; outdoor apparel and footwear; and nature-themed gifts.

Throughout the years, Johnny's name has become synonymous with conservation. His work and generosity have made him the recipient of numerous honors, including the Theodore Roosevelt Conservationist Award, the Sport Fishing Institute's "Fisherman of the Year," the International Association of Fish and Wildlife Agencies "President's Award," the National Wild Turkey Federation's Hunting Heritage Award, and many others. His efforts are based on the simple principle of inspiring people, especially youth and families, to love, enjoy, and conserve the great outdoors – the way his father taught him.

***Johnny Morris's father's Browning A5 shotgun**, used on many a quail hunt.*
Loaned by Johnny Morris.

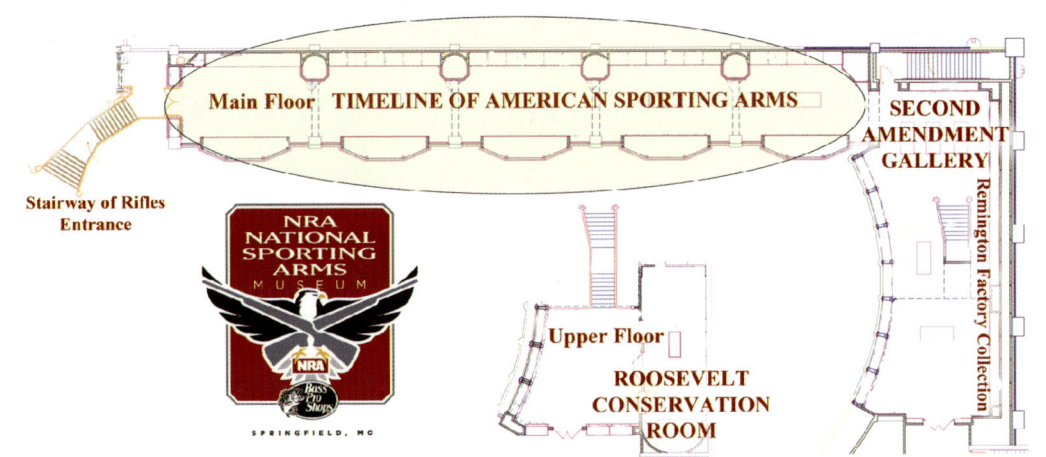

Main Floor   TIMELINE OF AMERICAN SPORTING ARMS

SECOND AMENDMENT GALLERY

Remington Factory Collection

Stairway of Rifles Entrance

NRA NATIONAL SPORTING ARMS MUSEUM

Bass Pro Shops

SPRINGFIELD, MO

Upper Floor

ROOSEVELT CONSERVATION ROOM

T I M E L I N E

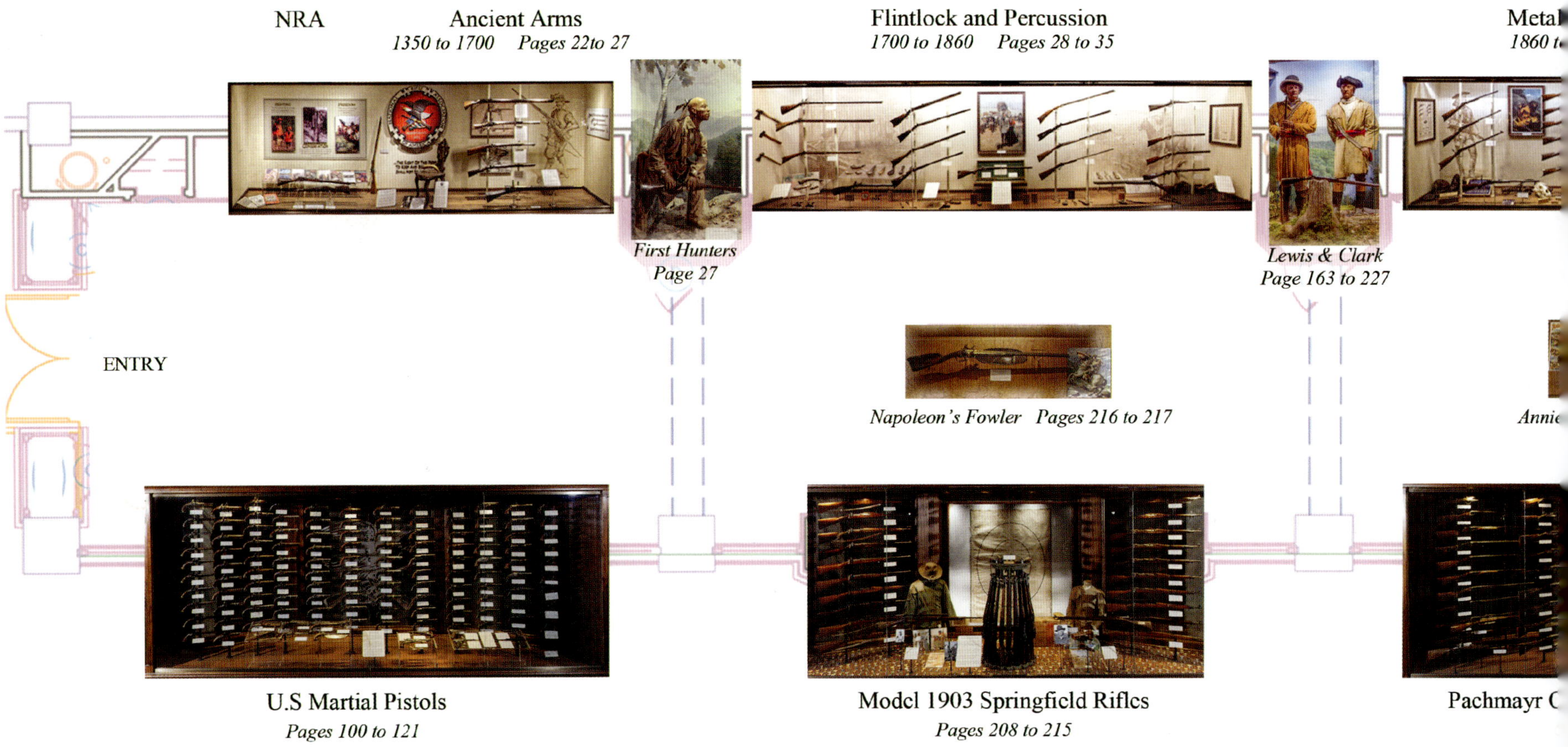

NRA

Ancient Arms
1350 to 1700   Pages 22 to 27

Flintlock and Percussion
1700 to 1860   Pages 28 to 35

Metal
1860 t

*First Hunters
Page 27*

*Lewis & Clark
Page 163 to 227*

ENTRY

Napoleon's Fowler   Pages 216 to 217

Annie

U.S Martial Pistols
Pages 100 to 121

Model 1903 Springfield Rifles
Pages 208 to 215

Pachmayr C

NRA NATIONAL SPORTING ARMS MUSEUM

MAIN LEVEL ENTRY HALL GALLERIES

OF AMERICAN SPORTING ARMS

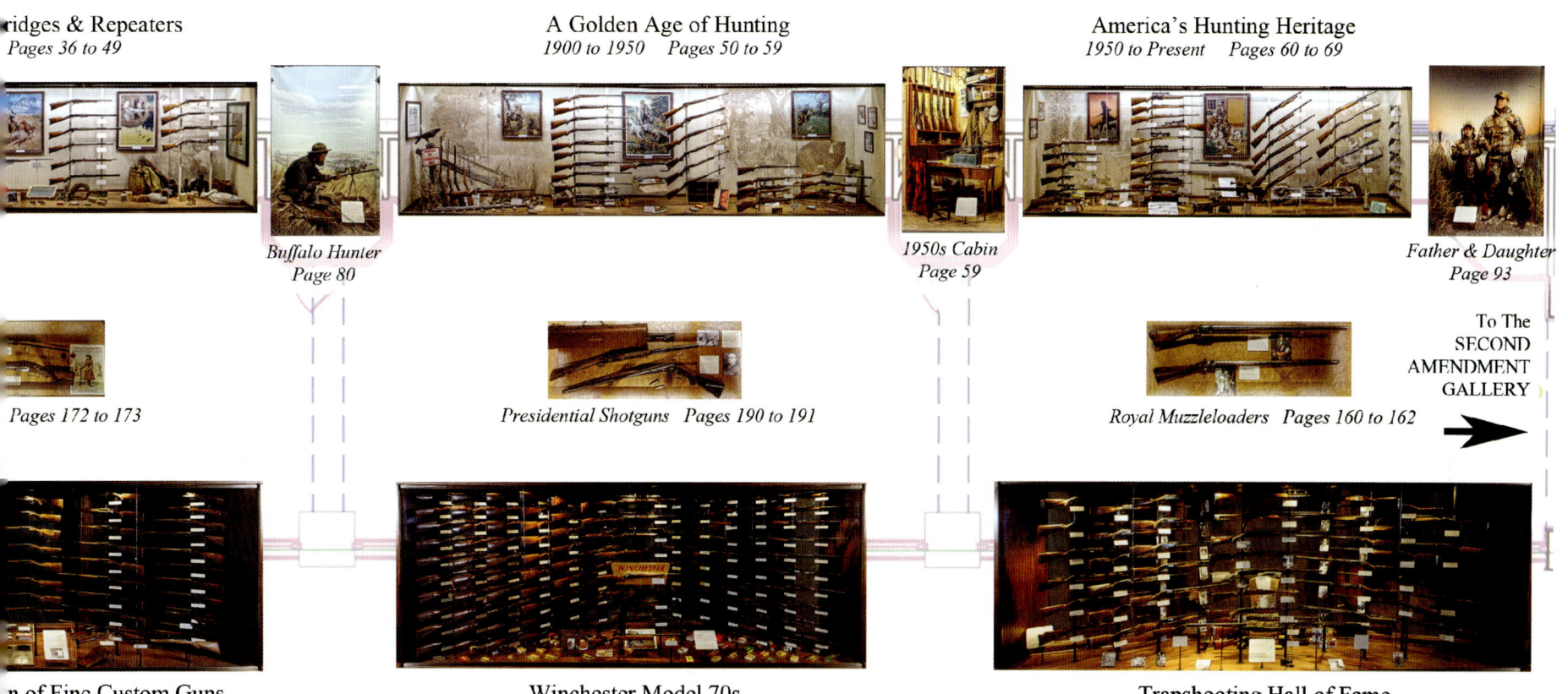

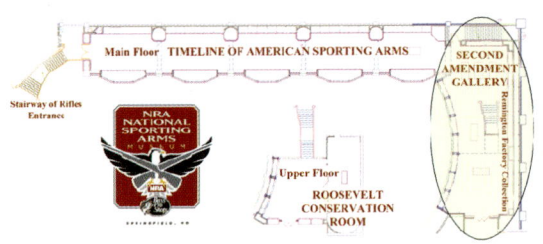

MAIN LEVEL
SECOND AMENDMENT GALLERY

To the TIMELINE of
AMERICAN
SPORTING ARMS

REMINGTON FACTORY COLLECTION

TABLE OF CONTENTS BY LOCATION IN THE MUSEUM

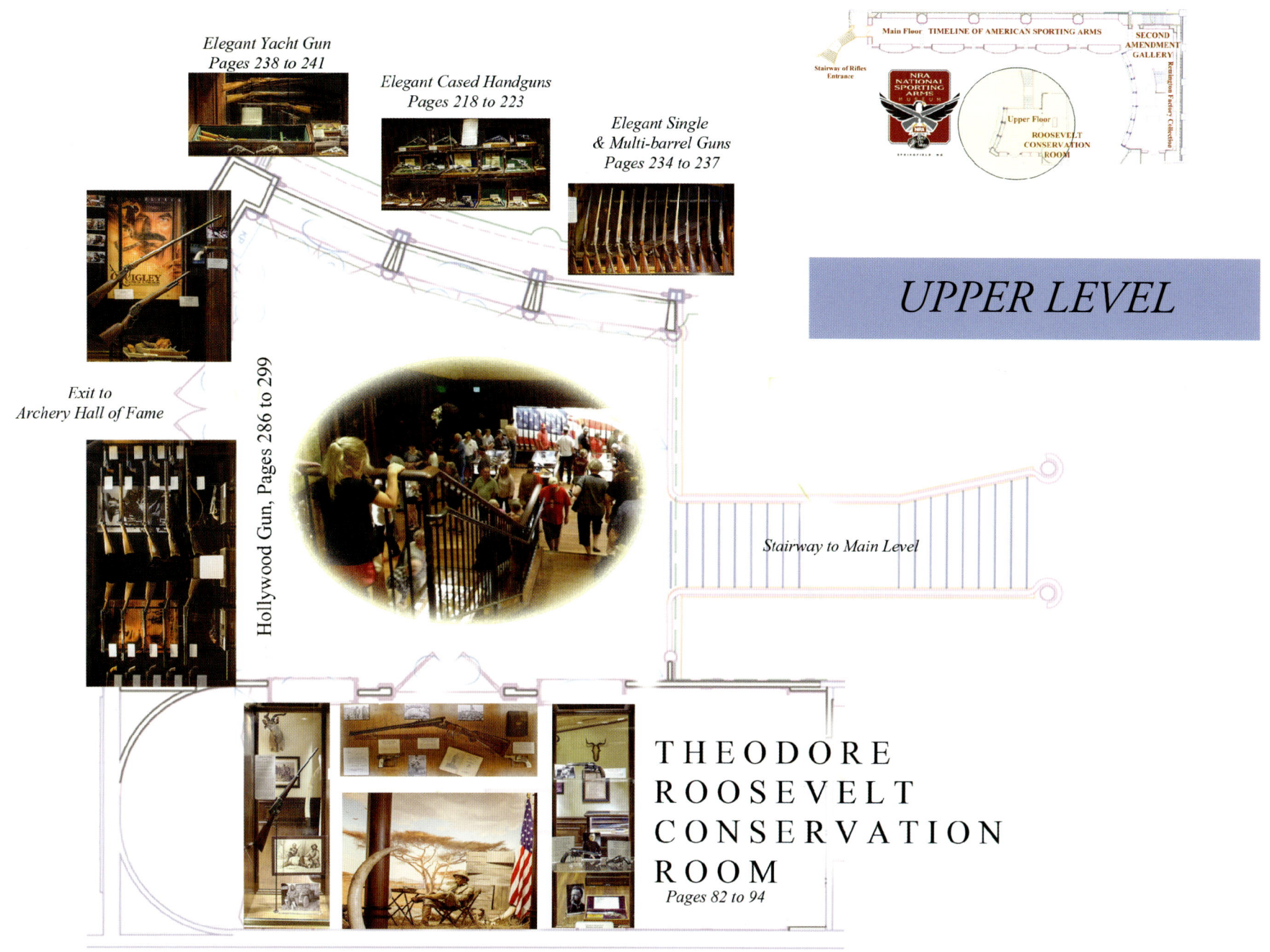

Main Floor TIMELINE OF AMERICAN SPORTING ARMS

SECOND AMENDMENT GALLERY

Stairway of Rifles Entrance

NRA NATIONAL SPORTING ARMS MUSEUM

Upper Floor
ROOSEVELT CONSERVATION ROOM

Remington Factory Collection

UPPER LEVEL

Stairway to Main Level

THEODORE ROOSEVELT CONSERVATION ROOM

HUNTING

AMERICA'S OLDEST TRADITION

For as long as there have been people, there have been hunters. It is a lifestyle that spans the world over and connects all people everywhere. In times past, hunting fulfilled basic needs such as providing food, clothes, and tools. Today, hunting is a wonderful way for friends and family to spend quality time together, reconnect with nature, and escape the demands of modern life.

Early hunters the world over used a variety of tools, including rocks, spears, atlatls, and bows and arrows. The animals they harvested were used fully – the meat for food, the bones for tools, the sinew for cording, and the hides for clothing and shelter.

Before the rise of agriculture, hunting was crucial to the survival of early hunter-

gatherer societies. In general, humans have shifted away from a subsistence existence of hunting and gathering. It still exists in some parts of the world, but it is no longer a predominant lifestyle. Over time, as people began to settle down and farm, the motivations, strategies, and rules governing hunting changed. Nonetheless, this noble tradition remained relevant and important by taking on a new role in American society.

The concept of sport hunting dates back to antiquity and the Romans. The practice spread across Europe and became commonplace. Once hunting was no longer a necessity in everyday life, the average commoners spent their days tending to their livestock and fields. They did not have the time to spend in the field hunting. Because of this shift in lifestyle, hunting game became a symbol of luxury for the upper class elites and royals.

For thousands of years, Old World tradition dictated that the rulers of various countries held title to all of the game in the land, which further prevented commoners from hunting. At the time the American Colonies were established in the 17th century, customs from England dictated that the King owned the land and the water and all of the creatures that lived in and on it.

This concept endured in the American Colonies until the Revolution. With the creation of the United States in the late

18th century, ownership of land and water in relation to wildlife had to be reevaluated. If the government owned it all, things would be no different than if a king claimed ownership. A new type of government demanded a new type of ownership for land and the wild game animals thereon.

In 1821, a Supreme Court of New Jersey case regarding oysters would set the precedent for wild game ownership in the fledgling United States. The judges ruled that the landowner did not have exclusive right to the oysters in the body of navigable water running through his land. Instead, they were part of the public trust and belonged to everyone.

This precedent of public trust now extends to all creatures and is the basis of modern hunting principles to this day in the United States. The idea that fish and wildlife belong to everyone is vastly different from the centuries-old European model. This American concept is part of a blueprint devised by our conservation forefathers that's known as the North American Wildlife Conservation Model.

The model also includes a tenet calling for democratic rule of law, which means hunting and fishing laws are created through a public process where everyone has a chance to contribute. Another important principle of this model ensures that every citizen has an opportunity, under the law, to hunt and fish.

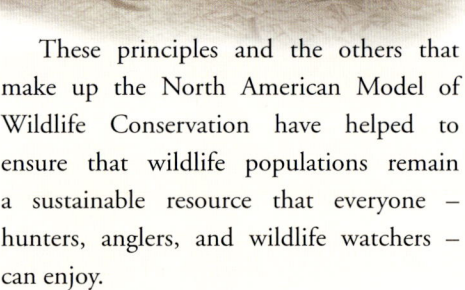

These principles and the others that make up the North American Model of Wildlife Conservation have helped to ensure that wildlife populations remain a sustainable resource that everyone – hunters, anglers, and wildlife watchers – can enjoy.

TYPES OF AMERICAN HUNTING

To this day, public land remains a vital resource for millions of hunters who pursue game. Private land is another option. Hunters may own the land, or seek permission from ranchers and farmers, or lease land for the chance to hunt.

Regardless of the type of land a hunter chooses, the concept of fair chase is paramount. Fair chase provides a balance between the hunter and the hunted. The idea is that hunters sometimes have a successful hunt, while at other times the quarry manages to avoid being taken.

Modern hunters are also committed

to safety. Thanks to hunter education for novices and hunters' ongoing commitment to safety, hunting is one of the safest outdoor activities that people can enjoy.

Over the centuries, hunting has branched out into a wide variety of types and styles. From deer to ducks, tree stands to bird dogs, and everything in between, there's a type of hunting for everyone in this country.

Hunting can be stationary and take place perched high in a tree stand or concealed in a ground blind. The idea is to scout areas before the hunt to better understand game animal behavior and travel patterns. On the day of a hunt, the hunter tries to remain incredibly still and wait for the deer or other game animal to come to the area. Hunters sometimes use food plots or natural food sources, scents, and sounds (such as locking antlers or game calls) to draw animals to an area.

The art of stalking – slowly making your way across the land – in search of game is also an effective way to hunt deer, elk or other game. This method can appeal to people who would rather not sit still and seek to take a more active role in the hunt.

The use of dogs for hunting in America dates back to 1650. Historians believe that the first hunting dogs came over from England with Robert Brooke, who settled in Maryland. Ever since, dogs have remained popular in many different types of hunting.

Bird dogs are often used for quail, pheasant, and other fowl. In this instance, dogs are used to cover the hunting area in front of hunters. The dogs' presence tends to flush birds out of their ground cover and up into flight. Shooting the birds while they are on the ground is considered unsportsmanlike behavior and is not allowed. Some dogs are also trained to go on point when they come across a game bird. Then, at the hunter's command, they flush the birds and retrieve those successfully taken.

Dogs are also used in waterfowl hunting. Instead of locating the game, they are trained to retrieve ducks or geese after the hunter shoots them.

Sometimes the dogs take a more active role in harvesting the game. Some breeds are trained to seek out animals and aid the hunters by treeing the game. Raccoon hunting is a good example of this technique.

In any case raising, training, and sharing the hunt with a good canine friend is a special joy of life for many hunters.

Some types of hunting combine many of the aspects mentioned previously. Just as deer hunters use blinds, they are also popular with duck hunters. Perched on the water's edge or covering a boat, the blind enables the hunters to lie in wait, undetected, for the flock to fly over their position. Then, once the birds have been harvested, the dogs are sent into the water for retrieval.

Hunting is a way for people to enjoy the outdoors and have the chance to feed their families nutritious meals. It is also an important tool for wildlife and pest management strategy. Certain animals, including prairie dogs, groundhogs, rats, squirrels, coyotes, foxes, and raccoons, can wreak havoc on crops, habitat and other wildlife species. Hunting is an important method for controlling wildlife populations and minimizing damage.

While hunting has been around for thousands of years, it has proven to be incredibly flexible and adaptive. From necessity to sport, royal privilege to the common man, the heritage hunting has prevailed. It has become an American tradition. In fact, one might say it is our oldest tradition, dating to long before the idea of America and the United States even existed.

Murals by John Wytock.

HUNTING - Timeline of American Sporting Arms

The Timeline of American Sporting Arms traces the history of hunting arms in America from the earliest days to modern times. Four of the five exhibit cases feature original century-old iconic paintings of classic sporting scenes, on loan from the Remington Factory Collection.

This first case in the series features NRA artifacts on the left and examples of the ancient firearms brought to the New World by explorers, conquistadors, and early settlers on the right side.

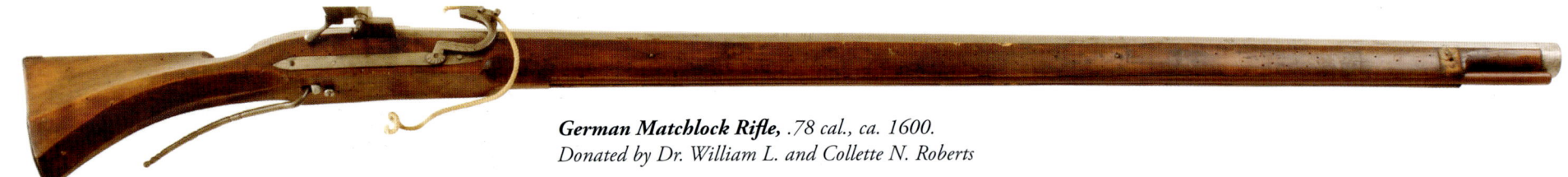

German Matchlock Rifle, *.78 cal., ca. 1600.*
Donated by Dr. William L. and Collette N. Roberts

THE MATCHLOCK

The matchlock firearm appeared sometime after 1450. It was the first type of gun to use a "lock" mechanism to ignite the powder charge.

A "serpentine" arm is mounted on the gun to hold a smoldering, chemically-treated cord - a "slow match." When the trigger lever is pressed, the burning slow match is lowered by simple mechanical linkage into a small pan of gunpowder mounted over the touch hole. This priming charge in turn ignites the main charge of powder inside the breech of the gun and propels the projectile down the barrel towards its target. The matchlock's simplicity and relative ease of manufacture kept it in use until the early 1700s, and even longer in parts of Asia.

Ancient Arms - 1350 to 1700

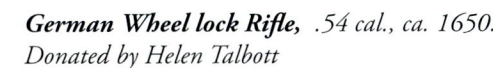

German Wheel lock Rifle, *.54 cal., ca. 1650.*
Donated by Helen Talbott

THE WHEEL LOCK

Despite its ease of operation, the matchlock had a serious disadvantage - wind and rain could render the smouldering slow match inoperable. This problem led to the development in the early 1500s of an intricate firearm called a wheel lock that used a self-contained ignition system.

This new system used a piece of pyrite or flint held in the vice-like jaws of the "dog." It could be lowered to rest against the edge of a spring-loaded serrated wheel that had been wound with a key like an old fashioned clock. Pulling the trigger released the coiled spring and wheel, causing the wheel to spin against the pyrite and create a shower of sparks that ignited the priming powder. Today's lighters work on the same principle of spinning a steel wheel against a small flint to create sparks that ignite the fuel to produce a flame.

Asian Miquelet Lock Wall Gun, *.55 cal., ca. 17th century. This Siamese wall gun was presented to Remington trade delegation while touring Asia in the late 1800s to attract foreign interest in their products. Loaned by Remington Arms Company*

Francisco Targarona Miquelet Escopeta, *.51 cal., ca. 1730–50.*
Donated by Dr. William L. and Collette N. Roberts

THE MIQUELET

As early as 1550, an early type of flint lock was developed - the snaphaunce. During the first quarter of the 17th century, the Spanish introduced an ignition system that had a snapping lock, similar to the snaphaunce, with the exception that the frizzen and pan cover combined into a single part. The miquelet, as the system came to be known, differed from later forms of flintlocks by its externally-mounted main spring and lock parts. It was used throughout the world and was particularly popular in Spain, the Near East and North Africa well into the 19th century. The external mounting of the spring and mechanism is reported to have been more amenable to field repairs than the internally mounted French flintlock mechanism.

Trade Fusil *- This flintlock is a .76 caliber fusil made for the Indian trade, ca. 1750. Note the bayonet lug, an unusual feature on a trade musket*

THE INDIAN TRADE MUSKET

Firearms were unknown to the Native Americans when Europeans began to establish permanent colonies in the Western Hemisphere following Columbus's discovery in 1492. Firearms made up a significant amount of the early trade between Europeans and Native Americans, and continued for nearly 250 years.

English, Spanish and French traders developed a special class of firearms commonly called "trade guns" that they freely exchanged with the tribes without restriction. By the mid-1700s many tribes had become quite proficient with the "thunder stick" of the settlers. Following the Lewis & Clark expedition in 1803 - 1806, a small cottage industry grew around providing "trade muskets" to the Indians. To trade a long arm with an Indian Chief was an ultimate symbol of respect and trust, and one not given lightly. Trade guns were an important tool in the developing economics and political environment that dominated western expansion from the colonial through the antebellum eras.

Typically, trade guns were civilian or sporting arms made to a lesser standard of quality than their Bond Street contemporaries. Trade guns were nominally between 46" and 64" in overall length and between .50 and .75 in caliber, or as per the period, between a 20 and a 12 bore. Traditionally these smoothbore flintlock muskets were fully stocked and most bore a serpent or dragon brass side plate.

The manufacture and trade of these guns continued well into the 19th century with the newly formed United States government actually contracting with various manufacturers to produce trade guns to fulfill treaty obligations with the tribes. No accurate count of the numbers of these guns produced exists but the survival rate is considerably smaller for similar guns of the same period due to the fact that they were used hard and kept in service until they were unable to function.

Artist's pre-construction concept of Museum dioramas, by Bob Sopchick

Indian scout with fusil.

EARLY ARMS IN AMERICA

Firearms were unknown to the Native Americans when Europeans began to establish permanent colonies in the Western Hemisphere following Columbus's discovery in 1492. By the mid-1700's many tribes had become quite proficient with the "thunder stick" of the settlers. Following the Lewis & Clark expedition in 1803 - 1806, a small cottage industry grew around providing "trade muskets" to the Indians.

Fusil - This flintlock is a .76 caliber fusil made for the Indian trade, ca. 1750. Note the bayonet lug, an unusual feature on a trade musket.

27

FLINTLOCKS AND PERCUSSION   1700–1860

During the early American Colonial period, firearms technology settled on a reliable firing mechanism, the flintlock. The flintlock ignition system became the standard until the mid-1800s. It was the system our colonial ancestors used to put food on the table and defend hearth and home from attacks. Ultimately, mounted on rifles and muskets, the flintlock secured America's independence.

A new system of ignition, known as the percussion system, became popular in the early to mid - 1800s. A hollow nipple was mounted leading into the breech of the barrel. A metallic percussion cap was mounted on this. When struck by the hammer, a chemical in the cap ignited and the spark travelled to the gunpowder charge to fire the gun. Percussion firearms offered a water resistant alternative to a flint and steel apparatus.

FLINTLOCKS & PERCUSSION 1700–1860

Early in this era gunsmiths developed the American Long Rifle, the first distinctly American firearm. As settlement moved West, the long rifle was modified for the needs of the Great Plains and Rocky Mountain regions, resulting in the Plains Rifle.

In the first half of the 19th century, firearms development accelerated with the development of breech loaders and eventually effective repeating firearms.

Spanish Blunderbuss, 1.25 in bore, ca. 1650
Although manufactured in Europe, this arm is believed to have been restocked and decorated by Spanish trained Native American craftsmen near Mexico City or Vera Cruz. Donated by Dr. William L. and Collette N. Roberts

THE AMERICAN LONG RIFLE

Commonly called the Kentucky Rifle, he American Long Rifle is the first distinctly American firearm. German gunsmiths settling in the colonies brought with them a style of hunting arm known as the Jaeger rifle. This evolved into the American Long Rifle to meet the needs of hunting on the new continent.

New features include a long slender barrel, reduced caliber of .45 to .50 cal., and an ornate brass patch box replacing the earlier sliding wood version. The stock extends full length to the muzzle, and features a slender wrist with a distinctive drop to the butt stock, and a raised cheek piece. The elaborate carving and inlay work make these guns works of art. The original Long Rifles were flintlocks, but they were later replaced with percussion ignition, and many flintlocks were converted to use percussion caps.

FLINTLOCKS & PERCUSSION 1700–1860

Top to bottom:

* **English Flintlock Fowler,** *.72 cal., ca. 1730–50.*
Most arms of the early colonists initially came from their home countries. Fowlers such as this have smooth bores in long thin-walled barrels for bird hunting.

* **Fordney American Long Rifle,** *.54 cal., ca. 1810–20.*
Melchior Fordney (1789-1846) was a noted flintlock and percussion riflesmith in Lancaster, PA. This examples shows the characteristics of the classic "Kentucky rifle."
Donated by Harmon Leonard

* **Southern Percussion Rifle, .***45 cal., ca. 1840–50.*
Less ornate than the American Long Rifle, the so-called Southern style of rifle was a popular hunting arm in the 19th Century.

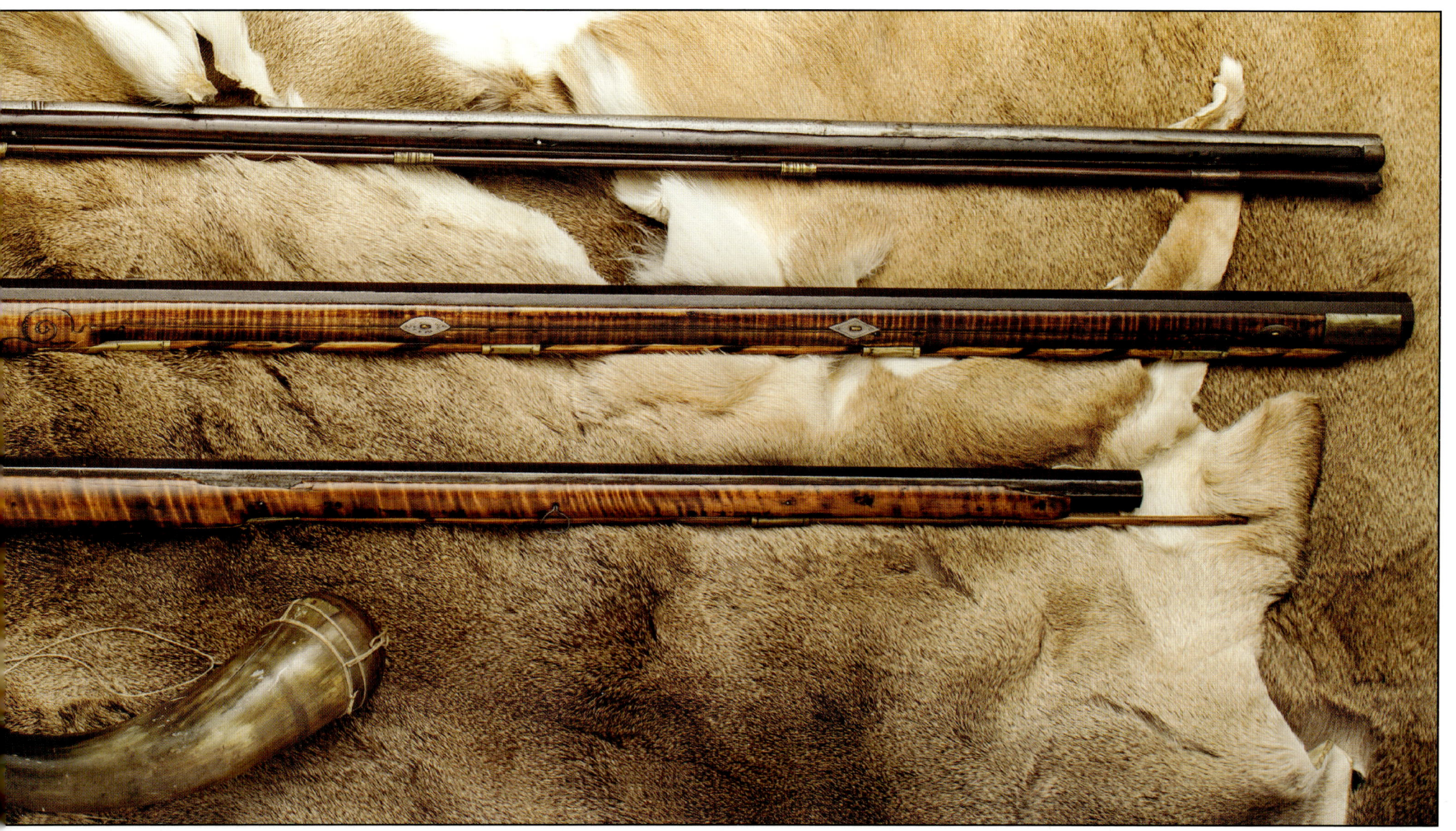

THE ST. LOUIS PLAINS RIFLE

As settlement pushed westward, the Great Plains and Rocky Mountains replaced the Appalachian Mountains as the American Frontier. Pilgrims heading into these wilds required a new style of rifle, which came to be known as the Plains Rifle. The calibers became larger, as appropriate for the big game of the West, such as buffalo, big bears, and elk. The barrel was made shorter for easy carry on horseback and to mitigate the weight of the heavy barrel. Half-stock wood was preferred over full-stock and the elaborate decoration of the Long Rifle was replaced by business-like simplicity for these percussion muzzleloaders.

St. Louis was the "Gateway to the West" in this era, and the natural place for Plains Rifle makers to set up shop. Gunsmiths such as Gemmer, Schaerff and, most famously, the Hawken Brothers provided rifles for mountain men, pioneers and buffalo hunters headed West from the 1820s to the 1860s.

Top to bottom:

* **Schaerff St. Louis Buffalo Rifle**, *.58 cal., ca. 1850*

* **St. Louis S. Hawken Gemmer Rifle**, *.50 cal., ca. 1849–50*

* **Wilmont, St. Louis Percussion Double Shotgun**, *12 ga., ca. 1850*

Loaned by Cletus Klein

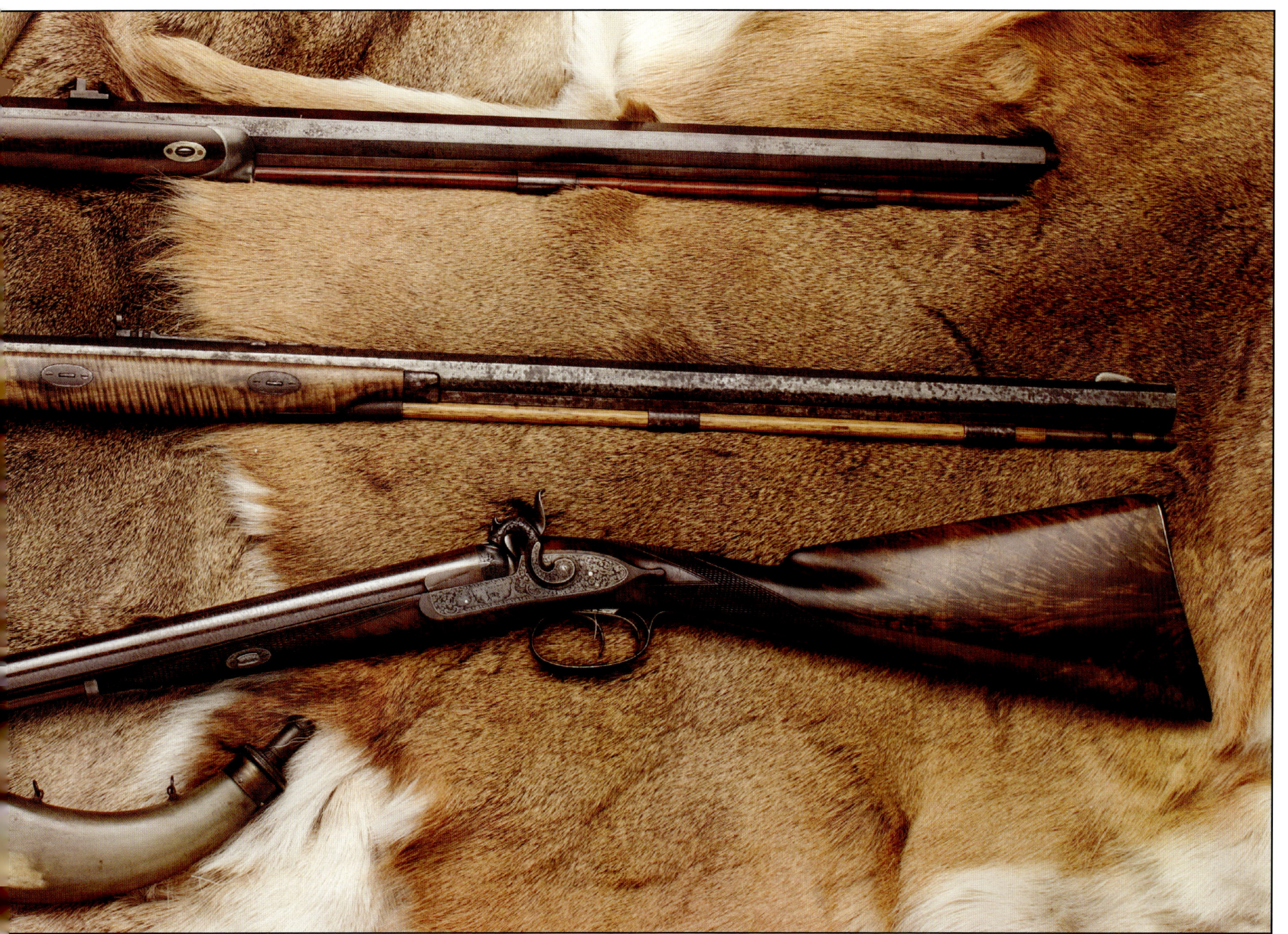

Lancaster Combination Gun *.52 cal. & 16 ga., ca. 1850*
Charles Lancaster (1820–1878) developed an oval bore rifling that was briefly adopted by the British military. This cased example has interchangeable rifle and shotgun barrels. It is accompanied by handwritten directions for use on Lancaster letterhead, numbered to gun, as follows:- "Oval Bore Double Rifle. The powder flask and accessories are set to the proper charge – coarse powder only should be used. Half a charge of powder should be fired before loading with ball. The rings around the tops of the ramrods denote the rifle to be properly loaded when they become flush with the muzzle of the barrel. The ball should not be rammed down hard or it will crush the grains of powder. The balls after being wrapped in paper the same size and thickness as that in the case should be dipped in Russian tallow (melted)."
Donated by the Estate of Jane R. Taylor

FLINTLOCKS & PERCUSSION 1700–1860

J. Henry & Son Percussion Shotgun *12 ga., ca. 1850*
Percussion smoothbores were utilitarian arms on the frontier, able to fire birdshot as well as buckshot at game. It would be unusual for a farm, ranch, or pioneer homestead to not have a muzzleloading shotgun as a basic and necessary tool for hunting, pest control, and defense if needed. A good argument could be made that the humble shotgun was truly "the gun that won the West."
Loaned by the Trapshooting Hall of Fame

Spanish Pinfire Shotgun *14 ga., ca. 1840–50*
An early type of metallic cartridge, the pinfire had the firing pin attached to the base of the round. They were the first cartridges that could be readily reloaded.
Donated by Elvin Drake

Kendall Underhammer Rifle *.50 cal., ca. 1850*
The underhammer system enjoyed some popularity for hunting in the Northeast. It was believed to provide faster and more reliable ignition, and to contribute to safe handling of the gun. Nicanor Kendall was a prolific maker, and contributed to the underhammer development around 1835.
Donated by Dr. William L. and Collette N. Roberts

Eight Gauge Chase & Sons Shotgun *8 ga., ca. 1860*
Big bore shotguns like this one made by William Chase & Sons, capable of firing at longer ranges, were popular choices for market hunters.

BREECHLOADERS

Long guns that could be loaded at the breech offered advantages over the earlier muzzleloaders. They could be reloaded significantly faster, and with less resistance from barrel fouling by previous shots.

Sharps Model 1853 Sporting Carbine, .52 cal., ca. 1854–57, s/n 10043.
Donated by the Kellert Trust

New Haven Arms Volcanic Carbine .41 rocket ball, ca. 1857–60. *The Volcanic was one of the earliest lever action repeaters. It was also an early attempt at a self-contained cartridge, with the gunpowder packed into the hollow base of the bullet.*
Donated by the Estate of Robert E. Petersen

EARLY REPEATERS

The development of the breechloading rifle, and eventually the metallic cartridge, created an opportunity for effective repeating firearms designs by the mid-19th century. An early but unsuccessful example was the Volcanic lever action repeater. It fired a "rocket ball" cartridge with the gunpowder packed in the hollow base of the lead bullet.

This pivotal design was initially created by the partnership of Horace Smith and Daniel B. Wesson. They abandoned the lever action mechanism to find success making metallic cartridge revolvers. However one of their investors, a shirt manufacturer named Oliver Winchester, saw promise in the design. With improvements by Tyler B. Henry, he introduced the Henry Rifle — the first in a long line of Winchester lever actions.

The Spencer was another early repeater that used a tubular magazine inside the stock to feed metallic cartridges. Both the Spencer and the Henry saw use in the Civil War, and opened new horizons for repeating rifles.

Top: *New Haven Arms Henry Rifle,* *.44 rimfire, ca. 1860–66, s/n 4985.*
Donated by the Estate of Max Shaeffer

Bottom: *Spencer Gemmer Sporting Rifle,* *.50 rimfire, ca. 1863–68, s/n 432. Sporting models such as this example are considerably more rare than the military versions used in the Civil War.*
Loaned by Doug Wicklund

METALLIC CARTRIDGES AND REPEATERS   1860–1900

The Civil War (1861–1865) ushered in a new era of firearms innovations and advancements in technology. The most significant included self-contained metallic cartridges and magazine -fed repeating arms.

New techniques of mass production gave birth to manufacturing firms whose names are still prominent today. Remington, Winchester, Colt, Smith & Wesson, and Marlin, as well as host of others, provided the average American with affordable and effective arms that not only put food on the table but offered protection as America moved West.

Metallic Cartridges & Repeaters 1860–1900

Single shot rifles were popular with hunters throughout this era. The lever action was the predominant repeating rifle for this era, although pump actions were also available. In shotguns, single and double barrels were most popular, although early repeaters began to appear even before the 1890s.

Late in the 19th century, smokeless powder began to replace black powder, making possible new advances in sporting arms design that are still considered state of the art today.

SINGLE SHOT RIFLES

Sturdy and accurate single shot rifles enjoyed a great popularity with hunters, from .22 rimfires for small game through large powder capacity .40, .44, .45, and even .50 caliber centerfire cartridges for buffalo and other large game.

Ball & Williams Ballard Conversion Rifle, *.44 cal., ca. 1870, s/n 15758.*
The Ballard design offered the ability to utilize either rimfire or centerfire cartridges.
Donated by Dr. Harold Cottle

Remington Rolling Block Rifle, *7mm, ca. 1885.*
This rugged reliable design was the most popular of the era.
Donated by David Savadyga

Winchester Model 1885 High Wall Rifle, *.32-40, ca. 1889, s/n 44170. Principally designed by John Moses Browning, this falling block action was Winchester's single shot hunting offering from 1885 to 1920. It was offered with high wall or low wall frame.*
Donated by David Savadyga

"FROM MY COLD DEAD HANDS"

Sharps Model 1874 Rifle, .44-90, ca. 1877

This 19th century antique Sharps is the rifle that NRA President Charlton Heston held aloft when he made this famous statement.

Donated by the Estate of Charlton Heston

CHARLTON HESTON (1923–2008)

Charlton Heston was a native of Illinois and a graduate of Northwestern University. He started his acting career in 1948 after serving in the US Army Air Corps during World War II and worked steadily until 2005. He was awarded two Oscars, two Golden Globes, and was nominated for three Emmy's. His portrayals of Moses (The Ten Commandments–1956) and Judah Ben-Hur (1959) won him world-wide fame and recognition. He served as President of the NRA for an unprecedented five terms (1998–2003) and was present at the grand opening of the National Firearms Museum in Fairfax, Virginia in May of 1998. He is, perhaps, most vividly remembered for his now iconic gesture of holding aloft a rifle and stating passionately, "From my cold, dead hands", visually bringing to life a popular tee shirt and bumper sticker slogan, "You can have my gun when you pry it from my cold, dead hands."

It was during a speech to the National Press Club in September 1997 that he admonished the gathered press about their relentless attacks on the 2nd Amendment and their continuing efforts to demonize firearms and their owners. Stating, "…that doorway to freedom is framed by the muskets that stood between a vision of liberty and absolute anarchy at a place called Concord Bridge. […] There can be no free speech, no freedom of the press, no freedom to protest, no freedom to worship your god, no freedom to speak your mind, no freedom from fear, no freedom for your children and for theirs, for anybody, anywhere, without the Second Amendment freedom to fight for it." He challenged the media to be more responsible in their coverage of firearms related stories.

From Major Dundee (1965) to El Cid (1961) to Planet of the Apes (1968) to the Omega Man (1971), Heston's acting range was remarkable and filled a catalog of work that spanned 60 years and over 130 film and television credits.

WINCHESTER LEVER ACTION RIFLES

Following the success of the Henry, Winchester developed a line of lever action rifles throughout the late 19th century that quickly became the dominant type of repeating rifle preferred by American hunters, beginning with the Model 1866, nicknamed "The Yellowboy" for its brass frame, it fired a .44 rimfire cartridge. It was followed by the Model 1873 which also introduced the early Winchester Center Fire (WCF) cartridges - .44-40, .38-40, and .32.20. Nearly 20 years later, the John Moses Browning designed Model 1892 offered a sleeker improved platform for the same class of cartridges.

While the 1873 and 1892 were effective repeaters with around 15 round capacities, the cartridges were not as effective for big game as some of the single shots of the era. This was initially addressed with the Model 1876 followed a decade later by the Browning designed Model 1886. These upscaled models chambered long cartridges with heavier bullets and significantly more capacity for gunpowder, offering significantly more power for hunting large animals.

Winchester Model 1866 Musket, .44 rimfire, ca. 1885, s/n 94399.
Donated by Loma O'Allen

Winchester Model 1873 Rifle, .32 WCF, ca. 1887, s/n 221638B.
Donated by Harry M. Townsley

Winchester Model 1876 Rifle, .40-60, ca. 1882-84, s/n 53295.
Donated by Harry M. Townsley

In the late 19th century, the introduction of smokeless powder meant that a smaller diameter bullet could be driven to higher velocities for performance comparable to the large caliber blackpowder loads. Winchester responded with the Browning designed Model 1894, which went on to become one of America's most popular deer rifles for over a century, along with the .30-30 cartridge designed for it.

Accompanying smokeless powder was a new pointed bullet design - the spitzer - that offered a much flatter trajectory over significantly longer range. However, the tubular magazines of Winchester lever actions to date risked accidental ignition by recoil of cartridges loaded with the point of a spitzer bullet resting against the primer of the round in front of it. Again, Browning responded with a new Model 1895 that used an integral box magazine allowing use of cartridges in the .30-06 class.

Winchester Model 1886 Rifle, .40-65, ca. 1892–94, s/n 86767.
Donated by the Estate of Max Shaeffer

Winchester Model 1892 Rifle, .32-20, ca. 1892, s/n 20618.
Donated by Harry M. Townsley

Winchester Model 1894 Rifle, .38-55, ca. 1910–15, s/n 806477.
Donated by the Estate of Max Shaeffer

Townsend Whelen's Winchester Model 1895 Rifle. .40-72, ca. 1900–03, s/n 38814.
Donated by the Estate of Colonel Townsend Whelen

COLONEL TOWNSEND WHELEN

Townsend Whelen was born March 6 1877, into a life of privilege, the son of a Philadelphia doctor. Townsend came from of a long line of professional men and was an unlikely candidate to become a professional soldier as well as a celebrated writer and outdoorsman.

In his youth he showed little interest in academics or athletics. On his 11th birthday things changed when his father gave him a Quackenbush air rifle. By the age of 13 he had graduated to a .22 Remington rolling block. In the summer of 1892 he won his first shooting contest. He continued to shoot competitively for the remainder of his life, winning his last match in 1960 in St. Louis, MO, at the age of 83.

Col. Whelen received a commission in the Regular Army and by 1917, when the United States entered WWI, he was assigned to the Army general staff. He eventually followed in the footsteps of his great-great grandfather, Israel Whelen, and took command of the Frankford Arsenal, where in 1804 his grandfather outfitted the Lewis and Clark Expedition. In 1929 he became the Director of Research and Development at the Springfield Armory. While there, he and his friend G.L. Wotkyns developed the .22 Hornet, based on the .22 WCF casing.

In 1936 at the age of 59, he retired from the military and launched his second career, becoming the nation's foremost outdoor writer, contributing to the most prestigious outdoor publications of the time including "The American Rifleman."

Colonel Townsend Whelen passed away on December 23, 1961. His capacity for hard work and his many years of experience in all phases of shooting, combined with an open and curious mind, earned him a worldwide reputation as a military officer, hunter, author, and firearms authority.

TOWNSEND WHELEN 1900

OTHER REPEATING RIFLES

Marlin's line of quality lever action rifles offered strong competition to Winchester from the 1880s through the 20th century. Whitney lever actions enjoyed some popularity in the late 19th century as well. The innovative Evans lever action used a spiral magazine in the buttstock with a capacity of up to 34 cartridges.

There were other repeating rifle mechanisms available at this time. Although not yet popular, bolt actions such as the Remington Keene were offered. Colt manufactured three sizes of pump action rifle, from a small .22 through a large frame for big game, with the medium size chambered for the .44-40 class cartridges.

Colt also very briefly offered lever action rifles. There is a story, never proven, that a Winchester representative visited Colt's offices with a sample of a Winchester revolver in hand, whereupon Colt decided to stick to sixguns and pump actions if Winchester would stay out of the revolver market.

Colt Medium Frame Lightning Rifle, *.32-20, ca. 1890, s/n 66747.*
Donated by Welton M. Modisette

Remington Keene Bolt Action Sporting Rifle, *.40-60, ca. 1880-83.*

Evans Repeating Rifle, *.44 Evans, ca. 1873–79.*
Utilizing a revolving magazine in the buttstock, these Maine-made rifles had ammunition capacity of 28 to 34 rounds.
Donated by Ruth Traxel

Whitney Burgess Kennedy Rifle, *.45-70, ca. 1880, s/n 724.*
Donated by the Estate of Kenneth "Tiny" Miller

Marlin Model 1881 Rifle, *.45-70, ca. 1882, s/n 1150.*
Donated by Farrel Owen

Marlin Model 1897 Rifle, *.22 rimfire, ca. 1909, s/n 412348.*
This example has a factory threaded muzzle that could accept a Maxim suppressor.
Donated by William Sternagle

HUNTING - TIMELINE OF AMERICAN SPORTING ARMS

BREECHLOADING SHOTGUNS

With the advent of self-contained shotshells, breechloading double barrel and single barrel shotguns gained in popularity throughout this era. They enjoyed popularity with bird shooters and small game hunters, for pest control on farms and ranches, and increasingly for competition and exhibition shooting.

Both elegant and inexpensive utilitarian foreign-made shotguns were popular. American makers such as Colt entered the market. However, it was the Parker Brothers that ultimately became known as the makers of the best double barrel U.S. made shotguns.

By the end of the 19th century, pump action repeaters came available and began to gain public acceptance.

Parker Brothers Lifter Hammer Shotgun, 12 ga., ca. 1877, s/n 26195.
The "Lifter" action opening mechanism was one of the first Parker shotgun designs offered.
Donated by Rupert Andrews

Colt Model 1883 Hammerless Shotgun, 12 ga., ca. 1885, s/n 1044.
Offered in both 10 gauge and 12 gauge, Colt's hammerless shotgun followed an earlier hammer gun model.
Donated by Francis E. Bailey

Spencer Shotgun, 12 ga., ca. 1900, s/n 16485.
Introduced in 1882, the Spencer was the first successful American pump action shotgun.
Donated by Bruce Catlin

Winchester Model 1897 Shotgun, 12 ga., ca. 1899, s/n 53627E.
Winchester's workhorse 1897 is a J.M. Browning designed hunting classic.
Donated by Alice Mary Willman

The Guide and the The Goose Shooter by Robert Wesley Amick, created for Remington advertising ca. 1905.
Loaned by Remington Arms Company

Rabbit Hunter by John Eads Collins, used as a Remington poster ca. 1910.
Loaned by Remington Arms Company

A GOLDEN AGE OF HUNTING 1900–1950

The turn of the century evokes images of big game hunts, safaris, and classic outdoor stories. This is the era when recreational shooting became popular and game hunting took on an important role in wildlife conservation efforts. Millions of Americans took to field and stream to enjoy the bountiful abundance.

In the late 19th and early 20th centuries, large scale market hunting of wild game and widespread habitat destruction resulted in the dramatic decline of some species. The bison population was estimated at over 60 million before the arrival of Europeans. It plunged to 750 by 1890, primarily as a result of commercial hunting. The passenger pigeon went from billions to extinction by 1914.

A Golden Age of Hunting 1900–1950

Theodore Roosevelt was a leader of the conservation movement in America. Responsible hunting regulations to ensure the preservation of game species and wild habitat grew throughout the first half of the 20th century, preserving America's wildlife and hunting tradition for future generations.

This era also saw the introduction of numerous new types of firearms. Many of the enduring classic sporting arms models got their start in this era. Doughboys returning from WWI wanted to hunt with bolt action rifles similar to their issue Springfield Model 1903s. GIs coming home from WWII looked for semi-auto hunting rifles, similar to their M1 Garands, or sporterized bolt-actions based on the Mauser type action.

Winchester Model 1890 Rifle, *.22 Short, ca. 1915, s/n 163682.*
The most popular rimfire pump-action rifle marketed by Winchester; this model was offered from 1890–1932.
Donated by Harry M. Townsley

Stevens "Crackshot" Rifle, *.25 rimfire, ca. 1920, s/n C797.*
Donated by David Savadyga

Winchester Model 1906 Rifle, *.22 LR, ca. 1927, s/n 511867B.*
John Browning's redesign of the 1890 to take short, long, and long rifle cartridges resulted in over 800,000 being produced.
Donated by Istvan Nemes

Winchester Model 99 Thumb Trigger Rifle, *.22 LR, ca. 1910.*
Made from 1902–1923, this unusual design was fired with the thumb.
Donated by David Savadyga

Quackenbush Rifle, *.22 LR, ca. 1910.*
Donated by Dr. William L. and Collette N. Roberts

Winchester Model 52 Rifle, *.22 LR, ca. 1928-30, s/n 11343.*
Produced from 1920–1980, this model was considered the premier smallbore target rifle.
Donated by C. R. Suydam

PLINKERS AND BOYS' RIFLES

Throughout the 20th century, by far the most used cartridge in America has been the humble .22 rimfire. It is used for small game hunting, target competition, and informal shooting widely known as "plinking." In the early 20th century, small scale .22 rifles enjoyed great popularity and were widely known as "boys' rifles." The inexpensive ammunition and low recoil made them popular for beginners guns and practice, as well as hunting for the pot and pest control, whether in single shot or repeating rifles. They ranged from the ubiquitous Stevens Favorite style single shots through Winchester pump repeaters and the unusual all-metal Quackenbush to full size precision adult target quality rifles such as the Winchester Model 52.

DOUBLE AND SINGLE BARREL SHOTGUNS

These simple yet functional designs remained popular for hunting and recreational shooting.

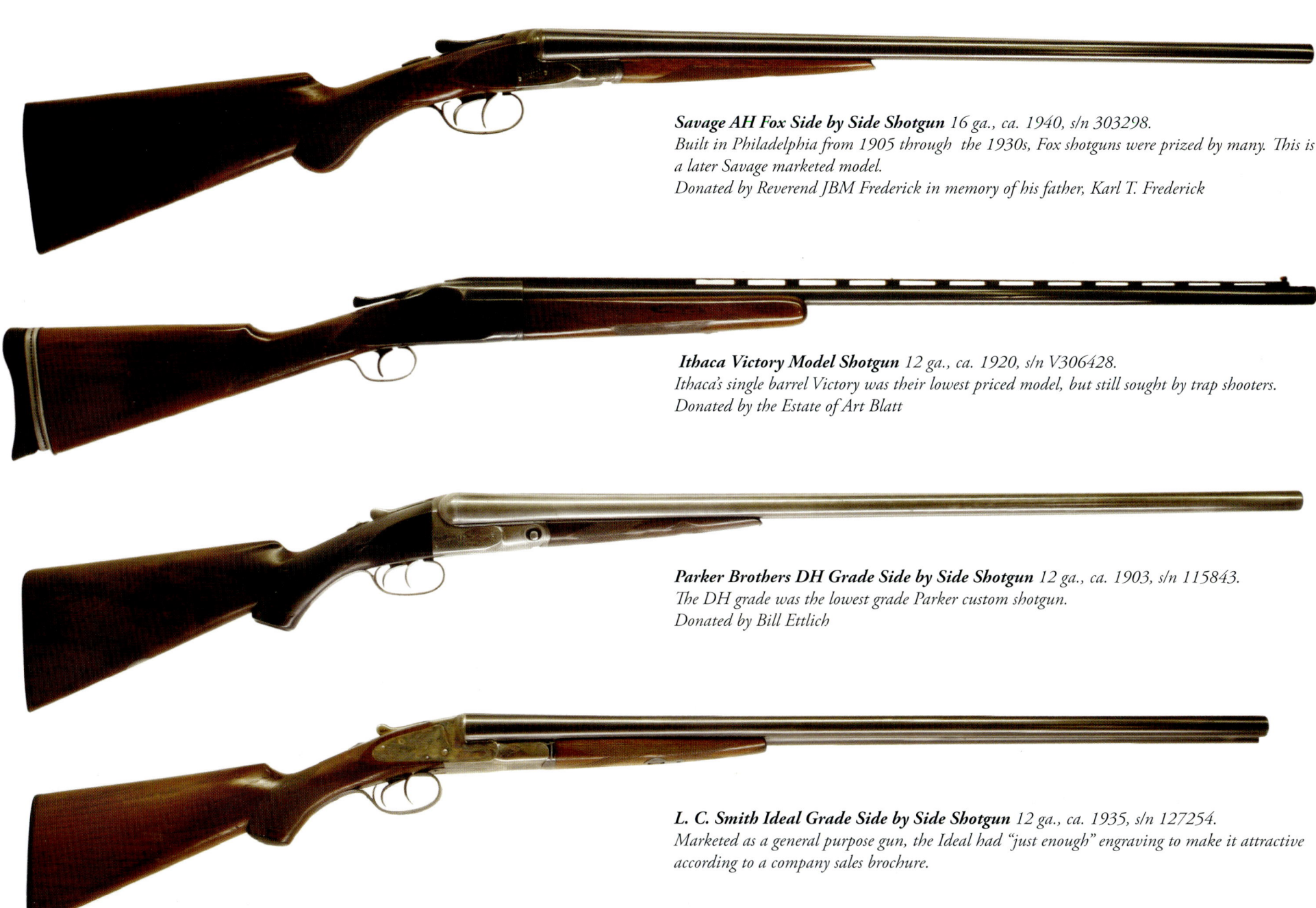

Savage AH Fox Side by Side Shotgun *16 ga., ca. 1940, s/n 303298.*
Built in Philadelphia from 1905 through the 1930s, Fox shotguns were prized by many. This is a later Savage marketed model.
Donated by Reverend JBM Frederick in memory of his father, Karl T. Frederick

Ithaca Victory Model Shotgun *12 ga., ca. 1920, s/n V306428.*
Ithaca's single barrel Victory was their lowest priced model, but still sought by trap shooters.
Donated by the Estate of Art Blatt

Parker Brothers DH Grade Side by Side Shotgun *12 ga., ca. 1903, s/n 115843.*
The DH grade was the lowest grade Parker custom shotgun.
Donated by Bill Ettlich

L. C. Smith Ideal Grade Side by Side Shotgun *12 ga., ca. 1935, s/n 127254.*
Marketed as a general purpose gun, the Ideal had "just enough" engraving to make it attractive according to a company sales brochure.

Winchester Model 12 Shotgun *12 ga., ca. 1970–73, s/n Y2013297.*
This pump shotgun introduced in 1912 is widely popular with hunters.
Donated by Dr. Sheldon Gilbert

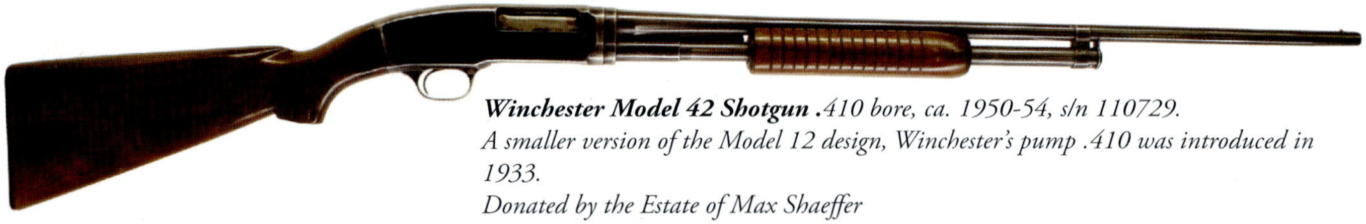

Winchester Model 42 Shotgun *.410 bore, ca. 1950-54, s/n 110729.*
A smaller version of the Model 12 design, Winchester's pump .410 was introduced in 1933.
Donated by the Estate of Max Shaeffer

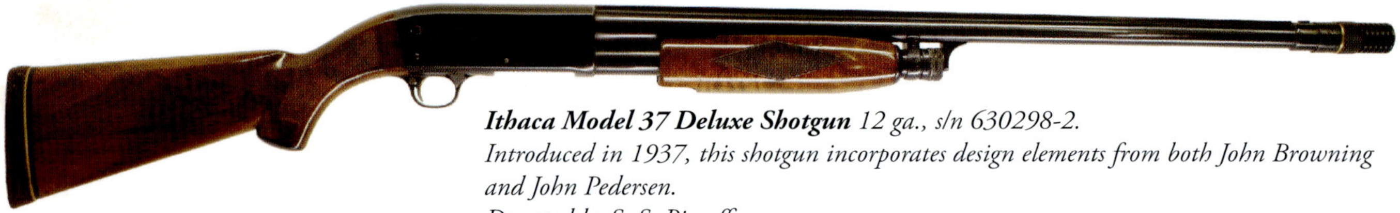

Ithaca Model 37 Deluxe Shotgun *12 ga., s/n 630298-2.*
Introduced in 1937, this shotgun incorporates design elements from both John Browning and John Pedersen.
Donated by S. S. Piroeff

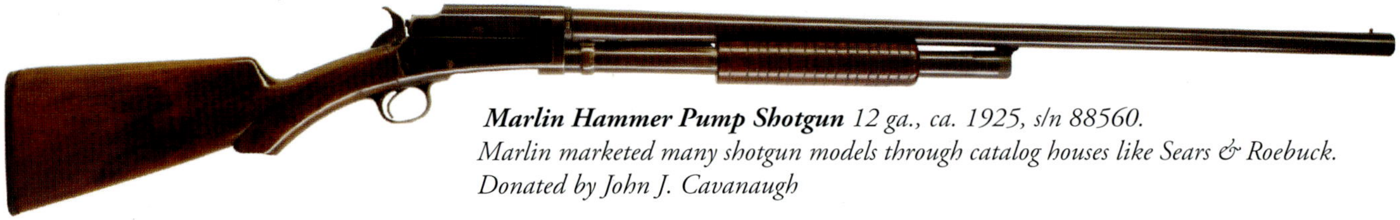

Marlin Hammer Pump Shotgun *12 ga., ca. 1925, s/n 88560.*
Marlin marketed many shotgun models through catalog houses like Sears & Roebuck.
Donated by John J. Cavanaugh

Browning Auto Five Shotgun *20 ga., ca. 1955, s/n C12139.*
This classic "hump-back" John Moses Browning design was introduced by FN in 1903. Variations were offered by Browning, Remington, and FN.
Donated by the Estate of Walter J. Burchan

Winchester Model 1911 Shotgun *12 ga., ca. 1912–20, s/n 14680A.*
Built from 1911 to 1925, this recoil-operated shotgun was Winchester's first autoloading model. A shell was chambered by grasping the barrel and pulling to the rear, a feature that could result in safe-handling issues.
Donated by Dorothy A. Briggs in memory of her husband Alfred Briggs

REPEATING SHOTGUNS

Semi-automatic self-loading shotguns began to see field use, along with increasingly popular pump actions.

COMBINATION GUNS

Combining a rifle barrel with a shotgun barrel, these versatile long guns offered the hunter an option for different types of game and shooting scenarios.

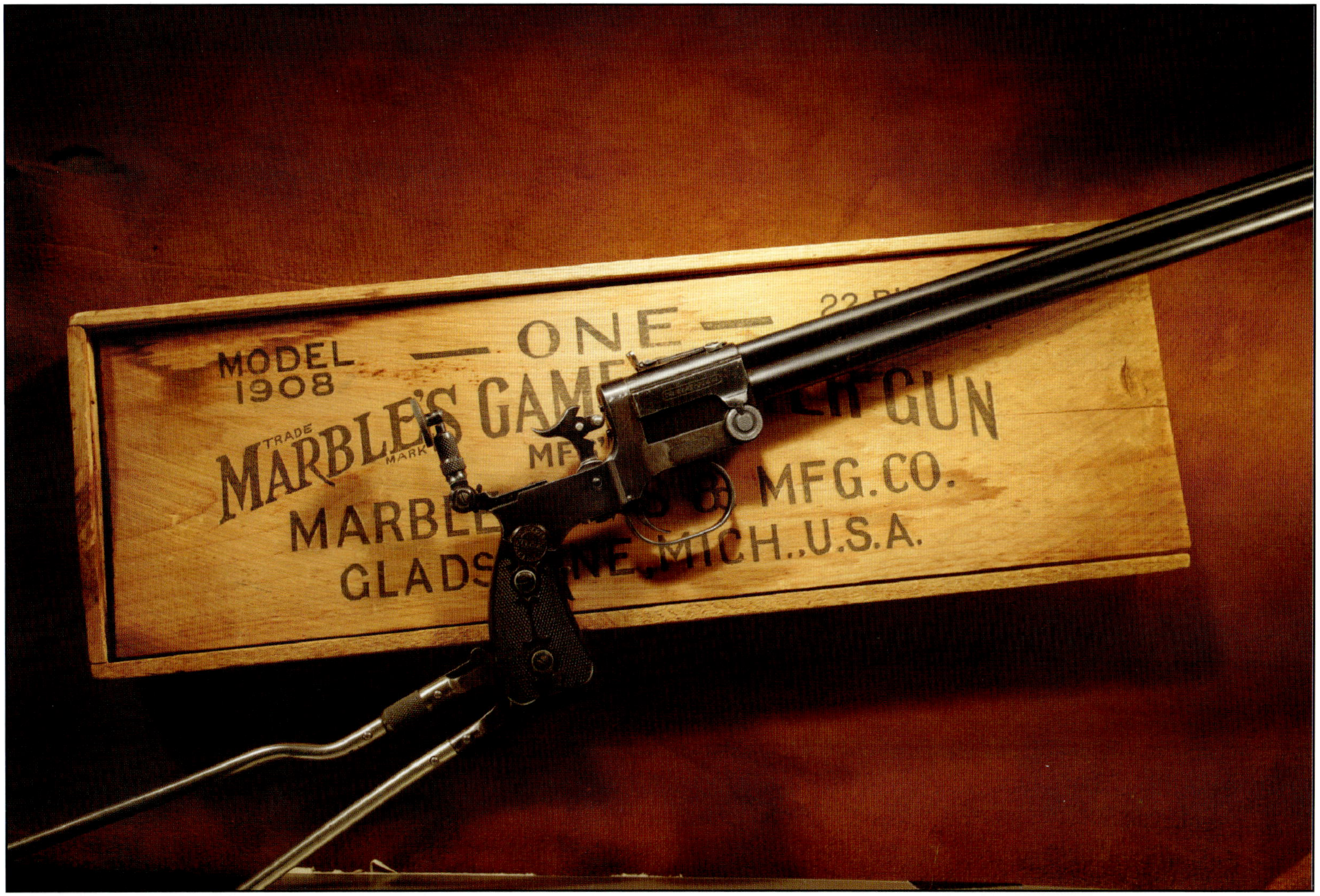

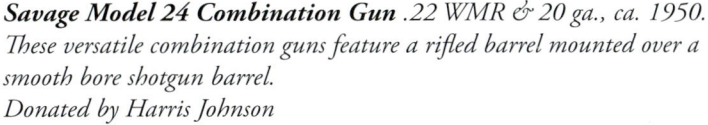

Marbles Game Getter. .22 rimfire & .44 shotshell, ca. 1918.
Made in Gladstone, Michigan, this handy combination rifle shotgun
features a skeletonized folding stock.
Donated by the Estate of Thomas Sefton

Savage Model 24 Combination Gun .22 WMR & 20 ga., ca. 1950.
These versatile combination guns feature a rifled barrel mounted over a
smooth bore shotgun barrel.
Donated by Harris Johnson

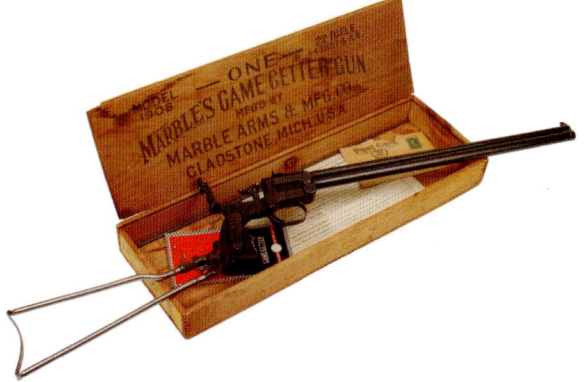

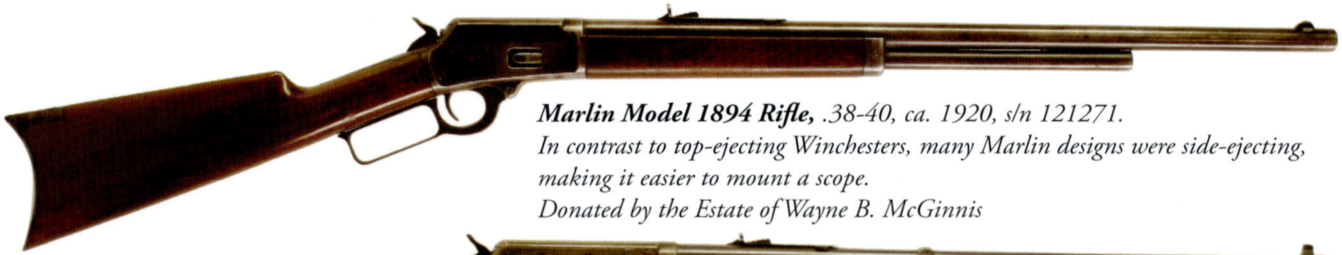

Marlin Model 1894 Rifle, .38-40, ca. 1920, s/n 121271.
In contrast to top-ejecting Winchesters, many Marlin designs were side-ejecting, making it easier to mount a scope.
Donated by the Estate of Wayne B. McGinnis

Marlin Model 36 Rifle. .32 Special, ca. 1940, s/n 8457.
Revamped with a two-piece firing pin, Marlin offered the lever-action Model 36 only until 1948.
Donated by Joseph Kerensky, Jr.

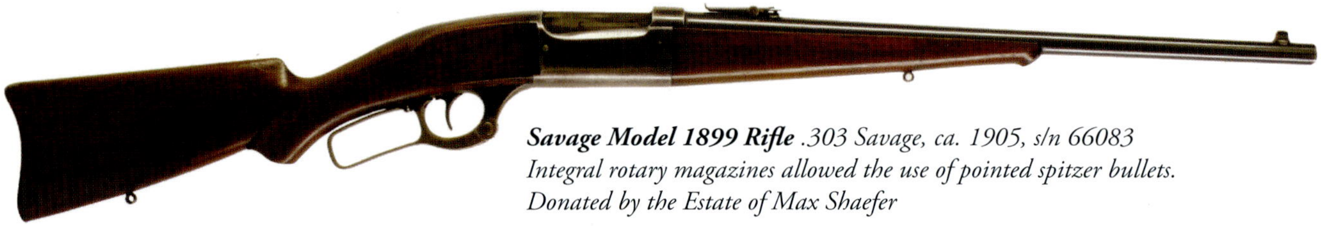

LEVER ACTION RIFLES

These slim handy rifles based on 19th century designs just continued to grow in popularity. A Marlin or Winchester "thutty-thutty" cradled in a gun rack in the rear window of a pick-up was a common sight in small town and rural America in the mid-20th century.

Savage Model 1899 Rifle .303 Savage, ca. 1905, s/n 66083
Integral rotary magazines allowed the use of pointed spitzer bullets.
Donated by the Estate of Max Shaefer

Winchester Model 64 Rifle .30-30, ca. 1950, s/n 1889024.
Produced from 1933 to 1957, this was to the Model 94 with a shorter magazine.
Donated by the Estate of Max Shaefer

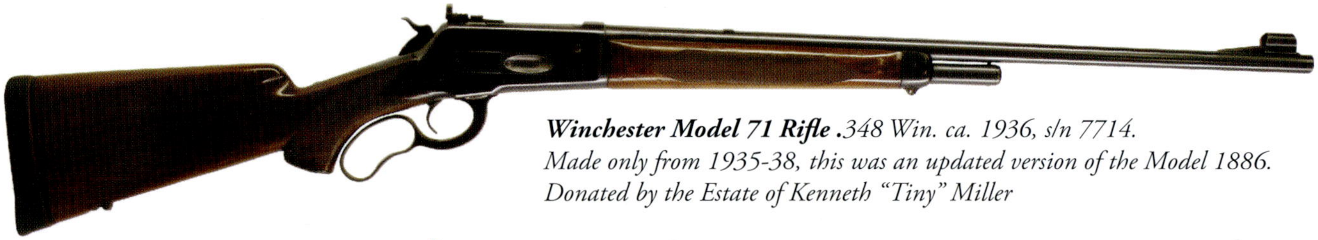

Winchester Model 71 Rifle .348 Win. ca. 1936, s/n 7714.
Made only from 1935-38, this was an updated version of the Model 1886.
Donated by the Estate of Kenneth "Tiny" Miller

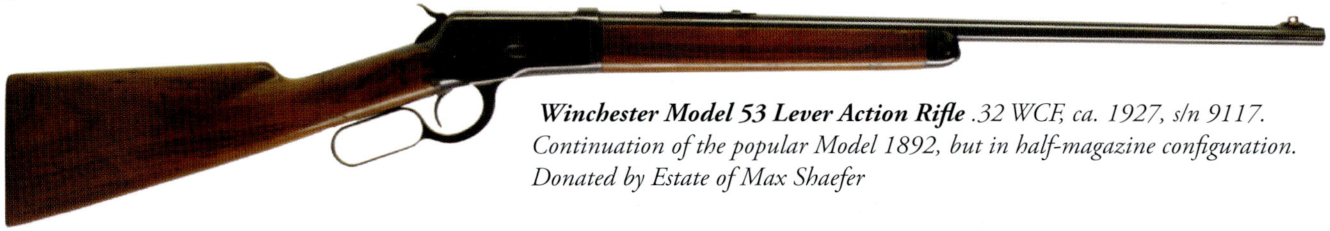

Winchester Model 53 Lever Action Rifle .32 WCF, ca. 1927, s/n 9117.
Continuation of the popular Model 1892, but in half-magazine configuration.
Donated by Estate of Max Shaefer

BOLT ACTION RIFLES

In the early 20th century, bolt action rifles began to make inroads with American hunters. The design allowed use of more ballistically efficient spitzer bullets and made mounting of scopes easier.

Mannlicher-Schoenauer Model 1903 Rifle *7mm, ca. 1920–30, s/n 18499.*
Donated by Carol Ann Palka

Winchester Model 54 Rifle *.30-06, ca. 1926–28, s/n 16085.*
Offered from 1919 to 1936.
Donated by Melvin Gordon

Remington Model 720 Rifle *.30-06, ca. 1942, s/n 42437.*
Remington began offering their 720 line in 1941, based on the earlier Model 1917 design.
Donated by Melvin Gordon

Mauser Sporter Rifle *8mm, ca. 1920, s/n 1565-2993.*
Many civilian sporters were built after the First World War using surplus military actions.

Sporterized Canadian Mk IV Military Rifle *.303 Brit, ca. 1950–55, s/n 52L1117.*
Sporterized after WWII by NRA Technical Staff as a gunsmithing project. Typical of military rifles turned into sporters by civilians postwar.

SELF-LOADING RIFLES

The earliest semi-auto rifles were designed and advertised for civilian sporting use, although they also gained popularity with law enforcement.

Remington Model 8 Semi-Automatic Rifle, *.30 Rem, ca. 1930, s/n 50297.*
This J.M. Browning design was recoil-operated and incorporated a rotating bolt head.
Donated by Dr. William L. and Collette N. Roberts

Winchester M1910 SL Semi-Automatic Rifle *.401 WSL, ca. 1913, s/n 2257.*
Donated by I. Earl Dubois, Jr.

Winchester Model 1905 Semi-Automatic Rifle *.35 WSL. ca. 1905–08, s/n 4541.*
Produced from 1905-1920, Winchester's blowback semi-automatic was reliable, but not powerful.
Donated by I. Earl Dubois, Jr.

THE HUNTER'S CABIN

Few things stir a hunter and outdoorsman's heart to warm memories of a cherished hunt more than the venerable hunter's cabin, so popular in the 1950s. Each cabin was usually filled with sparse but sturdy furnishings and all things necessary to the success of a classic hunt. You might find a pantry for canned goods and shelves of hunting books, coat racks and hooks for hunting vests and hats. There would be favorite boots, decoys, ammunition and cleaning gear for firearms, and of course the favorite and trusted firearms appropriate for a variety of game.

These cabins recall a time when the success of the hunt was measured as much by preparation, equipment, and camaraderie as by the game taken. It was a time when there was a certain established order to the hunt that, though never written, made the hunt a cherished event that became tradition for future generations of young hunters; a rite of passage. For the older hunters there is a nostalgia and comfort brought on by the memories of hunts gone by; the times when their fathers passed on the traditions and lore of the hunting cabin. The cabin was the base for operations, where the plans for each day's

hunt was made. It was a haven of warmth, cheer, and celebration at the end of each day's hunt. Success was marked by the renewal of friendships and the shared tales of the hunt.

When visitors view the hunting cabin diorama, memories of the cabins of their youth often bring remarks like, "my dad kept his favorite old plaid hunting jacket at the cabin," or "I remember my dad's friends talking about the hunting cabin they used for years when they were younger." Sometimes it stirs memories of "that old shotgun grandpa used to hunt quail." There were always the various cigar boxes, jars, and coffee cans used to store screws, springs, and other mysterious but valuable parts for future use. All these things draw us back to the rousing tales and jokes shared around a pot-bellied stove, while snow swirled outside, past frosty windows, or memories of hunt strategy being discussed around the table to the smell of coffee, while eggs and bacon sizzled on the wood-burning stove during the predawn darkness.

Times have changed, as has the modern hunting cabin. While camps with cabins are still found, today's hunters may be more concerned with cell phone reception or Wi-Fi. Blaze orange has replaced red plaid and nylon has replaced canvas. However, the longer the time spent in camp, the less these devices seem to be used and the more the traditions of the hunting camps of old return. Hopefully, the memories of these quaint, nostalgic little cabins will inspire a return to the wonderful times and honored values they represent.

59

AMERICA'S HUNTING HERITAGE   1950–PRESENT

The most recent decades of firearms development have brought numerous changes to the way we hunt and enjoy the shooting sports. Venerable arms companies such as Remington, Winchester, Smith & Wesson, and Colt have seen their share of challenges only to adapt and overcome, while the American public continues to enjoy recreational shooting, competition, and hunting in ever increasing numbers. New firms such as Sturm Ruger & Co. revolutionized manufacturing with investment casting and enabled millions to afford quality arms for sport and hunting.

AMERICA'S HUNTING HERITAGE 1950–PRESENT

New materials such as synthetic stocks, stainless steel, and lightweight alloys were applied to classic action types for improvements in durability, lightweight carry, weather resistance, and ease of care. Ergonomics have improved and design refinements enhance accuracy and reliability.

Optics have become standard on sporting rifles and many sporting handguns, beginning with telescopic scopes and progressing through a variety of electronic and specialty sighting systems.

RIMFIRES The ubiquitous, versatile .22 Long Rifle cartridge remains America's favorite round, chambered in a wide variety of modern rifles.

Ruger Model 10/22 Semi-Automatic Rifle *.22 LR, ca. 2010, s/n 234-96206.*
Introduced in 1964, this semi-auto with detachable 10 round rotary magazine has become an American favorite.
Donated by the Estate of Tom Kearns

Remington Nylon 66 Semi-Automatic Rifle *.22 LR, ca. 1962.*
The first mass-produced rifle with a synthetic stock.
Donated by Remington Arms Company

Armalite Model AR-7 Rifle *.22 LR, ca. 1970, s/n 52874.*
This semi-auto "survival rifle" will float if dropped from a boat, and can be taken down to be stored in its own stock.
Donated by the Thomas W. Sefton Trust

Marlin M70PSS Papoose Semi-Automatic Rifle *.22 LR, ca. 2009, s/n 4198937.*
Takedown stainless steel backpacking or survival rifle.
Donated by Edith Lauren in memory of Paul Martin Lauren

KSA Cricket Youth Rifle *.22 LR, ca. 2011, s/n 90630.*
Down-sized rifle designed as an introductory arm for young shooters.
Donated by the Estate of John Kozina

America's Hunting Heritage 1950–Present

BOLT ACTION RIFLES These rifles remain widely popular for their accuracy, reliability, and classic lines, even when updated with the latest technology.

Ruger Model 77 Rifle .220 Swift, ca. 2000, s/n 782-15187.
Designed by Jim Sullivan, these investment-cast receiver rifles follow classic Mauser lines.
Donated by Dr. Sheldon Gilbert

Weatherby Mark V Rifle .240 Weatherby Mag., ca. 1985, s/n H64438.
Introduced in 1957, Roy Weatherby's custom rifle line was built to accommodate high pressure proprietary cartridges.
Donated by Dayle McGaha

Browning High Power Rifle .30-'06, ca. 1969, s/n L69
Built in Belgium, this factory sporter was intended to compete with the many custom arms offered in the 1960s.
Donated by Browning

Winslow Arms Custom Rifle .243 Winchester, ca. 1976, s/n 20372.
Offered from 1963–1996, Winslow's custom bolt guns were built on FN Mauser actions.
Donated by the Estate of Tom Sciaca

Savage Model 110 Rifle .30-'06, ca. 1970, s/n 46777.
Nicholas Brewer, who created many Stevens and Savage arms, focused on a simple bolt-action design that was easy to produce.
Donated by Savage Arms

Anschutz Model 1813 Target Rifle *.22 LR, ca. 1985, s/n 210508.*
The top-of-the-line for smallbore target competition, featuring an ergonomically adjustable stock.
Donated by Anschutz

Knight MK85 Prototype Inline Rifle *.50 cal., ca. 1985, s/n 1.*
This is the prototype of the in-line design that revolutionized modern muzzleloading hunting.
Donated by William A. Knight

Browning Lever Action Rifle *.308 Win. ca. 1994, s/n 36790K72.*
The "BLR" is offered in several calibers and features a "rack-and-pinion" geared lever. The box magazine allows the use of pointed "spitzer" bullets which would be unsafe in a tubular magazine rifle.
Donated by the Estate of Bertha A. Baier

Remington Model 760 Rifle *.30-'06, ca. 1960, s/n 352161.*
Built from 1952 to 1961, this pump-action was offered in both rifle and carbine configurations.
Donated by Remington

Ruger Model Number 1 Rifle *.45-70, ca. 1994, s/n 130-00061.*
Based on the Scottish Farquharson falling-block action, this single shot was introduced in 1967.
Donated by the Estate of Bertha A. Baier

Remington M700 Left Handed Rifle *.270 Winchester, ca. 1988, s/n 6628405.*
Catering to the 7% of the population that are left-handed, Remington offers several LH models.
Donated by Titus Crow

Browning Automatic Rifle *.300 Win. Mag., ca. 2000, s/n 137PR27958.*
The "BAR" gas-operated design incorporates a hinged box magazine.
Donated by Dr. Sheldon Gilbert

Ruger Deerfield Semi-Automatic Carbine *.44 Mag., ca. 1975, s/n 102-94824.*
First marketed as the Deerstalker, this model was discontinued in 1985.
Donated by Jack Strader

Colt AR-15 Semi-Automatic Sporter Rifle *.223 Rem, ca. 1999, s/n CCH010959.*
The AR pattern rifle has become the most popular type of centerfire sporting rifle in America.
The straight-line stock and pistol grip minimize muzzle rise and allow better control.
Donated by Rick Steeley

SPORTING SHOTGUNS   The hunter's selection of effective and reliable shotguns has never been wider. While the pump action has probably proven the most popular in recent decades, semi-auto designs have come on strong. The classic side-by-side double barrel has mostly given way to over-under designs, bolt action shotguns have seen some limited success, and there is nothing the repeating designs can do that the humble single shot can't do equally well—(at least for the first shot!)

Remington Model 1100 Shotgun, *12 ga., ca. 1963, s/n 1234V.*
This gas-operated design replaced the long recoil system of the 11-48 shotgun.
Donated by Remington Arms Company

Winchester Model 59 Semi-Automatic Shotgun *12 ga., ca. 1960, s/n 2797.*
Incorporating an unusual glass fiber wrapped steel barrel, this was made only from 1959–1963.
Donated by the Estate of Walter J. Burchan

Franchi Semi-Automatic Shotgun *12 ga., ca. 1952, s/n D73883.*
Franchi began production of inertia-driven, long-recoil shotguns in the 1950s with the Model 48AL.
Donated by Jack Strader

High Standard C-200 Sportmatic Trophy Shotgun *12 ga., ca. 1960.*
High Standard, better known for handgun manufacture, entered into shotgun production in the 1950s.

TEN MILLIONTH MILESTONES FOR AMERICA'S MOST POPULAR SHOTGUNS

The pump-action Remington Model 870 and Mossberg Model 500 are the most popular smooth-bores in America. These are the 10 millionth made specimens of each.
The Remington 870 is the most manufactured shotgun in history. Introduced in 1951, this s/n 10,000,000 was made in 2009 and is on loan from Remington Arms Company.
The Mossberg 500 was introduced in 1961, and reached the 10 millionth milestone faster than any other shotgun, with this s/n U500,000 made in 2013 and donated to the NRA by Mossberg Arms.

J. C. Higgins M583-4 Bolt-Action Shotgun *12 ga., ca. 1965.*
The late 19th through mid-20th century saw large numbers of firearms made by gun manufacturers for large distributors and retailers, marked with the ultimate seller's "trade name," such as this High Standard made for Sears & Roebuck to market as their J. C. Higgins house brand.

Remington Model XP-100 Pistol, *.221 Fireball, ca. 1995, s/n B7504539.*
This bolt action single shot pistol was offered from 1963 to 1998. When introduced, the .221 Fireball was the fastest handgun round available.
Donated by Istvan Nemes

Harrington & Richardson M58 Topper Shotgun *12 ga., ca 1980.*
Available with interchangeable shotgun and rifle barrels.
Donated by the Estate of John Kozina

Wildey Semi-Automatic Pistol *.45 Win. Mag., ca. 2010, s/n 17168.*
Created by Wildey J. Moore, this gas-operated pistol utilizes a three-lug rotating bolt.
Donated by Veronica Walker

Beretta M686 Onyx Over/Under Shotgun *12 ga., ca. 2000, s/n P02805B.*
Featuring a standard automatic safety, this sporting version also has a longer stock length.
Donated by Dr. Sheldon Gilbert

Ruger Red Label Over Under Shotgun *12 ga., ca. 2000, s/n 410-19068.*
Features a cast stainless steel receiver.
Donated by Dr. Sheldon Gilbert

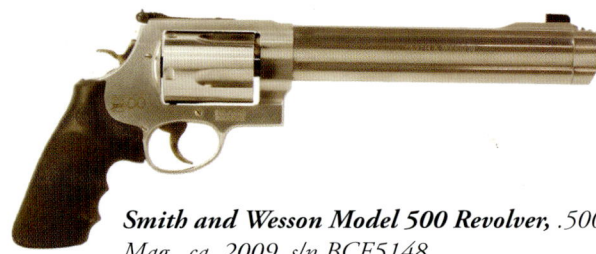

Smith and Wesson Model 500 Revolver, *.500 Mag., ca. 2009, s/n BCE5148.*
Considered the most powerful production revolver in the world, the M500 can generate over 3,000 ft/lbs of muzzle energy.
Donated by the Estate of William & Virginia Waterman

Antonio Zoli Z-90 O/U Shotgun. *12 ga., ca. 1979, s/n 193634.*
Produced in the Gardone valley of Italy.
Donated by the Estate of Art Blatt

HUNTING HANDGUNS

Although using full-size accurate .22 handguns for small game and pot hunting at close range had been a common practice for decades, it wasn't until the introduction of the powerful .44 Magnum cartridge in 1955 that handgun hunting of medium and large game became a serious and humane sporting pursuit. Since then a healthy range of hunting handguns has been produced.

Thompson Center Contender Pistol,
ca. 1969, s/n 9018.
Interchangeable barrels make this a single-shot pistol with multiple capabilities. This example is shown with quick-switch barrels for .357 Magnum., .45 Colt / .410 ga. shotshell, .223 Remington, & .256 Win.
Donated by Jack Strader

Ruger Blackhawk Revolver
.41 Mag., ca. 1983, s/n 47-04924.
A revamped version of the perennial single-action revolver, this model is offered in both rimfire and centerfire models.
Donated by Ryan McKillips

Ruger Target Model Pistol
.22 LR, ca. 1996, s/n 216-42009.
Variations of the Ruger .22 are probably the most popular rimfire pistol in America.
Donated by Ryan McKillips

Smith and Wesson Model 29 Revolver *.44 Mag. ca. 1984, s/n N786201.*
Donated by Jack Strader

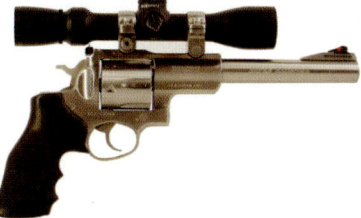

Ruger Super Redhawk Revolver
.44 Mag., ca. 1995, s/n 552-32358.
Donated by Judy Woodeson

HUNTING

WINCHESTER MODEL 70 BOLT ACTION RIFLE
Collection donated by Melvin Gordon

The Winchester Model 70 bolt action rifle has been called "The Rifleman's Rifle" as a tribute to the success and high regard that this remarkable gun has had since its introduction in 1936. Using elements from the Mauser bolt action design as well as its predecessor, the Winchester Model 54, the Model 70 quickly gained attention as one of the finest civilian bolt action rifles ever made. It was manufactured in three dozen calibers and offers the collector a myriad of variations, enhancements, and model types to collect.

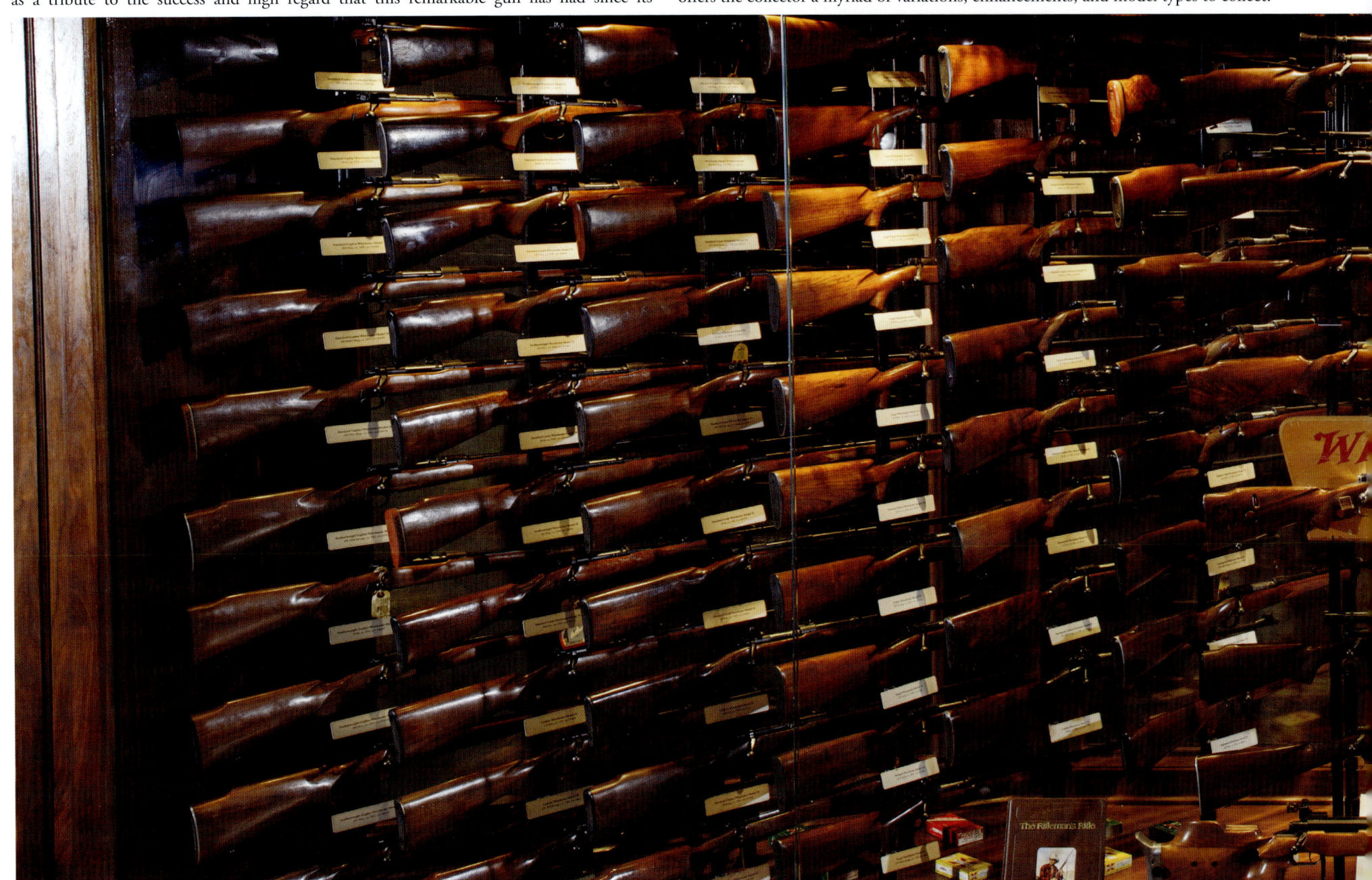

WINCHESTER MODEL 70

In 1964, with over 580,000 produced, the manufacturing process was streamlined and the Model continued in production through today. However, collectors eagerly seek out classic "Pre-64" Winchesters.

This stunning collection of Pre-1964 Winchester Model 70s includes every production caliber, numerous variations, and several prototypes, including the M70 Free Rifle and the unique radio-stocked Winchester.

WINCHESTER MODEL 70

Facing page -

EARLY WINCHESTER MODEL 70 RIFLES, left to right:

* ***Two digit s/n, .30-06, Standard Rifle Win. Mod. 70,*** *ca. 1935, s/n 17. First year production.*

* ***.220 Swift, Early Target Model Win. Mod. 70,*** *ca. 1939, s/n 19738.*

* ***.375 Holland & Holland, First Model Win. Mod. 70,*** *ca. 1936, s/n 674.*

THE RADIO RIFLE

Chrome Plated Radio Stock Win. Mod. 70, .308 Win., ca. 1956, s/n 385941.
Shortly after the invention of the transistor radio, Winchester experimented with building a radio into the buttstock. The feedback from the marketplace was clear - the American hunter did not need a highly reflective chrome-plated rifle playing "Rock Around the Clock" in the deer stand. As a result, this prototype is the only one in existence.

EXPERIMENTAL FREE TARGET RIFLE

.308 Win. Win. Mod. 70, ca. 1950, s/n 3.
Three free rifle concept guns were built for testing for specialized target competition. This is the only one that left the factory.

HUNTING

Basic configurations of the Model 70 - The Winchester Model 70 was manufactured in three primary configurations—Rifle, Carbine, and Featherweight. Each of these was offered in Standard Grade and Super Grade. Here are right and left side views of each configuration, listed top to bottom:

WINCHESTER MODEL 70

Top pair:
* Rifle, Standard Grade
* Rifle, Super Grade

Middle pair:
* Carbine, Standard Grade
* Carbine, Super Grade

Bottom pair:
* Featherweight, Standard Grade
* Featherweight, Super Grade

Winchester Model 70 Target Variations, top to bottom:

* *National Match,* .30-06, ca. 1950, s/n 159554.
* *Target Model,* .300 Savage, ca. 1949, s/n 121781. Rare caliber, only 362 made.
* *Bull Gun,* .22 Hornet, ca. 1953, s/n 265948.
* *Light Target Model,* .22 Hornet, ca. 1944-47, s/n 59838.

CALIBERS OF THE WINCHESTER MODEL 70

The Model 70 was made for a wide range of cartridges, from the diminutive .22 Hornet to the massive .458 Winchester Magnum (offered only as Super Grade African variation). Total production for each chambering ranged from over 208,000 for the .30-06 to only 362 for the .300 Savage.

Winchester Model 70

Standard production chamberings included (listed in order from most produced to fewest):

1.) .30-06	4.) .308 Win.	7.) .22 Hornet	10.) .375 H&H Magnum	13.) .250/3000 Savage	16.) .458 Win. Magnum
2.) .270 WCF	5.) .300 H&H Magnum	8.) .220 Swift	11.) .338 Win. Magnum	14.) .358 Win. Magnum	17.) .35 Rem.
3.) .243 Win.	6.) .264 Win. Mag.	9.) .257 Roberts	12.) .300 Win. Magnum	15.) 7mm	18.) .300 Savage

SPECIAL ORDER CHAMBERINGS

In addition to the standard offerings, a very limited number of Winchester Model 70s were manufactured for non-cataloged calibers.

Top - .25-35 Win., Standard Rifle, ca. 1940, s/n 28201.
This extremely rare chambering may be the only one ever made.

Bottom - .30-30 Win., Standard Rifle, ca. 1955, s/n 325615.
Extremely rare special order chambering.

WINCHESTER MODEL 70

METRIC CARTRIDGES

The 7mm was the only standard cataloged "metric" chambering for the Winchester Model 70. However, a very small number were made on special order or as experimental rifles for other metric calibers.

Top to bottom:

* ***9x57 mm, Standard Rifle,*** *ca. 1948, s/n 91199.*
* ***7.65x53mm, Standard Rifle,*** *ca. 1942, s/n 55613.*
* ***7.92x57mm, aka 8mm Mauser, R&D Standard Model,*** *ca. 1953, s/n 277802. This was a factory Research & Development rifle.*

EXPERIMENTAL NON-STANDARD CONFIGURATIONS

* *Top -* **27/65 Duplex Prototype Research & Development Win. Mod. 70,** *ca. 1954, s/n 314724. Rare experimental chambering.*

* *Bottom -* **Straight stock .358 Win., Featherweight Win. Mod. 70,** *ca. 1955, s/n 354183.*

CONSERVATION

HISTORY OF AMERICAN CONSERVATION

Since the arrival of the first humans, the North American continent has been home to hunters. From that time on, hunters have had significant positive and negative effects on wildlife populations. Uncontrolled and unregulated hunting pushed some species near and to extinction. However, recent conservation efforts supported and spearheaded by hunters have brought species back from the brink, created or enhanced wildlife habitat, and helped maintain the delicate balance between nature and human progress, thus ensuring the protection and proliferation of numerous species.

The earliest example of humans driving species to extinction occurred more than 10,000 years ago during the Quaternary extinction event. Throughout this time, the North American continent saw the disappearance of megafaunal land-dwelling animals including an ancient species of bison, the American mastodon, and ground sloths. One hypothesis for this mass extinction is that Paleo-Indians over-hunted these slow, vulnerable animals. Within 1,000 years of human arrival in North America, 80 percent of large mammal species had disappeared.

Modern humans did not fully recognize the need for conservation until the late 19th century when the passenger pigeon faced extinction. At the time of European contact, the passenger pigeon was the most prolific bird in the country, with numbers estimated from 3 to 5 billion. They were

extinct by 1914. Why? A combination of unregulated market hunting, habitat loss from westward expansion, and their unique need to roost in large groups. Highly social animals, passenger pigeons travelled in huge flocks only matched by swarms of locusts. These large groups made them easy targets for hunters. Once their numbers had fallen to a certain point, the breakdown of their social structure prevented them from breeding.

Their dwindling numbers did not go unnoticed. In the mid-1800s, conservationists tried to intervene to save the species by passing protective legislation that would limit the hunting of the bird. Many of the laws failed to pass and those that did were not enforced. Once the need for protection became obvious, it was too late. The numbers of the passenger pigeon had been so reduced that the birds could no longer mate. The last known passenger pigeon, Martha, died on September 1, 1914, at the Cincinnati Zoo where zoologists had tried to establish a breeding program for the species.

The second American conservation attempt, which was to save the American bison, had marked success by comparison. At the time of European contact, an estimated 60 million bison roamed the American landscape. By 1890, this number had dwindled to around a thousand. The animals were hunted mercilessly for their skins; the rest of the body was left to rot. Additionally, the U.S. government supported their mass slaughter as a way to garner more land for cattle, clear the

Photograph from the mid-1870s of a pile of American bison skulls waiting to be ground for fertilizer.

conservation efforts over the next century have helped to gradually increase the bison population. Currently, the once near extinct species has recovered to an estimated 400,000 animals. Granted many of those animals are not free roaming but instead raised for commercial purposes. However, the resurgence of the species nonetheless marks the first successful conservation campaign in North America.

The campaign to save the bison was part of the greater conservation movement in the United States, the height of which spanned from 1880 to 1920. During this time, conservationists sought to balance the success of society's industrial progress while still preserving the integrity of the all-sustaining natural environment. The clarion call was sent out to citizens and governments to conserve and protect America's wildlife, wild lands, and other natural resources that were potentially threatened by industrialization. Avid hunters were some of the first responders. In 1887, Theodore Roosevelt founded the Boone and Crockett Club, a hunter-conservationist organization that helped define hunting ethics, expanded and protected national parks, helped outlaw

commercial market hunting, and established funding mechanisms for future conservation efforts.

During this time the recognized need for conservation reached the federal government, thanks in large part to Theodore Roosevelt who is credited with the institutionalization of the conservation movement. With his guidance and urgings, the federal government established the National Park Service, National Forests, and numerous policies for protecting fish and wildlife. The Forest Reserve Act of 1891 allowed the President to set aside land in the public domain to expand National Forests. The Lacey Act of 1900 made it illegal to trade in wildlife, fish, or plants that had been illegally taken, possessed, transported, or sold. This reduced both market hunting and the introduction of non-native species. The Migratory Bird Act of 1918 made it illegal to pursue, hunt, take, capture, kill, or sell over 800 different species of birds.

In addition to legislation, conservation efforts led to the hiring of game wardens and conservation officers responsible for enforcing the new laws pertaining to hunting, fishing, and trapping. These

plains for railroad tracks, and weaken Indian populations by removing their main food source, thus pressuring them onto reservations.

Troubled by their declining numbers, conservationists and sportsmen alike became determined to save the bison. Such individuals included President Theodore

Roosevelt and zoologist William T. Hornaday who helped form the American Bison Society in 1905. The organization sought to raise public awareness of the decimated herds as well as money to form bison preserves. Both private and public

Sharps Model 1874 Rifle - *The buffalo hunter on the facing page is using the Sharps single shot rifle, considered by many to be the quintessential buffalo rifle. These are marked "Old Reliable" on the barrel and served for bison in .40, .44, .45 and .50 centerfire calibers. This one is chambered in .45-100 and was shipped to a trader in northern Texas, suggesting it was probably used as a buffalo rifle. The Remington Rolling Block was also widely used by buffalo hunters.*
Loaned by Doug Wicklund

state and local officials are responsible for a wide range of duties including ensuring proper licensing of hunters, assisting landowners in finding solutions to wildlife damage, teaching conservation and wildlife management classes to the public, keeping invasive species in check, monitoring animal populations, and many other duties that help to promote the balance between society and nature.

To those unfamiliar with modern conservation efforts, it may seem ironic that many species might not survive at all if it were not for the sportsmen who hunt them. Though hunting began as a primal survival need, it has since evolved into a recreational form of sustainable use that generates conservation stakeholders, incentives, and revenue. Ethical and regulated hunting has served as the most important conservation development and biggest contribution to conservation efforts in modern American society. Those who legally, safely, and ethically pursue their quarry are the most effective means of direct conservation efforts in the United States.

Woodchuck Shooting *by G. Ryder, Loaned by Remington Arms Co.*

Hunting generates billions of dollars through retail sales that help promote conservation. Many nonprofit conservation organizations sell hunting gear and memberships with a percentage of proceeds going to conservation efforts. Since 1937, Ducks Unlimited has conserved more than 11 million acres of wetlands and uplands using funds from the sale of memberships and hunting gear as well as donations. Other hunting retail companies form corporate sponsorships with nonprofit conservation organizations wherein a portion of the company's proceeds are donated to the nonprofit. For example, Bass Pro Shops partners with many nonprofit conservation organizations, including the National Fish and Wildlife Foundation, Ducks Unlimited, Rocky Mountain Elk Foundation, National Wild Turkey Federation, and Quality Deer Management Association. These mutually beneficial partnerships generate revenue for the nonprofit while the business gains exposure, contact, and recognition among the stakeholders of the nonprofit, thus attracting more customers.

Perhaps the biggest retail contributions to conservation come from the sale of ammunition and firearms. In 1937, Congress passed the Pittman-Robertson Act, also known as the Federal Aid in Wildlife Restoration Act, with strong hunter support and cooperation from state and federal government, conservation groups, and the firearms industry.

The Act and its subsequent amendments created excise taxes to help fund conservation efforts. These taxes include 11% of the wholesale price for long guns, ammunition, and archery equipment as well as 10% of the wholesale price for handguns. The tax applies to all commercial sales and imports. When sportsmen purchase such equipment, the revenue generated by the tax is appropriated to the Secretary of the Interior and deposited in the Wildlife Restoration Account. These earmarked dollars are then distributed to the states on a formula basis by the U.S. Fish and Wildlife Service through a grant program that pays up to 75 percent of cost-approved projects. Funds from the account are available to states in the form of grants, which support wildlife restoration projects, hunter education, and shooting range development. While hunters and target shooters are the primary source of funds for wildlife restoration, all U.S. citizens benefit from their contributions. Since the Pittman-Robertson Wildlife Restoration program began, the program has collected more than $7.15 billion in manufacturers' excise taxes and awarded this to states for wildlife conservation efforts, while states have provided their required match of over $1.78 billion.

In addition to Wildlife Restoration funds, hunters also contribute to conservation efforts by purchasing hunting licenses, permits, and tags each season, which generates millions of dollars for state wildlife management agencies. Purchases of the Federal Duck Stamp, required by the federal government to hunt migratory waterfowl, has produced more than $700 million. These funds are used by the government to buy and lease wetland for waterfowl refuges and production. Since the stamps were first issued in 1934, 5.2 million acres have been added to the National Wildlife Refuge System. Lottery hunting licenses also earn revenue for conservation. Many hunters will pay to enter lotteries for certain large game, but only a few will be offered the opportunity to purchase a hunting permit if selected. The two-pronged payment system generates revenue that is typically distributed to the state in order to conserve the habitats of the specified game and other species.

In addition to their monetary contributions, hunters have become essential components in wildlife management. By obeying bag limits set by state wildlife management agencies, hunters assist with population control and cull herds before they exceed carrying capacity, thus preventing winter die-off when food is scarce. They protect biodiversity and the delicate balance for the environment. With guidance from agencies, hunters also assist in removing invasive species from non-native environments. Hunters are a vital component to protecting and promoting America's biodiversity. With their financial and real-world contributions, these men and women ensure that the once-vital, turned-recreational pastime of hunting will be undertaken legally, ethically, and with deference to future generations of hunters.

The Scarecrow by G. Ryder.
Loaned by Remington Arms Co.

THEODORE ROOSEVELT:
CONSERVATIONIST

"We are prone to speak of the resources of this country as inexhaustible; this is not so."

– Theodore Roosevelt, Message to Congress, December 3, 1907.

Theodore Roosevelt, our 26th Chief Executive, was a man of many interests and pursuits. He was by far our most active and dynamic President. During his short 60 years of life, he wrote 39 books, 150,000 letters, visited every continent save for one, and fathered six children. He is the only person to be awarded both the Medal of Honor and the Nobel Peace Prize. The list could go on and on for many pages but we remember him here as a hunter and conservationist.

A true lover of the outdoors.

A sportsman with vision.

Some people today would be perplexed at how anyone who hunted with great zeal could be considered a conservationist and friend of wildlife. Are not the two at polar opposites from each other? Would it not be seen as hypocritical of someone to espouse publicly that they were a lover of wildlife and then proceed to go on a safari where he personally harvested an average of two animals a day, for an entire year?

Thankfully for our sake, Theodore Roosevelt lived and prospered in an age when the American public wasn't so easily duped into believing the worst about someone every time their name appeared in print. It was TR who truly began and mentored the fledgling movement of conservationists that today has paid rich rewards in dividends over 100 years later and has survived to fulfill many of the visions TR had for our future.

Young Theodore Roosevelt loved two things – shooting and hunting. The fact that he could combine the two activities was enough to fill him with boundless excitement. He established the Roosevelt Museum of Natural History in a corridor by his bedroom in the fashionable Gramercy Park brownstone where he'd been

Photograph showing Kermit Roosevelt and two men, one with a rifle, squatting around a dead animal as Theodore Roosevelt looks on.

On the great bear hunt - President Roosevelt after leaving Newcastle for the mountains - Colorado

born on New York City's East 20th St. He filled the museum with specimens that he had harvested and preserved via self-taught taxidermy – a skill at which he was quite proficient. He was the mini-museum's Director, Curator, Registrar, and chief donor.

He was not yet ten years of age.

So it is here, at the age of nine, that we see the first vestiges of the mindset that would guide him for the rest of his life, a mindset that still guides us today. Hunting was not something to be done for the mere sake of taking a life. It was here, in the back corridor of the brownstone, that the ethics of a hunter were formed.

Although TR never wore his religious convictions on his sleeve, he was a devout Christian and was more than familiar with this biblical passage from Genesis Chapter 9 –

And God blessed Noah and his sons and said to them, 'Be fruitful and multiply and fill the earth. The fear of you and the dread of you shall be upon every beast of the earth and upon every bird of the heavens, upon everything that creeps on the ground and all the fish of the sea. Into your hand they are delivered. Every moving thing that lives shall be food for you. And as I gave you the green plants, I give you everything. But you shall not eat flesh with its life, that is, its blood. And for your lifeblood I will require a reckoning: from every beast I will require it and from man.'

To young Theodore, as he interpreted the Old Testament passage, for every life taken, a debt is owed. It was the duty of the hunter to ensure that the hunted were given fair chase and that nothing was wasted. It was this morality that guided TR in his efforts to study nature and develop a sense of who and what he wished to become later in life.

THEODORE ROOSEVELT

He was not yet twenty years old when he and a fellow Harvard classmate wrote and published *The Summer Birds of the Adirondacks in Franklin County, N.Y.* He seemed destined to be a naturalist and it was sometime deep into his educational career at Harvard that he decided to abandon his naturalist pursuits for the more practical and financially stable field of law, public service, and eventually elected office.

Shortly after he married Alice Hathaway Lee in 1883, he ventured into the west to hunt an American Bison. It was during this hunt, and the difficulties that he encountered in even finding just one specimen to shoot, that he became aware

Theodore Roosevelt diorama at NRA National Sporting Arms Museum

of, and even alarmed at, the fact that a once thriving herd that numbered in the tens of millions had been reduced to near extinction. In his book, *Hunting Trips of a Ranchman*, written shortly after this experience, he lays out his thoughts on managed hunting and the responsibility hunters have, not only to the species of wildlife they hunt, but to future generations that will benefit from the continued prosperity of their kind.

These thoughts on wildlife are easily transferred, and the same logic applied, to all aspects of nature and natural resources. In 1887, TR co-founded the Boone & Crockett Club that has as its mission statement: "To increase humanities' awareness and understanding of wildlife and the ecosystems we all share and our influence on the

natural and cultural resources of these ecosystems."

After he became President in 1901, Roosevelt used his authority to protect wildlife and public lands by creating the U.S. Forest Service and establishing 51 Federal Bird Reservations, 4 National Game Preserves, 150 National Forests, 5 National Parks, and 18 National Monuments. During his presidency, Theodore Roosevelt protected approximately 230 million acres of public land.

TR brought the same full-speed-ahead robust enthusiasm to the presidency that typified his other pursuits. In 1903, President Roosevelt wanted to declare Pelican Island off the coast of Florida a federal wildlife refuge. With no statute authorizing the creation of wildlife refuges, Roosevelt had a government attorney investigate the status of any law that would allow him to create refuges.

Several days later, returning from the Justice department, the lawyer reported that no such law existed.

Roosevelt inquired, "But, is there a law to prevent it?"

The attorney responded that there was not.

"Very well," Roosevelt quickly added, "I so declare it!"

Pelican Island became the first of fifty-five wildlife preserves declared by the President. Since then, 500 others, in all the other states, comprise today's National Wildlife Refuge System.

Roosevelt also did much to popularize hunting. His famous 1902 bear hunt in Mississippi was so overstocked with reporters that a single cartoon about the trip launched a worldwide plush toy phenomenon that continues to this day – the Teddy bear.

The Inaugural Address of his successor, William Howard Taft, hardly had time to

settle upon those who heard it before Theodore was aboard the SS Hamburg and off to Africa for a yearlong safari on behalf of the Smithsonian Institution. His exploits were followed closely by the American public, first in the pages of Scribner's Magazine and then as a bestselling book entitled *African Game Trails*. In it he wrote:

"The mere size of the bag indicates little as to a man's prowess as a hunter, and almost nothing as to the interest or value of his achievement."

Here he again gave us a glimpse of the code by which he hunted. The hunt was not at all about the numbers killed, but the benefit that each cull had for the museum, the porters and the local community as well as the scientific community at large.

BEGINNING OF THE MILLENNIUM
The President says that on this trip west probably not a shot will be fired.

A PRACTICAL FORESTER
(A subject that had attention all through Mr. Roosevelt's Presidency.)
From the *Pioneer Press* (St. Paul)

Perhaps the best example of the mindset of TR and his quest to preserve and conserve is revealed in a quote from his speech dedicating the Grand Canyon as a National Park:

'In the Grand Canyon, Arizona has a natural wonder which is in kind absolutely unparalleled throughout the rest of the world. I want to ask you to keep this great wonder of nature as it now is. I hope you will not have a building of any kind, not a summer cottage, a hotel or anything else, to mar the wonderful grandeur, the sublimity, the great loneliness and beauty of the canyon. Leave it as it is. You cannot improve on it. The ages have been at work on it, and man can only mar it.'

As well as in a speech he gave a few years later, after his return from Africa:

'Conservation means development as much as it does protection. I recognize the right and duty of this generation to develop and use the natural resources of our land but I do not recognize the right to waste them, or to rob, by wasteful use, the generations that come after us... Moreover, I believe that the natural resources must be used for the benefit of all our people,

and not monopolized for the benefit of the few... Of all the questions which can come before this nation, short of the actual preservation of its existence in a great war, there is none which compares in importance with the great central task of leaving this land even a better land for our descendants than it is for us, and training them into a better race to inhabit the land and pass it on. Conservation is a great moral issue, for it involves the patriotic duty of insuring the safety and continuance of the nation.'

- Speech at Osawatomie, Kansas, on August 31, 1910

There has never been another like him, or even close for that matter. A hero in war, as well a generous peacemaker. An avid hunter and yet a conservationist. He was able to show the country then, as his example continues to show us today, that these were not virtues in conflict but ones that are essential to the well being and stability of the other.

HENRY CABOT LODGE's S&W New Model Number Three .44 Russian, s/n 21060.
This revolver was a gift from Theodore Roosevelt to Henry Cabot Lodge (1850 – 1924). A native of Massachusetts and graduate of Harvard, Lodge was a personal friend of Theodore Roosevelt and considered his closest political confidant.
Lodge served in the US House of Representatives prior to being elected Senator of Massachusetts in 1893, a seat he would hold for 30 years. He served as Senate Majority Leader as well as President Pro Tem during his career. He is perhaps best known for thwarting President Woodrow Wilson's hopes that the US Senate would ratify membership in the League of Nations.
Loaned by Jim Supica

CONSERVATION

LEONARD WOOD (1860 – 1927)

was Theodore Roosevelt's commander in the "Rough Riders" 1st U.S. Volunteer Cavalry. They became fast friends. Wood was one of only a handful of close advisors that TR would retain for his lifetime, and one who could speak candidly and even sternly to Roosevelt.

Upon graduating Harvard Medical School, he became an Army contract surgeon and was awarded the Medal of Honor in 1886 for carrying dispatches through hostile territory and leading hand to hand combat against the Apache in the last Geronimo campaign. In the 1890s he returned to graduate studies at Georgia Tech where he became the school's second head football coach, and then served as personal physician to Presidents Cleveland and McKinley.

After leading the Rough Riders, at the turn of the century he became Military Governor of Cuba and the U.S. military commander in the Philippines. By 1910, he was the Army Chief of Staff. He was one of the first patients to undergo successful brain surgery to remove a tumor.

Wood was a candidate for the Republican Presidential nomination in 1920, after which he served as Military Governor of the Philippines. When he died in 1927, he was buried in Arlington Cemetery, and his brain kept at Yale. Fort Leonard Wood in the Missouri Ozarks is named after him.

BRIGADIER GENERAL THEODORE ROOSEVELT JR.

(1887–1944) along with his brother Kermit (1889–1943) used this rifle to hunt Giant Pandas in the Himalayas for the Field Museum of Chicago. The two specimens they brought back were the first ever to be seen in the Western world and gave scientists much needed information about the panda that was previously unknown. Both bears are still currently on display.

Ted, as he was known to his family, graduated from Harvard in 1909, served with distinction during World War 1, became Assistant Secretary of the Navy, Governor of Puerto Rico, and Governor General of the Philippines. He was a founder of the American Legion. During the Second World War, he served as Assistant Division Commander of the 1st and 4th Divisions and was the only General Officer to hit the beaches of Normandy on D Day in the first assault wave. For his heroic accomplishments on Utah Beach he was awarded the Medal of Honor. He died of heart failure in France on July 12, 1944, just as he was promoted to Major General and given full command of the 90th Division.

Gen. Omar N. Bradley and Gen. George S. Patton referred to Ted as the bravest soldier they had ever known. Perhaps the greatest praise of him came from his father, who, when told that Ted always felt that he might not live up to expectations and be worthy of his father, the former President replied, "Worthy of me? Why I am so very proud of him. He has won high honor not only for his children but, like the Chinese, he has ennobled his ancestors. I walk with my head higher because of him."

GEN. LEONARD WOOD'S S&W REVOLVERS, *Smith & Wesson .44 Double Action, .44 Russian, ca. 1905, s/n 47550. and Smith & Wesson .38 Double Action, .38 S&W, ca. 1901, s/n 399155. Loaned by Jim Supica*

GEN. THEODORE ROOSEVELT, JR.'S WINCHESTER MODEL 1895, *.405 WCF, ca. 1925, s/n 419806.*
Loaned by Philip Schreier

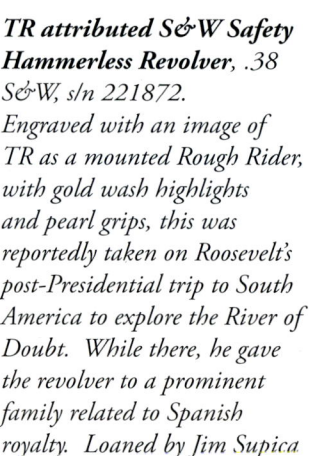

THEODORE ROOSEVELT'S S&W New Model Number Three, .38 U.S. Service caliber, ca. 1898, s/n 32661.
Roosevelt received this factory engraved revolver in May of 1898 just as he left New York for San Antonio to train the Rough Riders. It is one of only a handful of this model chambered for the then new .38 U.S. Service cartridge. It is believed he intended to take this revolver to Cuba in the Spanish American War. Photo by Paul Goodwin.
Loaned by Jim Supica

TR attributed S&W Safety Hammerless Revolver, .38 S&W, s/n 221872.
Engraved with an image of TR as a mounted Rough Rider, with gold wash highlights and pearl grips, this was reportedly taken on Roosevelt's post-Presidential trip to South America to explore the River of Doubt. While there, he gave the revolver to a prominent family related to Spanish royalty. Loaned by Jim Supica

ROOSEVELT'S WHITE HOUSE NIGHTSTAND PISTOL
FN Browning Model 1899, .32 ACP, ca. 1900, s/n 8664.
Theodore Roosevelt kept this pearl handled, banknote scroll engraved, gold inlaid pistol by his bedside both in the White House and at his Sagamore Hill home. Family legend holds that Mrs.
Roosevelt taught her grandchildren how to shoot with this pistol from the back porch at Sagamore Hill.
Donated by Cornelius Van Schaack Roosevelt III

THEODORE ROOSEVELT'S
*Frederick Adolph Double Rifle,
.500-450 Nitro Express, ca. 1910,
s/n 4108.*
*President Theodore Roosevelt was
given this rifle by noted German
arms maker Frederick Adolph. It
is engraved by Rudolph Kornbrath
and bears the seal of the United
States over each chamber.
Donated by Owen Albert, Courtesy
of Ron Peterson*

*Theodore Roosevelt and John Muir
(Founder of Sierra Club) on Glacier
Point, Yosemite Valley, California, in
1903*

THE FUTURE OF CONSERVATION

Today hunting is a staple of a vast network of wildlife biologists, outdoor enthusiasts, recreational shooters, conservationists, and those who enjoy the sport of fair chase. Billions of dollars are provided by hunters annually through licenses and fees to preserve and protect wildlife habitat and refuge areas. This much needed income comes from the hunters themselves and provides state departments of natural resources the necessary help to study wildlife and to better manage the ecosystems that we rely on for our own continued survival.

Here, the father carries a Weatherby Model 82, 12 ga. (*donated by Dr. Sheldon Gilbert*) while the daughter fields a Browning Magnum 20, 20 ga. (*donated by Joseph Kerensky, Jr.*).

AMERICAN MILITARY LONG GUNS

Firearms and freedom have been intermingled in America's history from the beginning. The Second Amendment to the Constitution (ratified in 1787) guaranteed Americans the right to keep and bear arms. That Amendment itself is just twenty-seven words: "A well regulated militia, being necessary to the security of a free state, the right of the people to keep and bear arms, shall not be infringed." Early American leaders including George Mason and Thomas Jefferson understood that the militia (and the arms held by these individuals) provided protection for the colonies, and were the bulwark against a government that went beyond its lawful powers and ruled by force.

More than two centuries later the U.S. Supreme Court in 2008 and 2010 affirmed that the American right to arms is an individual and personal right, and not a collective military right.

The military of the United States of America initially won American freedom and has preserved it since. It is founded on the personal role of individual volunteer armed citizens who formed the initial colonial militia units, and that tradition remains strong today.

It has been said that the 2nd Amendment is not about hunting and it goes far beyond target shooting as well. The consequences of the American Revolution and the resulting new form of government, based on the newly written Constitution and the Bill of Rights, were studied by many in other lands. In China, Mao Tse-Tung implicitly knew that his political power grew from the barrel of a gun and noted (in his little red book) that: "Our Principle is that the Party commands the gun, and the gun must never be allowed to command the Party."

The contrast with the founding of America is strong, where a revolution to establish a republic, overthrowing tyranny, came to be won and the individual right to bear arms held by individuals would uphold that change in power. In other political systems, firearms are feared by governments that seek to deny or take them away – for the right to keep and bear firearms is just the first of the many personal rights that any oppressive government will seek to remove.

This exhibit in the NRA National Sporting Arms Museum is a 21 gun salute to America's armed forces. From a flintlock musket actually used in the Revolutionary War through the types of guns carried by today's American heroes, it proudly displays some of the primary firearms that have been used to protect and preserve the United States.

The first exhibit in the Second Amendment Gallery is a 21 Gun Salute to America's Armed Forces.
These arms trace the history of the long guns of the American military from the Revolutionary War to today.

French Charleville Musket *.72 cal., ca. 1768.*
The French Charleville and the British Brown Bess were the predominant long guns of the American Revolution. This Charleville was carried by Edward Cox in the Revolutionary War.
Donated by Dr. William L. and Collette M. Roberts

U.S. Springfield Model 1808 Musket *.69 cal., ca. 1824.*
Early American military flintlock muskets followed the French Charleville design.
Donated by Dr. Harold Cottle

U.S. Harpers Ferry Model 1816 Musket *.69 cal., ca. 1835.*
This pattern was made at both Harpers Ferry and Springfield National Armories.
Donated by Mildred Gettings

U.S. Hall Model 1819 Breechloading Rifle *.52 cal., ca. 1837.*
The Hall was America's first military breechloading rifle.
Donated by the Estate of Major Gordon Bess, U.S.A.

U.S. Contract Percussion Conversion Musket *.69 cal., ca. 1846.*
To supplement government armory production, contracts were awarded to commercial gun makers for military arms.

U.S. Contract Model 1842 Musket. *69 cal., ca. 1847.*
Mexican War era.

U.S. Springfield Model 1855 Rifle *.58 cal., ca. 1855.*
Maynard tape priming system.

U.S. Model 1863 Rifle Musket *.58 cal., ca. 1863.*
Springfield Armory and many contractors produced
this type of rifle during the Civil War.

Enfield Pattern 1853 Rifled Musket. *.577 cal., ca. 1862.*
Considered to be the finest infantry arm in the world at the time of the American Civil War.
Used by both sides, it is estimated that nearly a million were imported.
Loaned by Doug Wicklund

U.S. Springfield Model 1868 Conversion Rifle *.50 cf, ca. 1869.*
Following the American Civil War, surplus percussion muskets were converted to breechloading
configuration for metallic cartridges.
Donated by the John & Mary McConnell Living Trust in memory of Robert M. McConnell

U.S. Springfield Model 1873 Rifle *.45-70, ca. 1884, s/n 514111.*
The "trapdoor" Springfield rifles and carbines were the standard issue arms throughout most
of the Indian Wars.
Donated by C. E. Gregg

U.S. Springfield Model 1870 Rolling Block Rifle *.50-70, ca. 1871.*
Both rimfire and centerfire breechloading Remington rolling block rifles were produced at Ilion, NY.
Donated by the John & Mary McConnell Living Trust in memory of Robert M. McConnell

U.S. Remington Lee Model 1879 Rifle *.45-70, ca. 1880, s/n 9282.*
Early bolt-action arms continued to utilize the same blackpowder cartridges used in the Springfield trapdoor single-shot arms.
Donated by Dr. Harold Cottle

U.S. Winchester Model 1895 Lee Rifle *.236 Navy, ca. 1897, s/n 12590.*
The straight-pull Lee was utilized by the U.S. Marines during the Boxer Rebellion in China and by many naval units.
Donated by Dr. R. A. Flanders

U.S. Springfield Model 1892 Krag Rifle *.30-40 Krag, ca. 1894, s/n 46301.*
The first American bolt-action to utilize both smokeless powder and jacketed projectiles, the Krag-Jorgensen was adopted from a foreign design.
Donated by David Savadyga

U.S. Springfield Model 1903 Rifle *.30-06, ca. 1917, s/n 593946.*
This bolt-action, based in part on the German Mauser design, was to serve with the American military through both World Wars.
Donated by Dr. Harold Cottle

U.S. Winchester Model 1917 Rifle *.30-06, ca. 1918, s/n 260017.*
Manufactured to supplement M1903 production, this shoulder arm was actually issued in greater numbers than the '03 during the First World War.
Donated by Kenneth L. Martin

AMERICAN MILITARY LONG GUNS

U.S. Winchester M1 Garand *.30-06, ca. 1944, s/n 379519.*
Called "the greatest battle implement ever devised" by General George Patton, the semi-automatic M1 Garand was widely distributed in both European and Pacific Theaters during WWII. It is credited with giving American troops a decisive advantage over adversaries armed with bolt-action rifles.
Donated by the John & Mary McConnell Living Trust in memory of Robert M. McConnell

U.S. Winchester M1 Carbine *.30 Carbine, ca. 1945, s/n 6706459.*
More than six million carbines were produced to serve as an arm that could be issued to personnel not requiring the full size rifle.
Donated by Mildred Gettings

U.S. M14 Style Rifle *7.62mm, issued ca. early 1960s, s/n 50114.*
Following the Korean conflict, American military arms designers developed an updated 7.62mm M1-based rifle with selective-fire capability that could utilize detachable box magazines. This is a semi-auto civilian version by Federal Ordnance.
Bequest of the Estate of James Beck

U.S. Colt M16 Style Rifle *5.56mm, ca. 1965, s/n SP00122.*
U.S. military design continued to evolve during the Vietnam conflict, with a lighter caliber selective-fire design still in service today. This is an early civilian version AR-15 semi-auto.
Donated by Colt

U.S. MARTIAL PISTOLS

Featuring the F. L. Starbuck Collection

Since its beginnings in 1775, the United States military has always relied on the bravery of its servicemen to secure and maintain our liberty. Those servicemen have always relied on their firearms to get their job done. Sidearms have been an essential tool for our armed forces since the first North & Cheney pistol was made in Berlin, CT, in 1799.

The vast majority of martial pistols in this exhibit are on loan from NRA member F. L. Starbuck. The Starbuck collection includes the many types, styles, and manufacturers of U.S. military side arms from 1799–1898. In addition to all standard issue sidearms from that century of U.S. service pistols, it includes a number of extremely rare variations and experimental models. This remarkable collection traces the evolution of pistols from flintlock to percussion to centerfire, as well as from hand hewn to factory made. The story of the rise of the United States as an industrial power can be traced through the development of these single shot and revolving handguns.

At the turn of the century, reliable semi-auto pistols became available. From 1900–1911, the U.S. military conducted an extensive set of field trials and tests to select an auto-loading pistol to replace the revolvers previously in service; ultimately resulting in the adoption of the Colt Model 1911 in .45 ACP. A group of actual pistols from these trials is shown here, along with successor 20th century U.S. military handguns.

Rare Simeon North Pistols

North was the first contract maker of U.S. military pistols. He also produced a very limited number of pistols for the civilian market. Surviving examples are extremely rare.
Top - Pair of .53 caliber duelling pistols. Although called duelers, these full size pistols are typical of the privately owned arms that might have been carried during the Revolutionary War.
Bottom - Over and under Simeon North double barrel percussion pistol. This is the only example of which the museum staff is aware. A flintlock version is also reported to exist.
Loaned by F.L. Starbuck

U.S. Martial Pistols

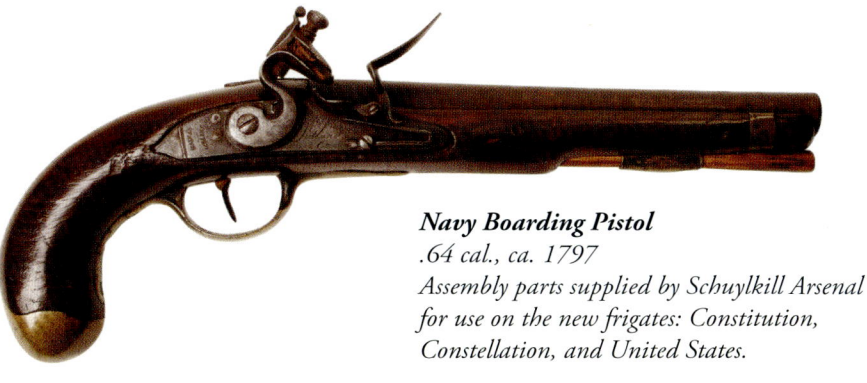

Navy Boarding Pistol
.64 cal., ca. 1797
Assembly parts supplied by Schuylkill Arsenal
for use on the new frigates: Constitution,
Constellation, and United States.

Robert McCormick Horseman's Pistol
.64 cal., ca. 1798.
This horseman's pistol is one of very few
known that bear Robert McCormick's name
on the stock flat.

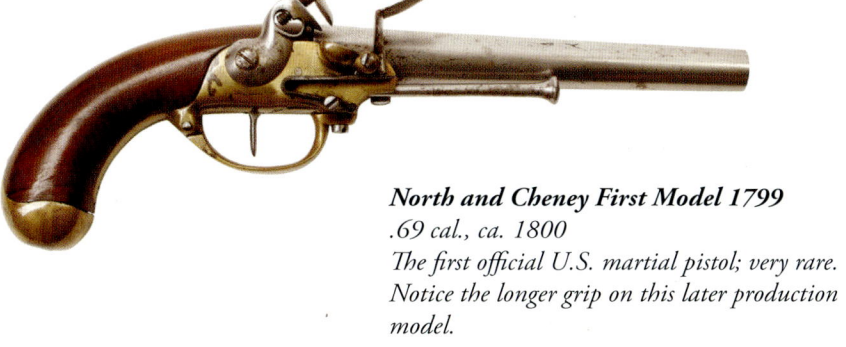

North and Cheney First Model 1799
.69 cal., ca. 1800
The first official U.S. martial pistol; very rare.
Notice the longer grip on this later production
model.

Harpers Ferry Armory Model 1805
.54 cal., ca. 1806, s/n 98.
This specimen, dated 1806, was one of the
first of this model produced.

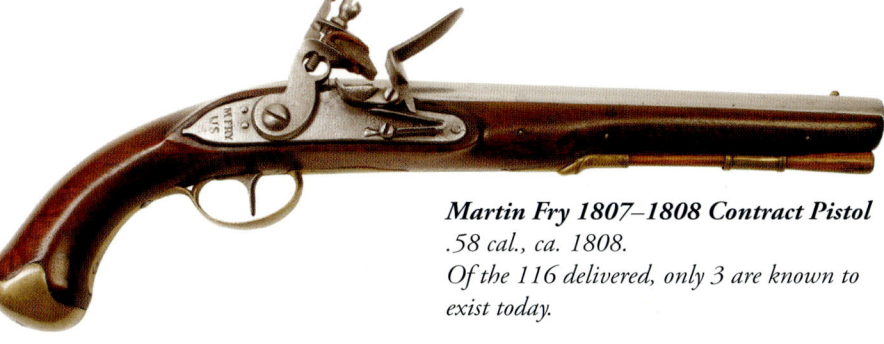

Martin Fry 1807–1808 Contract Pistol
.58 cal., ca. 1808.
Of the 116 delivered, only 3 are known to
exist today.

Simeon North Model 1808 Navy
.64 cal., ca. 1808–10.
Most of these pistols saw service in the War
of 1812.

Loaned by F. L. Starbuck

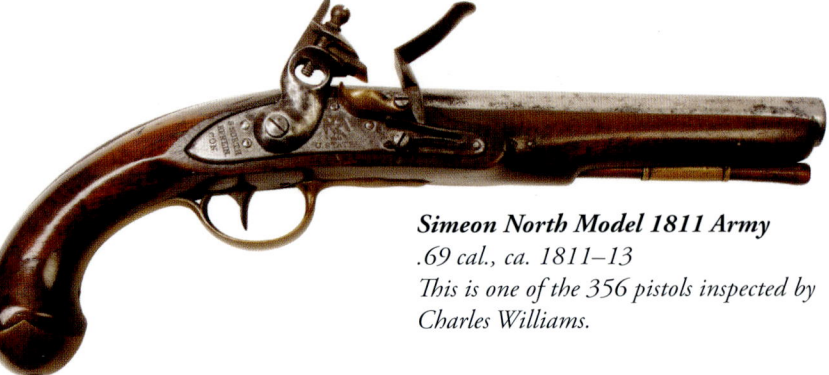

Simeon North Model 1811 Army
.69 cal., ca. 1811–13
This is one of the 356 pistols inspected by Charles Williams.

J. Henry Navy Contract 1813-14 Ships Pistol *.54 cal., ca. 1813–14.*
These pistols were used in the War of 1812.

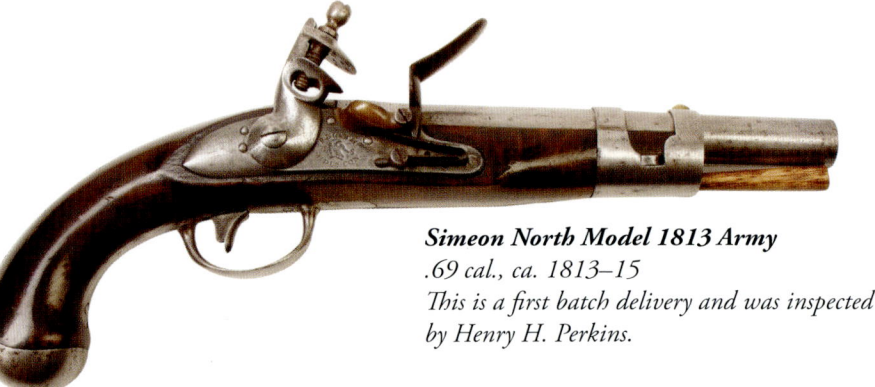

Simeon North Model 1813 Army
.69 cal., ca. 1813–15
This is a first batch delivery and was inspected by Henry H. Perkins.

Simeon North Model 1813/16 Navy
.69 cal., ca. 1813–16.
Notice the extended forestock. This may be the only known example of this type.

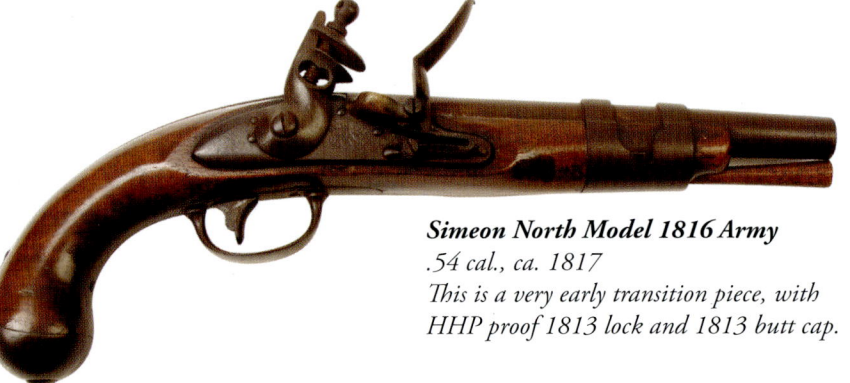

Simeon North Model 1816 Army
.54 cal., ca. 1817
This is a very early transition piece, with HHP proof 1813 lock and 1813 butt cap.

Springfield Model 1817 Type I
.69 cal., ca. 1817–18.
This is 1 of 400 pistols with a gooseneck hammer. Originally called the Model 1807, production began in 1808, but was then discontinued. They were completed in 1818.

Springfield Model 1817 Type II
.69 cal., ca. 1817–18.
This is the second type lock with the reinforced hammer. 600 of this type were made to complete the production of 1000 flintlock pistols.

Simeon North Model 1819 Army
.54 cal., ca. 1819–23.
This is the first pistol to have a swivel ramrod and unique safety bolt.

W.L. Evans Flintlock Navy Model 1826
.54 cal., ca. 1830–31.
Dated 1831.

Asa Waters Model 1836
.54 cal., ca. 1836–44.
Dated 1841.

Percussion Conversion Model 1836
.54 cal., ca. 1847–50.
Cone-in-barrel style conversion from flintlock to percussion.

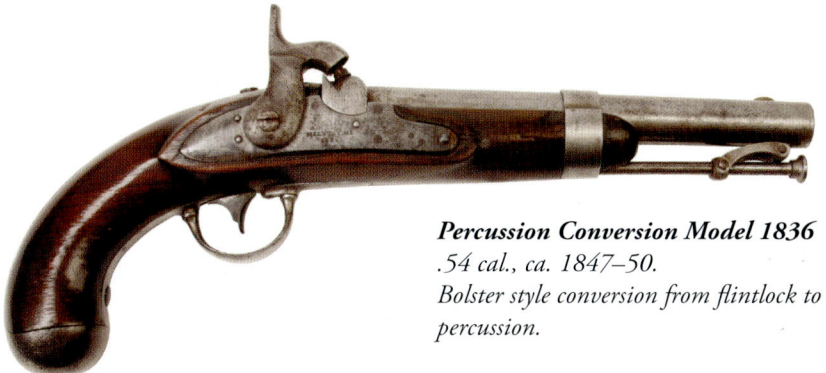

Percussion Conversion Model 1836
.54 cal., ca. 1847–50.
Bolster style conversion from flintlock to percussion.

Loaned by F. L. Starbuck

Elgin Cutlass Pistol
.53 cal., ca. 1838.
150 of these were made for the US Navy to outfit the
South Sea exploring expedition.

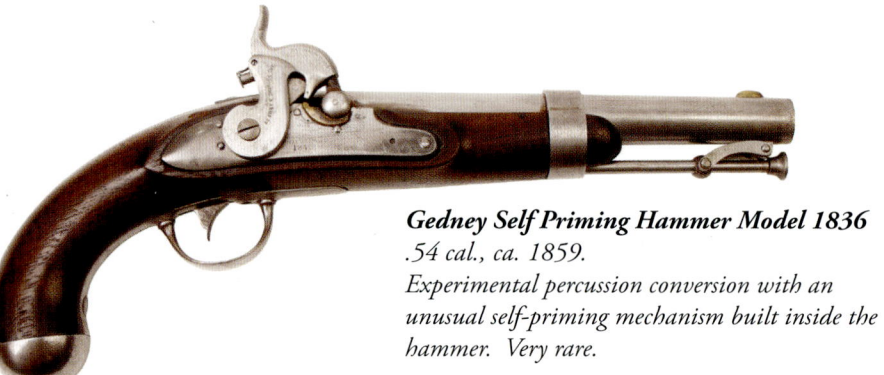

Gedney Self Priming Hammer Model 1836
.54 cal., ca. 1859.
Experimental percussion conversion with an
unusual self-priming mechanism built inside the
hammer. Very rare.

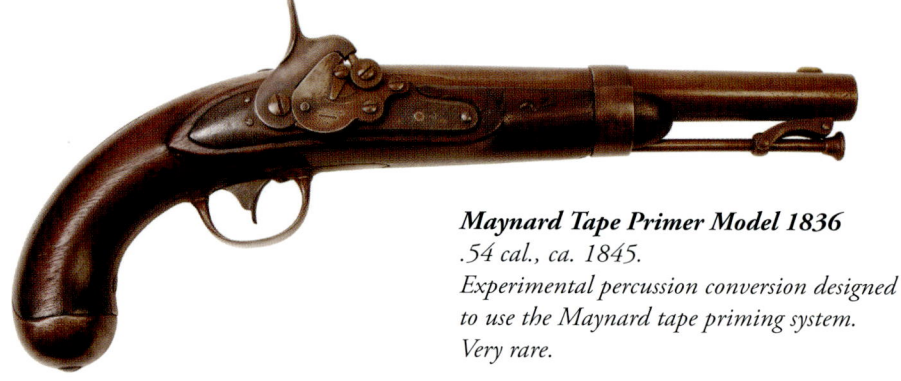

Maynard Tape Primer Model 1836
.54 cal., ca. 1845.
Experimental percussion conversion designed
to use the Maynard tape priming system.
Very rare.

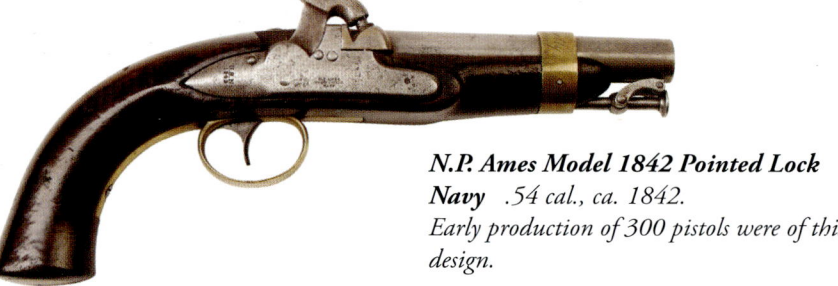

N.P. Ames Model 1842 Pointed Lock
Navy *.54 cal., ca. 1842.*
Early production of 300 pistols were of this
design.

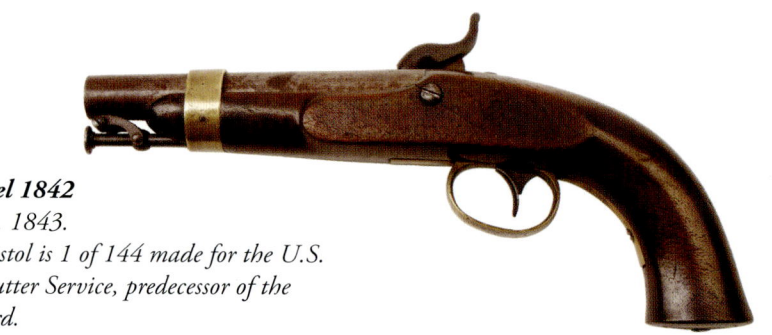

USR Model 1842
.54 cal., ca. 1843.
This rare pistol is 1 of 144 made for the U.S.
Revenue Cutter Service, predecessor of the
Coast Guard.

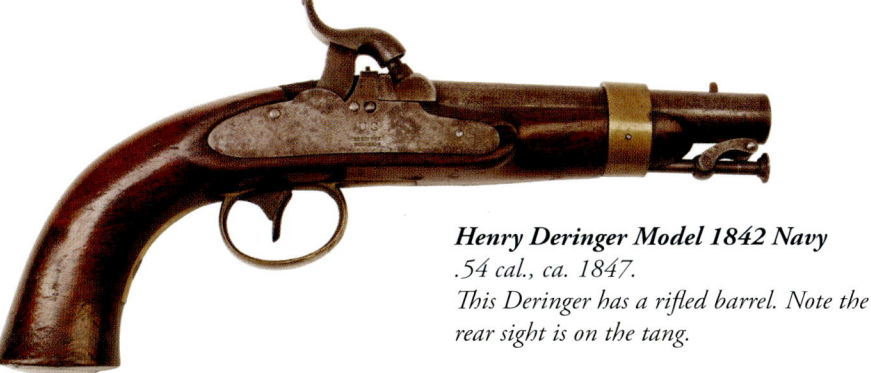

Henry Deringer Model 1842 Navy
.54 cal., ca. 1847.
This Deringer has a rifled barrel. Note the
rear sight is on the tang.

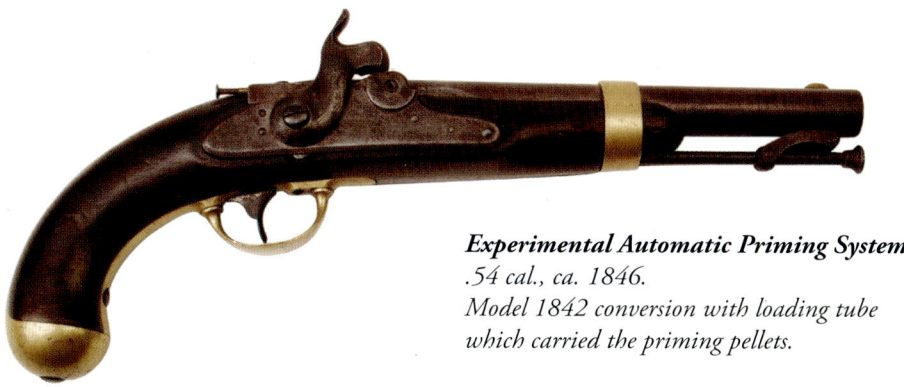

Experimental Automatic Priming System
.54 cal., ca. 1846.
Model 1842 conversion with loading tube
which carried the priming pellets.

Henry Aston Model 1842 Army
.54 cal., ca. 1845-52.
This was considered to be the best military
pistol of its time. 1850 date with "H. Aston"
marking.

I.N. Johnson Model 1842 Army
.54 cal., ca. 1853-55.

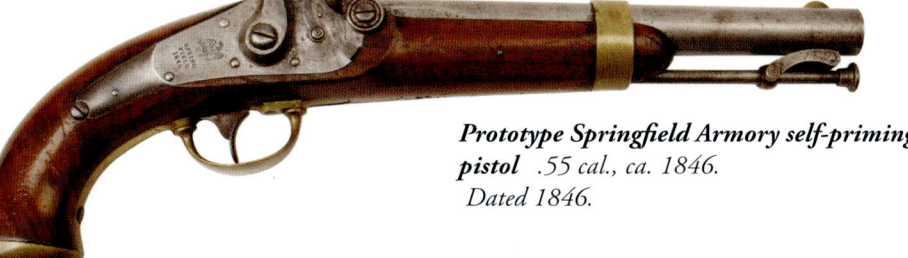

Prototype Springfield Armory self-priming
pistol *.55 cal., ca. 1846.*
Dated 1846.

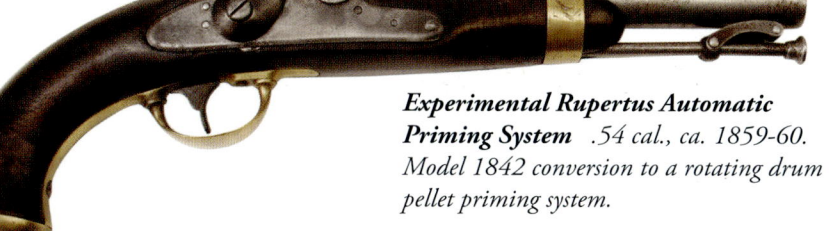

Experimental Rupertus Automatic
Priming System *.54 cal., ca. 1859-60.*
Model 1842 conversion to a rotating drum
pellet priming system.

Loaned by F. L. Starbuck

COLT PATERSON & WALKER REVOLVERS

From 1823 through the latter part of the 19th century, America was settling and defending the Western Frontiers between the United States and Mexico. The settlers were under nearly constant threat from various Indian nations, with the Comanche Nation being the largest and most aggressive of the era. A Comanche warrior could launch, from horseback, ten arrows into the air, before the first struck the ground. Their horsemanship and skills with the bow and arrow gave them a decided advantage over the frontier settler's single-shot muzzle-loading pistols and muskets. The frontiersmen would locate an enemy, dismount, and fire in volleys, with some reloading while others were firing. This plan of attack left them at a severe disadvantage when confronted with a mounted, rapid firing, and rapidly moving aggressor.

A new weapon and combat strategy was needed. This changed in the 1840s under the command of Ranger Col. John (Jack) Coffee Hays, the first Ranger to gain fame for his mixture of fearlessness and innovative fighting techniques.

In 1837, Samuel Colt had introduced the first widely successful repeating firearm with his revolving pistol design. This five shot folding trigger .36 caliber revolver is known today as the "Paterson Colt," after the location of the New Jersey facility where they were manufactured.

The new gun was used to good effect by Col. John Coffee "Jack" Hays' Rangers battling Comanche warriors in Texas. Armed with early Colt's repeaters and adopting the Indian style of mounted warfare, the Rangers were more than a match for the Comanche raiders.

Despite its obvious advantages, the Colt Paterson revolver had initially been a commercial failure. The cost of a pair of single shot flintlocks was between $6 and $9 in 1835 while the cost of a single new Colt revolver was $26. The reluctance of the military to absorb the additional costs, combined with a national depression in 1837 led to the 1843 failure of Colt's first company, The Patent Arms Manufacturing Company of New Jersey.

By the spring of 1846, Capt. Samuel Walker of the U.S. Mounted Rifles was dispatched by Col. Hays to Washington to locate Sam Colt and expedite the delivery of 1,000 Patterson revolvers to be used in the defense of the frontiers of Texas. While meeting with Colt, Walker described how Colt's revolvers were turning the tide in the battles for the frontier and expressed a desire for a more powerful revolver with six shot capacity. Walker and Colt became immediate friends and as a result of their conversations, the Walker model .44 caliber five-shot revolver was introduced by Colt's new manufacturing company.

The massive new revolver was bigger and more reliable than its Paterson predecessor. Perhaps most importantly, the .44 Colt Walker was a real man stopper. In fact, it proved to be too powerful for the metallurgy of the times, and the few surviving specimens of the 1,100 manufactured are often found with cracked or shattered cylinders.

Colt addressed this issue by shortening the cylinder on the redesigned Dragoon model, requiring a reduced powder charge, and the new line of Colt percussion revolvers soon became a huge success with both the military and civilian market.

Captain Samuel Walker

Colonel Samuel Colt

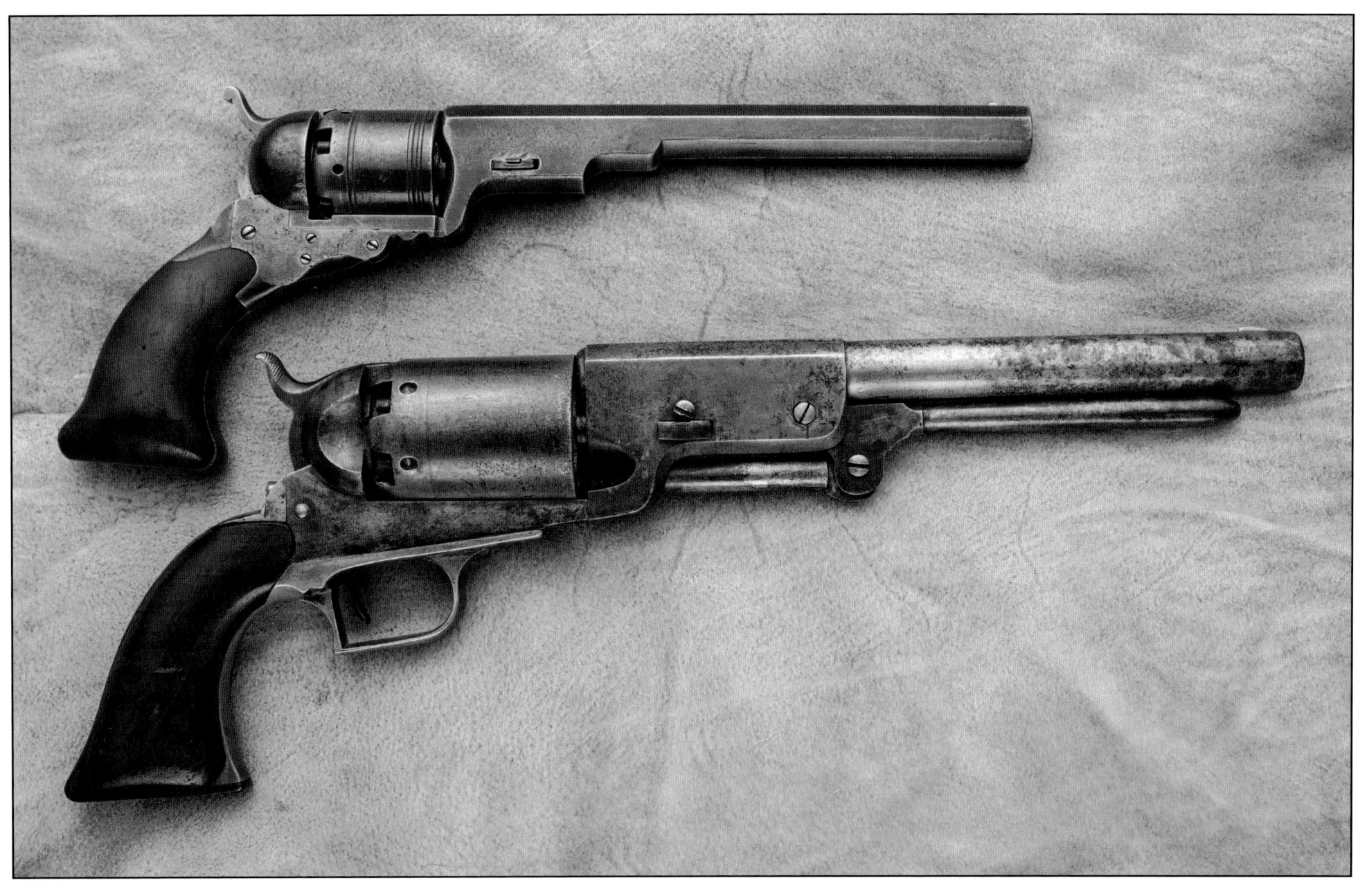

*Top - **Colt Texas Paterson Revolver,** .36 cal., ca. 1838-40, s/n 636.*

*Bottom - **Colt Walker Model 1847 Revolver,** .44 cal., ca. 1847, s/n D Co. 158.*

Loaned by F. L. Starbuck

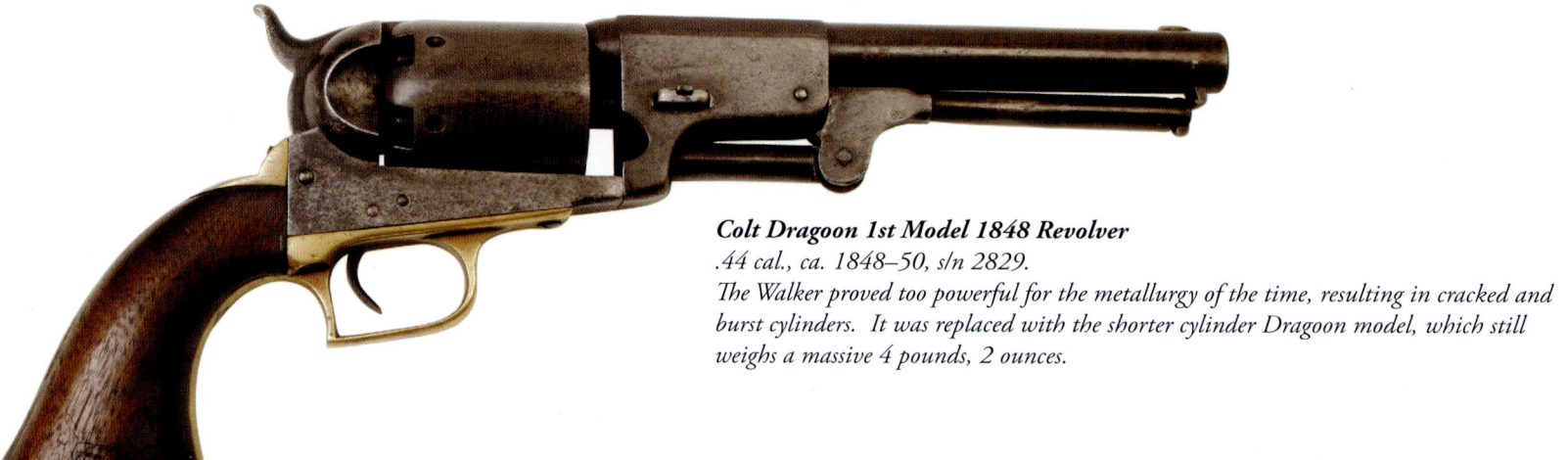

Colt Dragoon 1st Model 1848 Revolver
.44 cal., ca. 1848–50, s/n 2829.
The Walker proved too powerful for the metallurgy of the time, resulting in cracked and burst cylinders. It was replaced with the shorter cylinder Dragoon model, which still weighs a massive 4 pounds, 2 ounces.

Colt Model 1849 Revolver
.31 cal., ca. 1863, s/n 204555.
Purchased by the Union Defense Committee and given to the Navy for use of the steamer Quaker City.

Colt Model 1860 Army Revolver
.44 cal., ca. 1860–65, s/n 47521.
This was the major pistol in use during the Civil War.

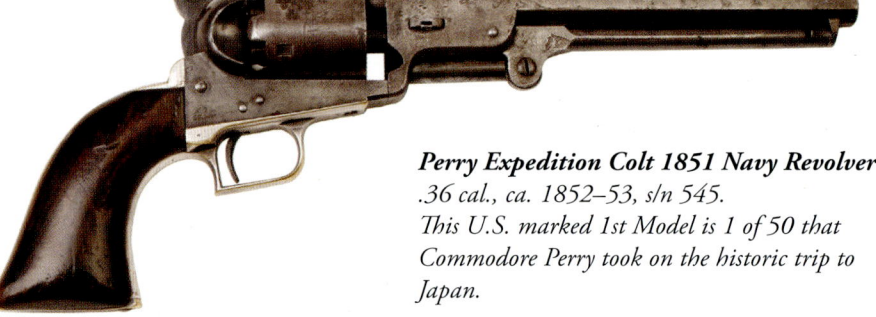

Perry Expedition Colt 1851 Navy Revolver
.36 cal., ca. 1852–53, s/n 545.
This U.S. marked 1st Model is 1 of 50 that Commodore Perry took on the historic trip to Japan.

Colt Model 1861 Navy Revolver
.36 cal., ca. 1861–65, s/n 3358.
Limited quantities of this streamlined pistol were used during the Civil War.

EARLY STOCKED MILITARY HANDGUNS

In the mid-19th century, attachable shoulder stocks for military handguns saw limited usage. The theory was that the arm could be carried and deployed as a handgun with the stock detached, or provide a more stable platform for better aimed fire with the pistol mounted to the stock, to the extent that it could serve the same role as a carbine. This was considered an advantage for cavalry and other mounted troops.

Springfield Model 1855 Pistol Carbine
.59 cal., ca. 1855–57.
A novel design with a Maynard primer and detachable shoulder stock.

Colt Dragoon Model 1848 Revolver
.44 cal., ca. 1848–50, s/n 17741.
With detachable shoulder stock.

Colt 1860 Army with Canteen Stock
.44 cal., ca. 1862–63, s/n 86872.
Detachable shoulder stock serves as a canteen.

Loaned by F. L. Starbuck

Unidentified cavalry soldier in Union frock coat with Remington New Model Army revolver

Massachusetts Arms Co. Adams Navy
.36 cal., ca. 1857–61, s/n 407.
500 of these were made under government contract.

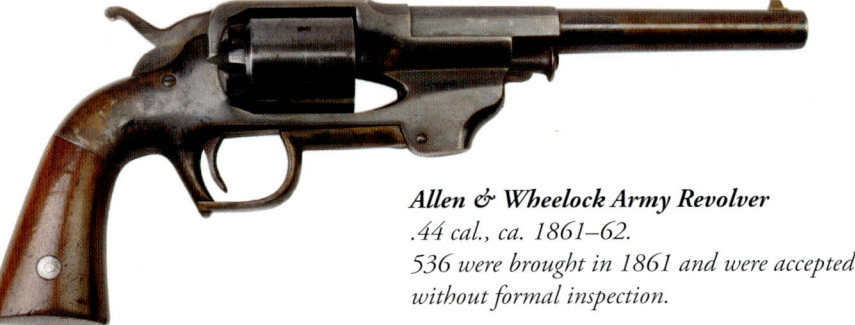

Allen & Wheelock Army Revolver
.44 cal., ca. 1861–62.
536 were brought in 1861 and were accepted without formal inspection.

Remington-Beals Army Model Revolver
.44 cal., ca. 1861–62.
Martially marked pistols are rare with only a few hundred purchased.

Remington-Beals Navy Model Revolver
.36 cal., ca. 1861–62.
About 500 were sold to the U.S. Army and have martial markings.

Benjamin Joslyn Army Revolver
.44 cal., ca. 1861–62, s/n 1445.
Of the 1500 bought most were purchased on the open market and not formally inspected.

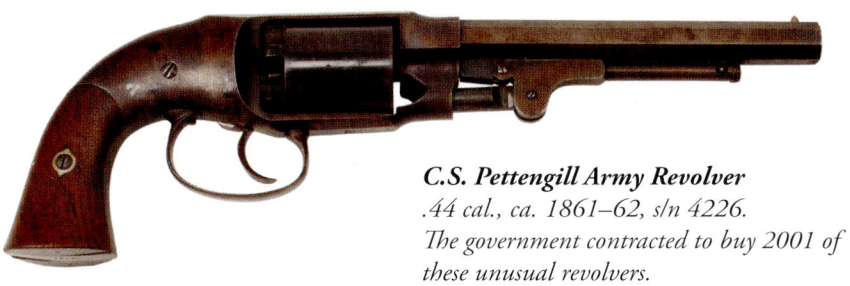

C.S. Pettengill Army Revolver
.44 cal., ca. 1861–62, s/n 4226.
The government contracted to buy 2001 of these unusual revolvers.

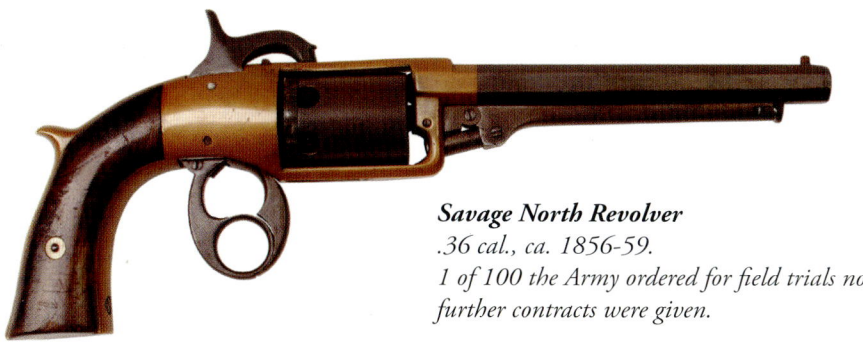

Savage North Revolver
.36 cal., ca. 1856-59.
1 of 100 the Army ordered for field trials no further contracts were given.

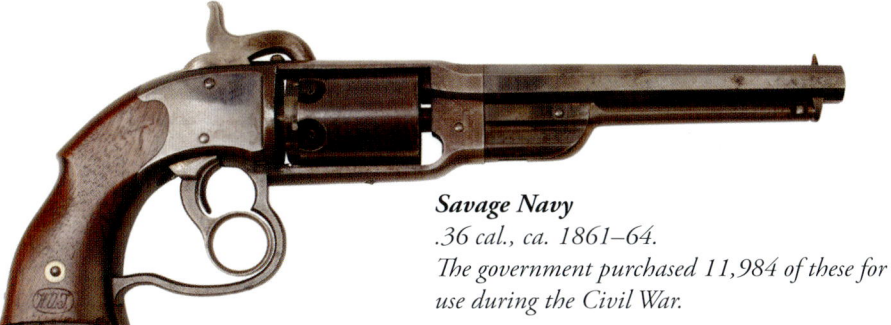

Savage Navy
.36 cal., ca. 1861–64.
The government purchased 11,984 of these for use during the Civil War.

Rogers & Spencer Army Revolver
.44 cal., ca. 1865, s/n 3495.
Contract deliveries were too late for Civil War service.

Remington Model 1861 Army Revolver
.44 cal., ca. 1862, s/n 7964.
Made in 1862 these are also known as the "Old Model Army."

Remington Model 1861 Navy Revolver
.36 cal., ca. 1862, s/n 16183.
Made in 1862 these are also known as the "Old Model Navy."

Loaned by F. L. Starbuck

Remington New Model Army Revolver
.44 cal., ca. 1863–65, s/n 110771.
This model was one of the major handguns of the Civil War.

Remington New Model Navy Revolver
.36 cal., ca. 1863–65, s/n 36196.
The U.S. Navy purchased 4300 of these revolvers.

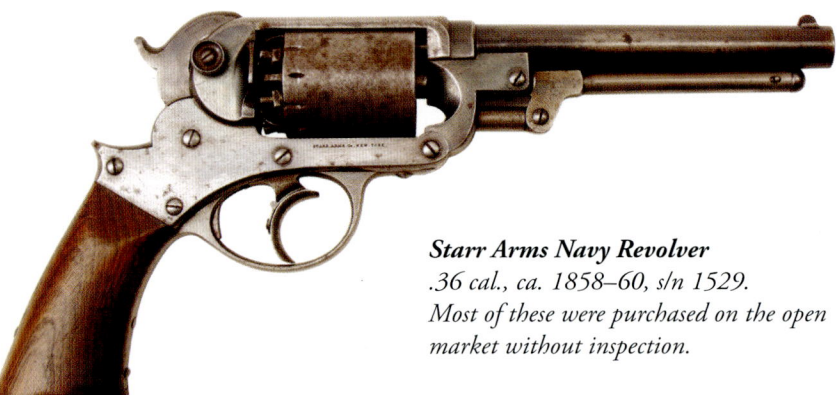

Starr Arms Navy Revolver
.36 cal., ca. 1858–60, s/n 1529.
Most of these were purchased on the open market without inspection.

Starr Arms Co. Double Action Model 1858 Army
.44 cal., ca. 1858–63, s/n 20000.
The double action mechanism was unusual on American revolvers of this era.

Starr Arms Co. Single Action Model 1863 Army
.44 cal., ca. 1863–65, s/n 39254.
Starrs were the third most used revolver brand during the Civil War, behind only Colt and Remington.

Whitney-Navy Revolver
.36 cal., ca. 1859–62, s/n 27624.
This popular revolver was inspected by Guert Gansevoort and bears his P/GG mark.

Model 1869 Breech-Loading Pistol
.50 cal., ca. 1869.
This experimental trial trapdoor pistol is the product of Springfield Armory.
After field test failures interest ended.

Remington Rolling Block
Model 1865 Navy Pistol
.50 rimfire, ca. 1866–70, s/n 6141.

Remington Rolling Block
Model 1867 Navy Pistol
.50 centerfire, ca. 1870–72, s/n 1057.
Basically a model 1865 with a trigger guard
and a center fire breech block.

Remington Rolling Block
Model 1871 Pistol
.50 centerfire, ca. 1872–88.
This pistol is the last of the single shots.

Loaned by F. L. Starbuck

Troop K, 1st Cavalry 1888 at Jefferson Barracks, Missouri

Colt 1851 Navy Conversion Revolver
.38 cartridge, ca. 1871–72, s/n 89845. These conversions were done in the early 1870s.

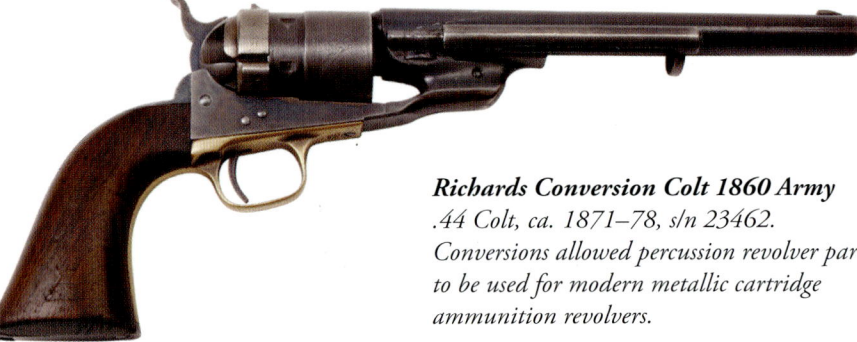

Richards Conversion Colt 1860 Army
.44 Colt, ca. 1871–78, s/n 23462. Conversions allowed percussion revolver parts to be used for modern metallic cartridge ammunition revolvers.

Colt 1861 Navy Conversion Revolver
.38 cartridge, ca. 1875, s/n 2875. Like the Model 1851 these conversions were done in the early 1870s.

Hopkins & Allen Test/Trials Revolver
.44 rimfire, ca. 1879, s/n 121. A U.S. marked .44 rimfire.

The Cavalier. The young soldier and his horse on duty at camp Cheyenne.

Smith and Wesson American 1st Model Revolver
.44 American, ca. 1870–72, s/n 1467.
Made 1870 - 1872. The Army ordered 1000 of these top-break revolvers.

S&W Schofield Kelton Safety 1st Model
.45 Schofield, ca. 1875, s/n 2631.
1 of the 25 equipped with the experimental Springfield Arsenal Kelton thumb safety device.

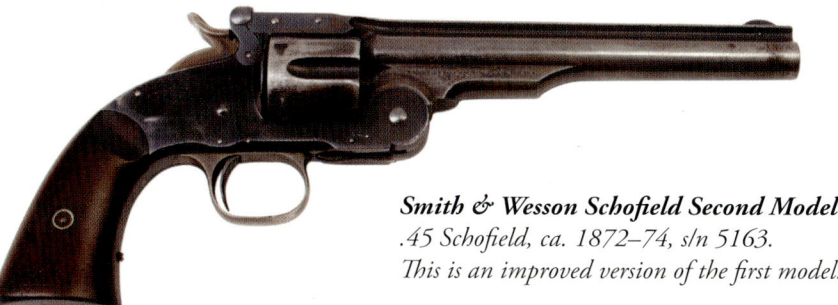

Smith & Wesson Schofield Second Model
.45 Schofield, ca. 1872–74, s/n 5163.
This is an improved version of the first model.

S&W US Revenue Service New Model Number Three
.44 Russian, ca. 1890, s/n 25833.
Issued to the Revenue Cutter Service, predecessor of the Coast Guard.

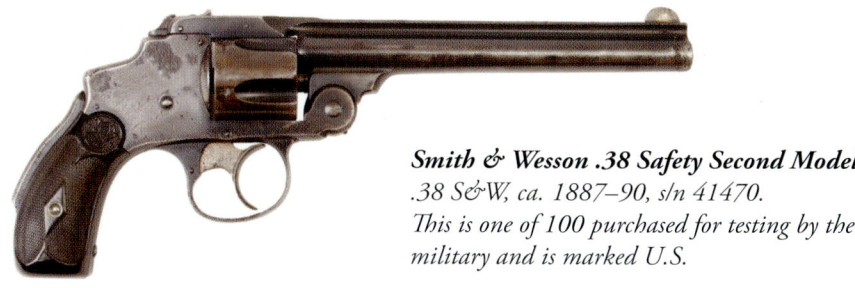

Smith & Wesson .38 Safety Second Model
.38 S&W, ca. 1887–90, s/n 41470.
This is one of 100 purchased for testing by the military and is marked U.S.

Loaned by F. L. Starbuck

Colt Model 1889 Navy
.38 Colt, ca. 1889–94, s/n
20856.
These .38 caliber revolvers
were the first with a swing out
cylinder.

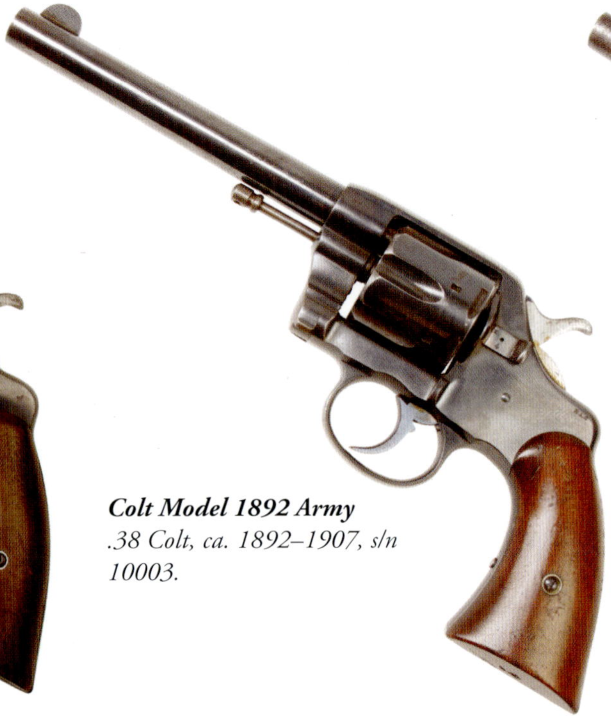

Colt Model 1892 Army
.38 Colt, ca. 1892–1907, s/n
10003.

Colt Model 1894 Army
.38 Colt, ca. 1895–97, s/n 6367.
These .38 caliber revolvers were an
improvement over earlier models.

Gen. Hatcher's Smith and Wesson Victory Model Revolver
.38 Special, ca. 1942, s/n V0442.
The Victory Model is a WWII continuation
of S&W's .38 Hand Ejector Model, first
used by the military in 1901. This one has
a clear side plate, made as a demonstration
model for Gen. Julian Hatcher.
Donated by the Estate of Thomas W. Sefton

Colt Model 1911 Pistol
.45 ACP, ca. 1917, s/n 155432.
Adopted by the military in 1911 and considered by some to be the finest military pistol ever made, this John Moses Browning design is still in use for special applications today, over a century later.
Donated by the Estate of Thomas W. Sefton

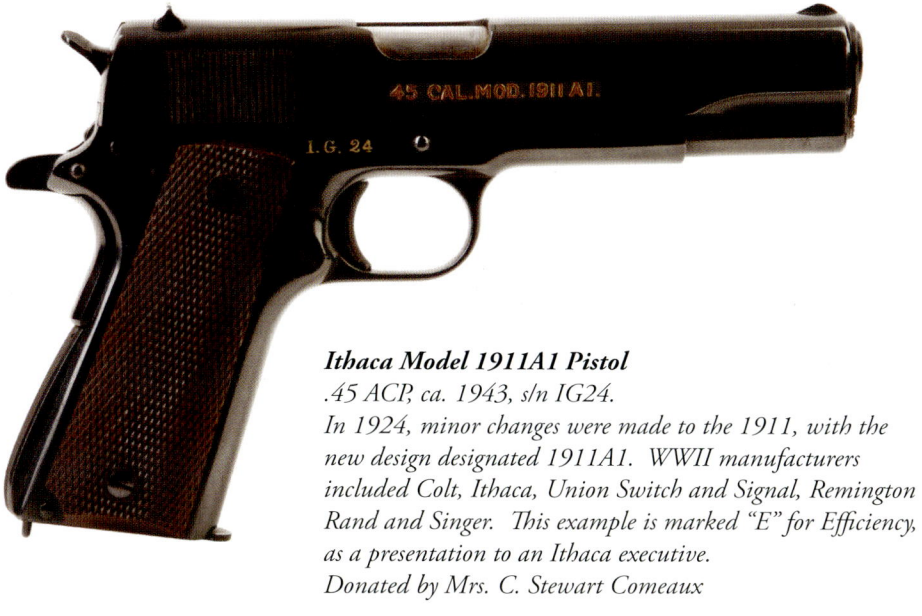

Ithaca Model 1911A1 Pistol
.45 ACP, ca. 1943, s/n IG24.
In 1924, minor changes were made to the 1911, with the new design designated 1911A1. WWII manufacturers included Colt, Ithaca, Union Switch and Signal, Remington Rand and Singer. This example is marked "E" for Efficiency, as a presentation to an Ithaca executive.
Donated by Mrs. C. Stewart Comeaux

Beretta M9 Pistol
9mm, ca. 1998, s/n M9-5426.
Today's standard military issue pistol, first adopted in 1985.
Loaned by Doug Wicklund

AN AUTO-LOADING PISTOL FOR THE ARMY

With the development of effective "auto-loading" (semi-automatic) pistols at the beginning of the 20th century, the U.S. military began a search for a new issue sidearm. The .38 caliber double action revolver had recently replaced the venerable .45 caliber single action revolvers, but the round was considered to lack "stopping power." The army decided to look for a semi-auto with a detachable box magazine of .45 caliber

The selection process lasted from 1900 to 1911, beginning with trial issues of Lugers and proceeding through requests for handgun manufacturers to submit pistols for rigorous testing. In 1907, the finalists came down to the John Moses Browning designed Colt and the Savage pistol, both in .45 ACP. In the head-to-head shootout in 1911, the Colt was found superior and it became the U.S. sidearm. It is still widely used today, over a century later, with many believing it to be the finest combat handgun ever designed.

These are four pistols actually used in the U.S. military handgun selection trials.

Donated by Bailey and Taz Brower

Left to right:

***Luger Model 1901 American Eagle**, 7.65mm, ca. 1901, s/n 6873.*
One thousand Luger pistols, including this example, were purchased for initial testing by the U.S. cavalry in 1901. They were marked with an American eagle over the chamber. The German design was rejected in favor of a larger caliber, but these Lugers were among the first auto-pistols field tested by U.S. troops.

***Colt Model 1907 Pistol**, .45 ACP, ca. 1907, s/n 134.*
One of only 200 Colt Model 1907 pistols that were manufactured exclusively for the U.S. military pistol trials. They were issued to cavalry units in Minnesota and the Philippines. Colt's modifications from their first .45 ACP, the Model 1905, included introduction of the grip safety on the Model 1907.

***Savage Model 1911**, .45 ACP, ca. 1911, s/n 4.*
This is one of only four Savage Model 1911's ever made as the final modification of the original 1907 design. It is likely that this is the exact gun that was used in the final head-to-head 1911 endurance test shoot-out between the Colt and Savage designs to select the next U.S. service pistol.

***Grant Hammond Model 1917, Serial Number One**, .45 ACP, ca. 1917, s/n 1.*
Shortly after the adoption of the U.S. Model of 1911, the Grant Hammond was tested as a possible replacement. It was rejected, in part due to the fact that the magazine is ejected automatically after the last round is fired. Only 13 were ever made.

THE REMINGTON FACTORY COLLECTION

From the beginning, the Remington factory maintained a collection of its arms products on hand in Ilion, NY, to show off to prospective customers as well as an archive of formal contract samples/ documentation for firearms produced for the government. Guns produced for specific family members, elaborately embellished guns, arms used as assembly line patterns for testing and evaluation, and notable serial number examples - all formed the Remington Factory Collection, housed at Ilion, NY.

It was not until 1977 that the company opened its own museum as part of the Ilion facility, showcasing 250 firearms dating from the 1820s. Like most museums, only a small fraction of the holdings could be placed on exhibit. Reference storage areas held other prototypes and variations with many of these items still seeing active usage for new firearms design and production.

In 2013, a special selection of seventy-five pieces from the Remington Factory Collection, chosen by NRA National Firearms Museum staff, were transferred to the new NRA National Sporting Arms Museum at Bass Pro Shops in Springfield, MO. This marked the first time that these Remington collection treasures were offered on daily exhibition together to the general public outside of Ilion, New York.

REMINGTON ARMS COMPANY

America's oldest gunmaking business began humbly in 1793 with the birth of Eliphalet Remington II in Herkimer County, NY. It was 23 years before the young Remington started his career by forging his first rifle barrel and later, with enough orders from neighbors on hand, moving the family operation to a hundred-acre plot near the newly dug Erie Canal. As the Mohawk Valley became a significant commercial region, this small water-powered enterprise flourished. The small town that grew up around the Remington business was to be called Ilion.

For the first forty years, the product line that came out of Ilion was primarily rifle barrels – each stamped "REMINGTON" near the breech. While other components including lockplates were manufactured overseas, most of the company's barrels went to other gunsmiths in the region for assembly, with only a limited number of completed arms being created directly by the Remington family, which now included sons Philo, Samuel, and Eliphalet III.

The Mexican War soon changed that business model. Several contractors including John Griffiths and William Jenks turned to Remington to have rifles and carbines made for fulfillment of their government orders. Meeting government standards for parts interchangeability and acquiring needed machinery from other established firms – including N.P. Ames – Remington quickly became one of the leading private firms, its output supplementing the two national armories, in the north at Springfield, MA and in the south at Harpers Ferry, VA.

The American Civil War marked a shift in Remington's product line, with several percussion handgun models made at Ilion becoming standard issue sidearms for Union cavalry and infantry forces. Other government contracts were let to Remington for thousands of rifle-muskets with the final fulfillment on these arms being delivered nearly a year after the hostilities had ceased. On the commercial market, Remington's target arms found ready application in national match competition at Creedmoor and Sea Girt.

These postwar years marked Remington's transition into metallic cartridge arms and smokeless ammunition with its rolling block action line of rifles and carbines receiving enthusiastic domestic interest. The millions of arms represented by foreign orders funded expansion into new repeating rifle designs and enabled the company to become an international success. The old Ilion factory space continued to be the nexus of the company, but supplementary factories were created in Bridgeport, CT, and Eddystone, PA,

as ammunition products from the Union Metallic Cartridge Company, and later the Peters Ammunition Company, also came under the Remington corporate umbrella.

Through two world wars, domestic and Allied military orders kept Remington in expansion mode. Bolt-action rifles made during one conflict also were retained for usage in the second war. This continued growth segued into increased civilian sales, and development of a broad line of sporting rifles, shotguns, and handguns that was to flow for decades out of the state of New York across America. An ammunition plant was built in Arkansas and a clay target plant was built in Georgia.

More recent developments at Ilion have included Remington becoming a major part of the Freedom Group and participating in an acquisition program that has also brought Bushmaster, DPMS/Panther Arms, H&R Firearms, Marlin, and Parker Gunmakers together in the largest American gunmaking conglomerate to date.

Wood Model Prototypes of Experimental Designs
ca. 1870–90. In the days before CAD/CAM designing, wooden models were used to derive part placement and manufacturing fixtures.

Early Remington Percussion Target Rifle *.42 cal., ca. 1845–50.*
Fewer than 100 heavy barrel rifles were made.

Early Remington Percussion Combination Rifle-Shotgun, *.50 cal. & 30 ga., ca. 1850–60.*
One barrel is rifled; the other smoothbore.

Remington Beals Revolving Rifle, *.36 cal. Ca. 1855–60.*
Remington produced both revolving rifles and handguns utilizing similar designs.

U.S. Contract Sample Remington Zouave U.S. M1863 Percussion Rifle, *.58 cal., ca. 1863.*

REMINGTON FACTORY COLLECTION

Prototype Remington Split Breech Rifle, Type I *.40 cal, ca. 1863–66.*
Remington's first cartridge long gun.

Remington Split Breech Carbine, Type II *.50 rimfire, ca. 1865.*
Nickel plated receiver, marked "U.S." on butt plate.

Foreign Brass Frame Rolling Block Copy *.45 cal., ca. 1870–1900.*
The Remington Rolling Block was the most popular single shot cartridge rifle design from the 1860s to the early 20th century. It was widely copied.

Detachable Stock Remington Rolling Block Pistol *.22 rimfire, ca. 1873–75.*
Remington's pistol carbine utilized a rolling block pistol and a detachable skeleton wire stock.

Remington Rolling Block Cadet Rifle w/ Bayonet *.22 rimfire, ca. 1913–23.*

Training rifle produced for military schools.

REMINGTON ROLLING BLOCKS

At the close of the American Civil War, government officials found themselves inundated with an overload of outmoded muzzleloaders and many varieties of breechloaders. Standardizing and simplifying on Remington's new single-shot action design patented by factory supervisor Joseph Rider, both the U.S. Navy and the U.S. Army ordered thousands of carbines, pistols, and rifles. Remington provided actions to Springfield Armory to be then fitted to existing parts to create expedient military arms at lower costs. New York State National Guard regiments also chose the Remington rolling block rifle as their standard.

On the civilian side, the Remington rolling block action was found to be well-suited as a target rifle foundation. National Rifle Association sponsored teams competed successfully overseas in Ireland and at home on the Creedmoor range on Long Island in long-range competitions that established the merits of this design. Centerfire and rimfire variants allowed the rifle design to also be used for informal target work (plinking) as well as hunting roles.

Out on the western plains, Remington rolling blocks were popular choices for buffalo hunters. Chambered for the same range of .40 to .50 caliber cartridges employed in the sidehammer Sharps guns, Remington rifles had fewer parts and offered a sturdy receiver for extended firing of stout-recoiling ammunition.

ELEGANT AND UNUSUAL REMINGTON SINGLE SHOTS
Top to bottom:

Prototype Remington Rolling Block Sporting Rifle #2, *.30 cal., ca. 1872-73.*

Ida Remington Squire's Remington-Beals Rifle, *.32 rimfire, ca. 1866-70.*
Specially engraved for Philo Remington's daughter, Ida. Fewer than 800 made.

Remington Vest Pocket Pistol w/ Stock, *.22 rimfire, ca. 1865-88.*
Rare long barrel version of the Vest Pocket Pistol with a detachable wire stock.

REMINGTON HEPBURN RIFLES

Leaving his former career as a nearby muzzleloading gunsmith, Lewis L. Hepburn (1832–1914) turned his hand to breechloaders as the superintendant of Remington's mechanical engineering department, resulting in a new falling-block action that was introduced to shooters in the 1880 factory catalog. Hepburn had been a noted competitive shooter on the American Creedmoor team and his simple, side-lever actuated rifles were ideal for prone target work. The strong Hepburn action could also accommodate smokeless ammunition that was introduced during its thirty-year production period.

Top -
Remington Hepburn Scoped Rifle,
.44 CF, ca. 1880-1907, s/n 4777.
This rifle was used by Lewis Hepburn, Remington's supervising engineer, to verify factory ammunition accuracy.

Prototype Remington Birdshead Butt Model 1875
.44 CF, ca. mid 1870s, s/n 1875. One-of-a-kind experimental model.

Bottom -
Remington Hepburn Creedmoor Rifle,
.44 CF, ca. 1880-1907, s/n 7542. The internal hammer Hepburn offered great accuracy for Creedmoor and other competitions.

REMINGTON MILITARY PROTOTYPE AND TRIALS RIFLES

In the 1870s through 1890s, Remington was active in developing new rifle designs for consideration by the U.S. military, as reflected by these four guns.

Army Trials Remington Elliott Rifle, *.45 cal., ca. 1872.*
One of 15 designs submitted by various manufacturers for the U.S. Army rifle trials of 1872.

Prototype Remington Keene Rifle, *.45 cal., ca. 1880–83, s/n M0068.*
This prototype still reflects the 1868 single shot rifle hammer and receiver profile. A later version was considered by the Army in their 1882 trials, and purchased by the Navy and U.S. Indian Department.

Prototype Remington Cook Rifle, *.40 cal., ca. 1894.*
Made for U.S. Navy tests.

Prototype Remington Lee Rifle, *6mm, ca. 1872.*
Made for U.S. military trials. Non-standard chambering.

REMINGTON PUMP RIFLES

Prototype Remington Model 14 Pedersen Rifle,
.44 cal., ca. 1914.

Remington Gallery Special Cartridge Counter,
.22 LR, ca. 1910–15, s/n 318353. Intended for use in shooting galleries, featuring a
device built into the stock to count the number of rounds.

Remington Breech Loading Hammer Shotgun
.12 ga., ca. 1885, s/n 22332.

Remington Parker 8 ga. Shotgun,
ca. 1937, s/n 171734.
Remington bought the Parker factory in 1934. They resumed manufacture of new shotguns under the Parker name in 1937 in Meriden, CT.

Prototype Remington Model 11-48
.410 Shotgun, .410 ga., ca. 1948, s/n 000000.

Facing page - **THE PISTOL THAT REPLACED THE 1911 (Almost)**

In 1918, the U.S. Navy held a head to head pistol trials competition between the current issue Colt 1911, the Grant Hammond, and the Remington Model 53, all three chambered for .45 ACP. After a 5,000 round torture test, the Remington was deemed superior, and the Navy requested a bid for 75,000 from Remington to replace all existing 1911 pistols and all revolvers for the U.S. Navy and Marine Corps. Remington, who had just received a contract to build 150,000 1911 pistols for WWI usage, submitted a bid that the Navy considered too high. Although a second request for bids was placed, the war was winding down and the contract was never awarded. This Model 53, pictured with a factory-cutaway smaller Model 51, is the only surviving example of what was almost the replacement for the 1911.

Model 53 Military Prototype
Remington-Pedersen .45 Pistol,
.45 ACP, ca. 1917.
Provisionally accepted by the Navy; only known specimen.

The Safe Automatic

Caliber .380

REMINGTON .UMC

Pistol

Takes the Standard
.380 Caliber Automatic
Pistol Cartridge Ob-
tainable Anywhere.

The Self-Aiming Automatic.
Fits the Hand Right.
Lies Flat in the Pocket.

Protects the Home
Without
Risk of Accident.

SAFE Completely.

Has *a positively locked breech when firing.*
Requires *one trigger pull for each shot.*
Can not *be fired without gripping handle.*
Has *a safety you can lock at will.*
Impossible *to fire a live cartridge left in the barrel when magazine is removed.*

An Exclusive
Remington UMC
Improvement.

Especially Designed for Quick Straight Shooting.

THE REMINGTON ARMS UNION METALLIC CARTRIDGE COMPANY, Inc.
Largest Manufacturers of Firearms and Ammunition in the World.
WOOLWORTH BUILDING.   NEW YORK CITY.

Remington Model 51 Pistol factory cutaway,   .380 ACP, ca. 1918–33, s/n PA1743. Designed by John Pedersen. 65,000 were produced.

WWI SECRET WEAPON

The Remington Pedersen Device,
.30 cal., ca. 1918, s/n 1034502.
While the Springfield 1903 five shot .30-06 bolt action rifle was an ideal military weapon for engaging the enemy at long ranges, when machine guns and poison gas slowed WWI combat to a brutal close quarters trench warfare ordeal, the military needed a faster firing, higher capacity, lower recoiling alternative. The Pedersen Device replaced the bolt in a modified Springfield 03 to convert it into a high capacity semi-auto for close combat trench warfare. Although 65,000 were made, they came available after the war's end. They were never issued and were ordered to be destroyed.

REMINGTON U.S. MILITARY SNIPER RIFLES

Top - **Remington M700/M40 with Redfield Scope,** *7.62mm, ca. 1968, s/n 314169. During the Vietnam conflict, Remington received a contract to produce a modified Varmint Model 700 as a sniper rifle for the U.S. Marine Corps.*
Bottom - **Remington Model 1903A4,** *.30-06, ca. 1943, s/n 3407107. Remington received a contract during WWII to produce an expedient sniper rifle based on the M1903A3 currently in production.*

EXPERIMENTAL LAW ENFORCEMENT CONFIGURATIONS

*Top - **Remington Double Hand Gripped Model 870***, *12 ga., ca. 1980, s/n T277084V.*
This dual-gripped 870 shotgun variant was considered for law enforcement sales.

*Bottom - **Remington Folding Stock Model 7600 Rifle***, *6mm, ca. 1977, s/n 7479460.*
Another law enforcement "might have been," the folding stock on this rifle offered portability.

A TWENTY-TWO OF A DIFFERENT COLOR - The Remington factory experimented with variations in color, branding, and other cosmetics on their popular line of .22 rifles.

Above - **Remington Flag Stocked M552 Rifles,** *.22 LR, ca. 1957-88, s/n's D1400164, B1605067 & B1604872. Experimental flag motif stocks, possibly for the Bicentennial.*

At left, top to bottom:

* **Experimental Remington Model 572 Teal Color Pump Rifle,** *.22 LR, ca. 1958–62.*

* **Remington White Stocked Nylon 66 Rifle**, *.22 LR, ca. 1959, s/n A2124085.*

* **Black Widow Remington Nylon 66** *Serial No. 10, .22 LR, ca. 1959, s/n 00000010.*

TOM FRYE'S BLOCKBUSTER
Remington Nylon 66 Rifle, .22 LR, ca. 1959.
Exhibition shooter Tom Frye broke Ad Topperwein's aerial shooting record with this rifle over a 13-day stint, firing at 100,010 hand thrown wooden blocks, missing only 6. The photo of Frye sitting on a mountain of wood blocks became a staple advertising image for Remington in the early 1960s.

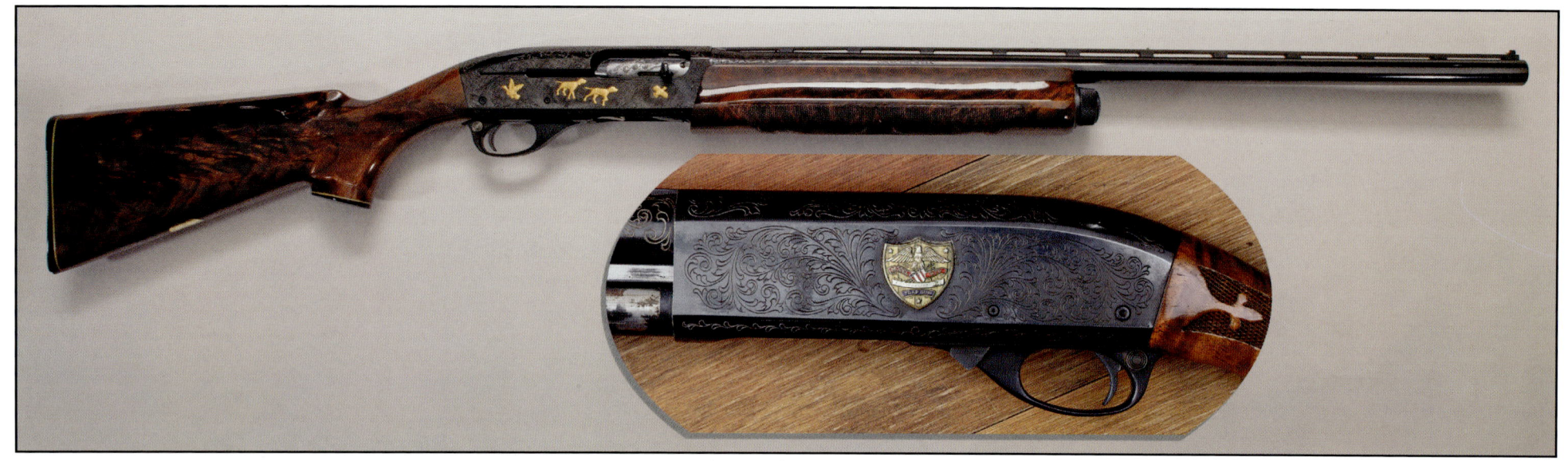

Experimental Remington Model 870 Trap Gun, *12 ga., ca. 1970, s/n S400504V.*
Prototype trapshooting variation.

Remington Model 40 Rifle, serial number one, *.22 LR, ca. 1956, s/n 00001.*
The first example of this precision rimfire target rifle.

Prototype Remington Model 31 LTC Trap Shotgun, *12 ga., ca. 1935, s/n 110509.*

REMINGTON MILESTONES

Top - **The First Remington Model 3200 Over Under Shotgun**,
12 ga., ca. 1973, s/n OU40000.
First production gun of this model.

Bottom -- **The Ten Millionth Remington**
This Remington Model 58 Shotgun 12 ga., ca. 1963, s/n 36758, is marked as the 10 millionth
Remington sporting firearm manufactured.

The First Remington Model 870 Pump Shotgun,
12 ga., ca. 1948, s/n 000.
It is believed that this may be the first production Remington Model 870, which was destined to become probably America's most popular shotgun. Zero serial number guns were usually factory first production run pieces, built for exhaustive ammunition, function testing, and evaluation.

The First Remington R15 Semi-Automatic Rifle,
.223 Rem., ca. 2008, s/n RA000001.
The first production gun of Remington's AR pattern rifle. The modern ergonomic features, reliability, and accuracy of this type of semi-automatic have made it the most popular style of sporting rifle in America.

REMINGTON FACTORY CUTAWAYS

Loaned by Remington Arms Company, LLC.

Portions of these guns have been cutaway to show how the guns work. These sectionalized arms may be used by factory gunsmiths and others to observe or demonstrate the inner works, to train armorers and as sales demonstration models. Factory cutaways are very rare.

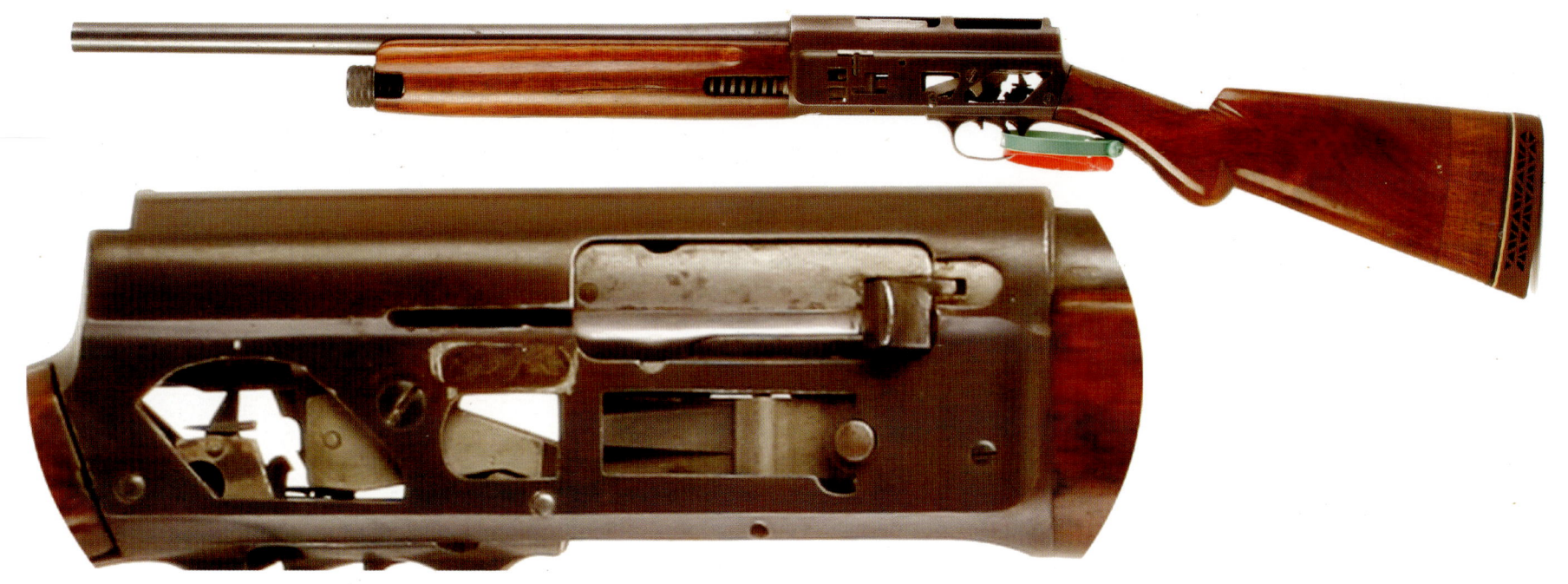

Cutaway Remington Model 11 Shotgun
12 ga., ca. 1940, s/n 61307.

Cutaway Remington Model 1903A1 Rifle
.30-06, ca. 1942, s/n XC1631.

Cutaway Remington Model 14 Rifle
.30 Rem., ca. 1920, s/n C23711.

Cutaway Remington Model 7400 Rifle
.270 Win., ca. 1990, s/n 8166484.

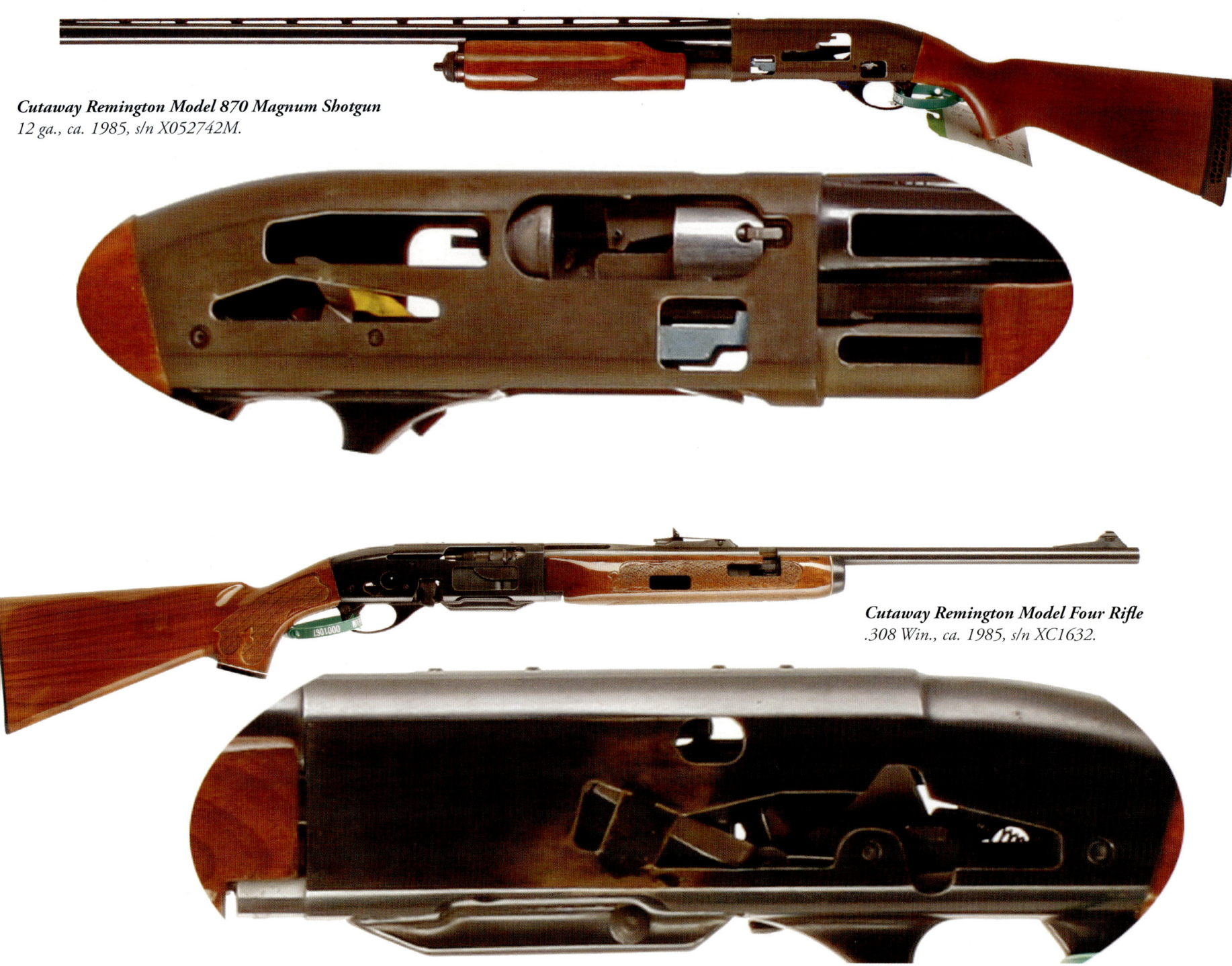

Cutaway Remington Model 870 Magnum Shotgun
12 ga., ca. 1985, s/n X052742M.

Cutaway Remington Model Four Rifle
.308 Win., ca. 1985, s/n XC1632.

Cutaway Remington Model 3200 Shotgun
12 ga., ca. 1973, s/n OU4246.

Cutaway Remington Peerless Shotgun
12 ga., ca. 1970, s/n 00001.

Cutaway Remington Model 1100 LT-20 Shotgun
20 ga., ca. 1983, s/n N901392K.

Cutaway Remington Nylon 66 Rifle
.22 LR, ca. 1970, s/n A2109528.

Cutaway Remington Viper 522 Rifle
.22 LR, ca. 1960, s/n 3013879.

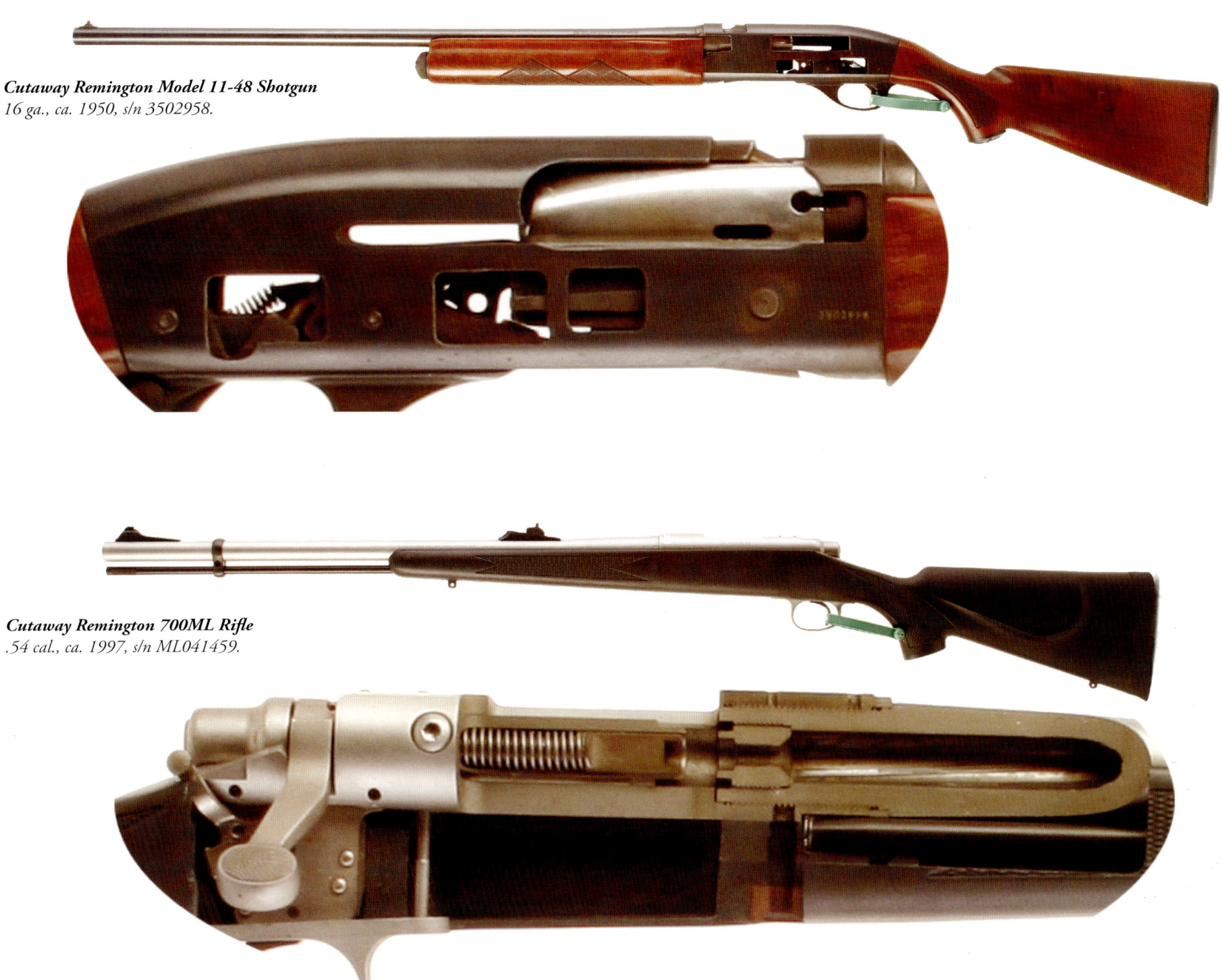

Cutaway Remington Model 11-48 Shotgun
16 ga., ca. 1950, s/n 3502958.

Cutaway Remington 700ML Rifle
.54 cal., ca. 1997, s/n ML041459.

REMINGTON ART COLLECTION

Manufacturing a fine product was only part of the Remington strategy and throughout its long history, the company commissioned artists to produce outdoor and sporting motif artworks that could be utilized in advertising, calendars, and prints. Quality was not stinted and Remington's artistic legacy includes works from classic American painters including Philip R. Goodwin, Maynard Reece and N.C. Wyeth. The resulting collection has been called the single largest holding of sporting and wildlife-related art in the world. Part of this iconic artwork has been housed at the museum/corporate offices at the New York factory and in North Carolina. In 2013, sixteen original oil paintings that had been widely used for advertising by Remington were carefully evaluated by a conservator before being transferred to the NRA's National Sporting Arms Museum at Bass Pro Shops in Springfield, MO. These treasured paintings, now shown in conjunction with period arms, provide a priceless exhibition of the American outdoor sporting lifestyle.

Swift Approach by Frank Tenney Johnson, published as a Peters Cartridge Co. poster.

Yukon Trouble by Lynn Hunt Bogue, used to promote the Remington Model 8 semi-auto rifle in a poster ca. 1910s.

Painting of covered wagon train by Robert Wesley Amick, ca. 1920s or 1930s.

One Down by Robert Wesley Amick, used in Remington advertisements ca. 1920s.

The Pistol Shooter by Frank Xavier Leyendecker.

Portrait of a Gentleman by Frank Xavier Leyendecker, ca. 1910.

A Chancy Shot by H. G. Edwards

Dangerous Bend *by N.C. Wyeth, ca. 1910–1912, used as an advertisement for Remington Arms UMC, including advertising the Remington Model 8 semi-auto rifle, ca. 1924.*

Tribute to a Dog by Lynn Bogue Hunt, published as a Remington poster ca. 1929. The text is from attorney, and later U.S. Senator from Missouri, George Graham Vest. ca. 1855.

The best friend a man has in the world may turn against him and become his enemy. His son or daughter that he has reared with loving care may prove ungrateful. Those who are nearest and dearest to us, those whom we trust with our happiness and our good name may become traitors to their faith. The money that a man has, he may lose. It flies away from him, perhaps when he needs it most. A man's reputation may be sacrificed in a moment of ill-considered action. The people who are prone to fall on their knees to do us honor when success is with us, may be the first to throw the stone of malice when failure settles its cloud upon our heads.

The one absolutely unselfish friend that man can have in this selfish world, the one that never deserts him, the one that never proves ungrateful or treacherous is his dog. A man's dog stands by him in prosperity and in poverty, in health and in sickness. He will sleep on the cold ground, where the wintry winds blow and the snow drives fiercely, if only he may be near his master's side. He will kiss the hand that has no food to offer. He will lick the wounds and sores that come in encounters with the roughness of the world. He guards the sleep of his pauper master as if he were a prince. When all other friends desert, he remains. When riches take wings, and reputation falls to pieces, he is as constant in his love as the sun in its journey through the heavens.

If fortune drives the master forth, an outcast in the world, friendless and homeless, the faithful dog asks no higher privilege than that of accompanying him, to guard him against danger, to fight against his enemies. And when the last scene of all comes, and death takes his master in its embrace and his body is laid away in the cold ground, no matter if all other friends pursue their way, there by the graveside will the noble dog be found, his head between his paws, his eyes sad, but open in alert watchfulness, faithful and true even in death.

HISTORIC ARMS

A gun with a known historical association is a tangible connection to our collective past, and such connections are rare and precious things.

Some historic guns may be associated with an event or special circumstances. Accordingly, included here are guns used in the Civil War and serial number one guns which represent milestones in firearms design and manufacture.

However, foremost among the firearms at the NRA National Sporting Arms Museum — those that most capture the attention and fire the imagination — are most likely those that are attributed to a specific historic figure. It takes a cold soul and dearth of imagination not be stirred by a shotgun that a president or king took hunting, a sixgun that a desperado or lawdog carried on his hip, or a firearm used by America's first female superstar to bedazzle adoring crowds with feats of unprecedented marksmanship.

When contemplating such treasures, it's worth asking the question, "How do you know..?" The answer is seldom cut and dried.

Researching an historic gun's pedigree and evaluating its provenance is sometimes more art than science. A good story and a stack of newspaper clippings make for an enjoyable tale, but the diligent researcher will always ask, "How do we know that this particular gun belonged to this particular individual?"

Numerous factors may be considered. The most convincing support will be documentation produced contemporaneous to the gun that definitively connects a specific firearm to the person in question. Factory shipping records or court documents that identify the gun by make, model, and serial number are excellent examples.

The vast majority of historically attributed firearms will not enjoy this degree of specificity in their documentation. At this point, the researcher digs into the material that supports the story and evaluates the gun itself. Family legends are carefully examined. Especially helpful are documents from previous generations that specifically identify who used the gun when, and the chain of ownership down through the generations. The credibility of the documents themselves are carefully considered. If available, factory shipping information may be checked to see if it is compatible with the gun's claimed history. Inscriptions will be carefully examined to see if they appear to be authentic and from the gun's era of use, or are possibly a later embellishment.

In a court of law, there are varying degrees of proof. A criminal defendant must be found guilty "beyond a reasonable doubt." A civil case, on the other hand, may be decided by "the preponderance of the evidence," examining the question of which side is better supported by the facts that can be proven and carefully weighing the comparative credibility of the evidence each side offers.

Each of the historic guns on exhibit has been reviewed with these standards in mind and each found worthy of presentation for the reader's consideration, with authentication generally ranging from ironclad to highly probable.

Here are the guns, and here are the stories of the men and women who used them.

KING JAMES II's John Cosens Flintlock Fowler
10 ga., ca. 1600.

Bearing the royal cipher of King James II (1633–1701) of England, this 10 ga. fowling piece was made by John Cosens around 1685 and was once in the collection of the Duke of Argyll. King James II was the last male of the Stuart line to hold the throne of England, Scotland, and Ireland, which he lost during the Glorious Revolution of 1688 after a three-year reign. This piece was reportedly taken from the royal baggage train after James fled England.

KING JAMES II (1633–1701)

James II was the shortest reigning King of England during the Stuart period. The second son of Charles I, he inherited the throne after his older brother died without leaving a legitimate heir. James would rule for three years before being driven out of the country.

James was Catholic at a time of religious turmoil in Great Britain initially set in motion by Henry VIII more than 100 years prior. During this time, England was decidedly Anti-Catholic, excluding practitioners from holding any influential public office. James tried to change this by issuing the Declaration of Indulgence, which granted broad religious freedom but also allowed the king to suspend laws passed by Parliament, essentially rendering James an absolute monarch.

Concerned by his sweeping reforms and unchecked exercise of power, a group on English nobles conspired with William of Orange to invade England and seize the throne from James. William was chosen because he was the husband of James' oldest daughter, Mary, who had been raised as an Anglican. When William invaded, James fled England, but not before allegedly throwing the Great Seal of the Realm into the River Thames. Parliament decreed that James' flight and disposal of the Seal amounted to his abdication, leaving the throne vacant. At this time, Mary was declared Queen. James II lived out the rest of his days in France and died of a brain hemorrhage in 1701.

THE DUKE OF YORK's *John Manton Flintlock Fowler*

16 ga., ca. 1760.

This fowler was made by John Manton of London and was owned by Frederick Augustus (1763–1827), the Duke of York, second son of King George III. Made in the early 1800s, the gun exhibits tastefully understated decoration, but with elegant flourishes, such as a gold touch hole and pan.

FREDERICK AUGUSTUS, DUKE OF YORK (1763–1827)

Frederick Augustus, also known as Prince Frederick and the Duke of York and Albany, was the second son of King George III of England. He is best remembered for his military innovations and reforms. Frederick joined the British military at 17, was promoted to full general at 30, and made Commander-in-Chief at 32. During his tenure, he was responsible for implementing administrative and structural reforms still in use today. He established systems of merit-based promotion, curtailing jobbery and nepotism in officer appointments. To ensure that officers were properly trained, he supported the founding of the Royal Military College. He also saw to it that public funds were set aside for uniforms, ending the tradition of colonels being responsible for clothing their troops. Though Frederick never inherited the throne, he served as England's heir presumptive following the death of his niece and father. His older brother, King George IV, outlived him by three years.

LEWIS & CLARK

For over a decade prior to his election as president in 1800, Thomas Jefferson had wanted to learn about the country west of the Mississippi River. Captain Meriwether Lewis and his family had been friends and neighbors of Jefferson for many years, so when Jefferson needed a personal, presidential secretary, he recruited Lewis. Soon after, Lewis and the President began planning an expedition to explore the West, with hopes of finding an all-water route to the Pacific Ocean. While drafting the plans, it became apparent to Jefferson that Lewis was the obvious choice to lead the expedition.

They were concerned that a large number of men on the expedition could be considered an aggressive force by France and Spain, who at the time controlled parts of the territory to be explored. They first planned to take between 12 and 15 men. However it soon became obvious they would need more and Lewis asked to have a co-commander in the person of Captain William Clark. Lewis and Clark had served together in the military. Soldiers and civilian interpreters were recruited as they finalized plans. When the party departed from St. Louis in the spring of 1804 , there were just over 30 men.

There was no way to estimate the duration of the exploration and the equipment and supplies list was extensive. They would need to provide for health and safety as well as the arms necessary for hunting and defense.

The commanders were armed with their personal rifles, pistols, tomahawks, and knives. Captain Lewis also had a fowling piece and a pair of cased duelling pistols. Captain Clark carried his personal hunting rifle, a "Kentucky style" in .36 cal. He referred to it in his journal as his "small rifle." Both Captains carried a horse pistol and each had an espontoon. The standard U.S. military pistol of the era was the model 1799 .69 cal. flintlock made by North and Cheney. The espontoon was regarded throughout the military as the "distinguishing arm of an officer" and a symbol of authority. It was described as a half pike, being about 6 feet in length with a spear-like point roughly 6-8 inches long with a cross bar just below. These were used as a weapon, a gun rest, or as a walking stick. Each of the other members were armed with a rifle or musket, knife, tomahawk, powder horn, and a possibles bag with extra flint, shot, and ball. While buying supplies in Philadelphia Captain Lewis purchased an air rifle and, while in St. Louis, two swivel mounted blunderbusses and a swivel mounted cannon.

The most impressive and unusual firearm used on the expedition was the Girardoni Air Rifle. The air rifle was built in Austria by Bartholomaus Girardoni, in about 1779 and had been used effectively by the Austrian army during the Napoleonic wars. This weapon had somehow found its way to Philadelphia when

Captain Lewis was purchasing supplies for the expedition.

It is a .46 caliber 22 shot repeater that is powered by compressed air stored in a steel tank that also serves as the shoulder stock on the gun. The tank was removed by unscrewing it from the receiver and attaching it to a hand pump, similar to a bicycle pump of today. It took about 1500 strokes to bring the tank to 800 PSI. A hopper on the right side of the rifle would hold 22 round lead balls that were gravity -fed into the breech. Captain Lewis was an excellent showman and used the air rifle to impress the tribes they encountered, who reacted with amazement and awe at the show of "big medicine" by the Captain.

Whenever they encountered a new tribe in the journey, they would arrange a council. A speech would be given, mostly written by President Jefferson, indicating how the great white father in the east would aide their people if they would stop warring with neighboring tribes and trade with the United States of which they were now a part. At the conclusion of the speech, Captain Lewis would give medals and gifts, then conduct his "magic" show by showing the compass and how the needle would always point north and, weather permitting, a magnifying glass would be used to ignite a fire.

The final act was to demonstrate the air rifle. A target would be set up and the rifle shot six to ten times. The natives were never allowed to see the air tank being filled or the hopper loaded. They were careful to never disclose that there was only one air rifle. They left the impression that the

rifle could be shot all day and that every member of the party had one available.

Many guns have been credited as "the gun that won the West." Most often, this is the classic Colt Single Action Army revolver or Winchester lever action rifle. Some thoughtful analysts might say the buffalo rifle for its role in decimating the herds of the Great Plains, opening that area to railroads and settlers and forcing Native Americans onto reservations. Others might point to the Springfield trapdoor rifle carried by the U.S. Army in the Indian Wars, or even the humble double barrel shotgun, a tool as common as the axe or plow for homesteaders, ranchers, and settlers.

However, an excellent argument could be made that if one were pick a single individual gun that "won the West," it

would be the Italian repeating air rifle that Lewis & Clark carried on their epic journey. This small Corps of Discovery crossed and began to chart a vast unknown continent and returned, losing only one man. They encountered new tribes - friendly, hostile, and unknown.

It was by demonstration of the Girardoni that Lewis & Clark silently conveyed the message that the smart course of action would be to send this group on their way upriver and let the next tribe worry about them. It was peace through the illusion of superior firepower… and it set the stage for the opening of the American West.

The air rifle on display in the National Sporting Arms Museum is the Girardoni-Style

Air Rifle, made by Ernst August Stormer of Herzberg Germany.

GIRARDONI AIR RIFLE

Among the arms of the Lewis and Clark expedition was one of these remarkable rifles. It is a .46 caliber air rifle. The buttstock serves as an air reservoir and is charged by a hand pump. It launches a nearly half inch diameter lead ball with great accuracy and enough power to penetrate a one inch plank at 100 yards with no smoke and virtually no sound. It is also a 20-shot repeater, with follow up shots available on demand - an amazing feature in an era of single shot muzzleloading flintlocks. The Corps of Discovery made a point of demonstrating the prowess of this rifle to every tribe they sat down to meet with on their cross country voyage.
Donated by Michael Carrick

CIVIL WAR CARBINES AND HANDGUNS

The period of national strife from 1861 to 1865 went by many names, and nowhere else in the country was there a more divided area than here in Missouri. Whether you refer to it as the War Between the States, the Civil War, or even the Late Unpleasantness; no matter if you are a Northerner or a Southerner, rebel or Yankee; the war cost the country four years of unparalleled destruction and grief, with over 600,000 casualties. The rifles, muskets, revolvers, and pistols from this time period bear silent witness to this national tragedy.

The war taxed the abilities of the two national armories to produce enough arms to supply the hundreds of thousands of recruits that swelled the ranks of both sides in the spring of 1861. Both sides relied on private contractors and imports to supplement what they each could produce domestically.

It was an era of rapid development in firearms design, with breechloaders, metallic cartridge arms, and repeating long arms coming into use. Cavalry and other mounted units used revolvers and short carbines, such as these, which proved handy and effective from horseback or when quickly mounting and dismounting.

U.S. military issue sidearms of the Civil War are shown in the U.S. martial arms chapter. In addition to issue arms, many Civil War handguns were privately purchased by individual soldiers from commercial offerings. Some of those examples are shown here.

Top to Bottom

Gallagher Carbine .50 cal., ca. 1860s, s/n 16766.
17,000+ made, both percussion and cartridge.
Donated by Helen Hansen

Maynard 2nd Model Carbine .50 cal., ca. 1858-65, s/n 24036.
Maynards were used by both sides.
Donated by the John & Mary McConnell Living Trust in memory of Robert M. McConnell

Starr Percussion Carbine .54 cal., ca. 1862-65, s/n 21934.
Over 20,000 made; used by the Union in the West.
Donated by the Kellert Trust

Smith Carbine .54 cal., ca. 1861-65, s/n 19281.
30,000 made; fifth most issued Union carbine.
Donated by the John & Mary McConnell Living Trust in memory of Robert M. McConnell

HISTORIC ARMS

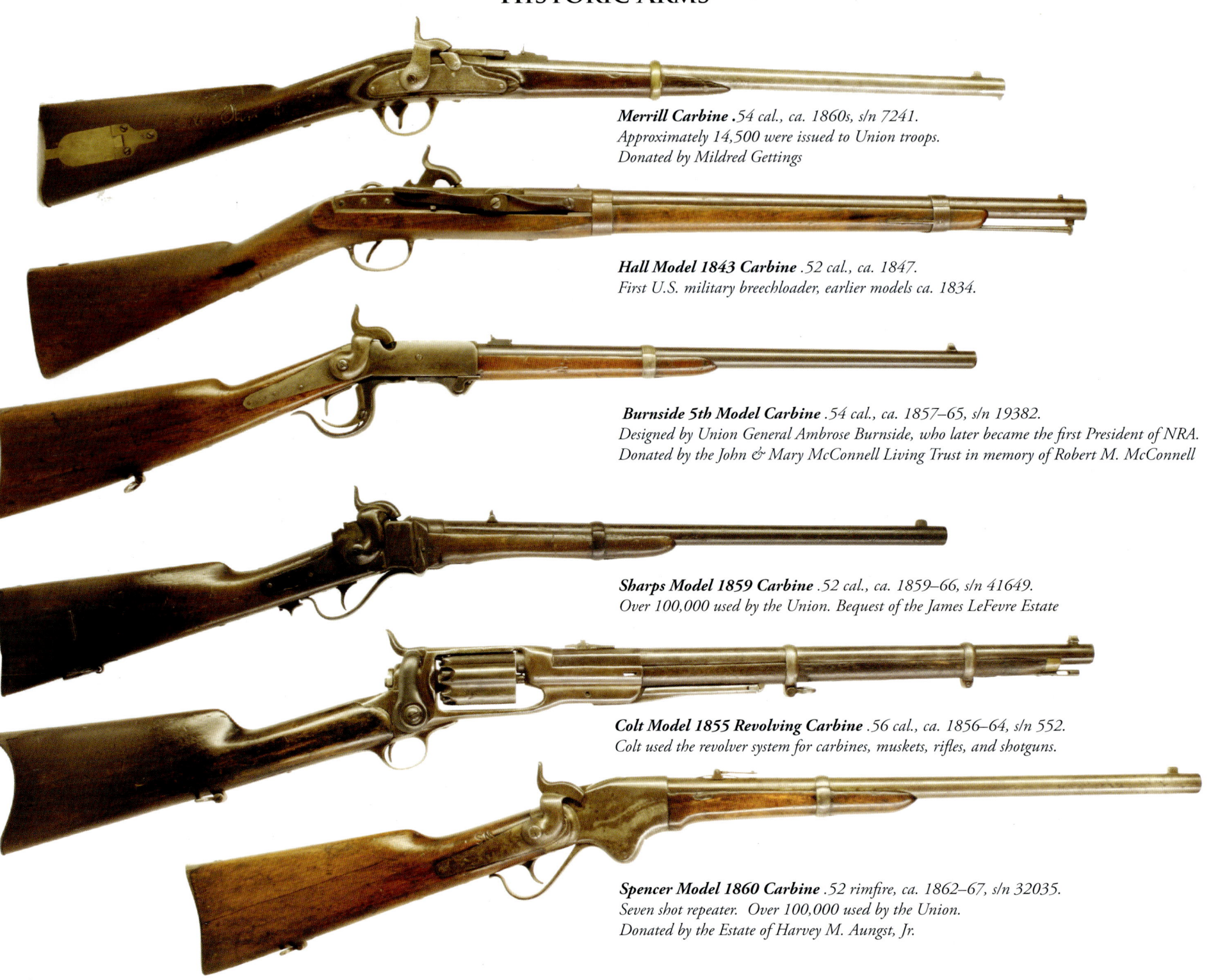

Merrill Carbine .54 cal., ca. 1860s, s/n 7241.
Approximately 14,500 were issued to Union troops.
Donated by Mildred Gettings

Hall Model 1843 Carbine .52 cal., ca. 1847.
First U.S. military breechloader, earlier models ca. 1834.

Burnside 5th Model Carbine .54 cal., ca. 1857–65, s/n 19382.
Designed by Union General Ambrose Burnside, who later became the first President of NRA.
Donated by the John & Mary McConnell Living Trust in memory of Robert M. McConnell

Sharps Model 1859 Carbine .52 cal., ca. 1859–66, s/n 41649.
Over 100,000 used by the Union. Bequest of the James LeFevre Estate

Colt Model 1855 Revolving Carbine .56 cal., ca. 1856–64, s/n 552.
Colt used the revolver system for carbines, muskets, rifles, and shotguns.

Spencer Model 1860 Carbine .52 rimfire, ca. 1862–67, s/n 32035.
Seven shot repeater. Over 100,000 used by the Union.
Donated by the Estate of Harvey M. Aungst, Jr.

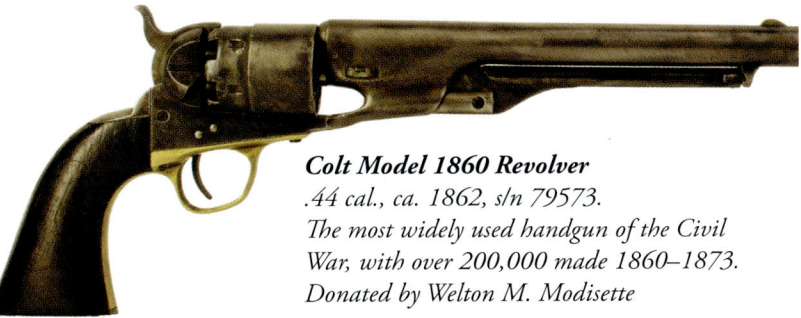

Colt Model 1860 Revolver
.44 cal., ca. 1862, s/n 79573.
The most widely used handgun of the Civil
War, with over 200,000 made 1860–1873.
Donated by Welton M. Modisette

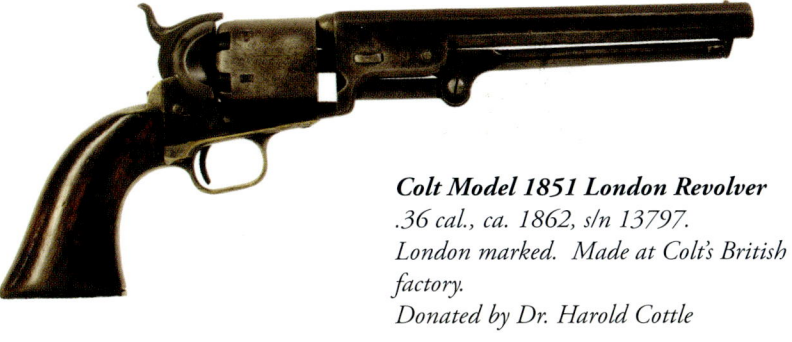

Colt Model 1851 London Revolver
.36 cal., ca. 1862, s/n 13797.
London marked. Made at Colt's British
factory.
Donated by Dr. Harold Cottle

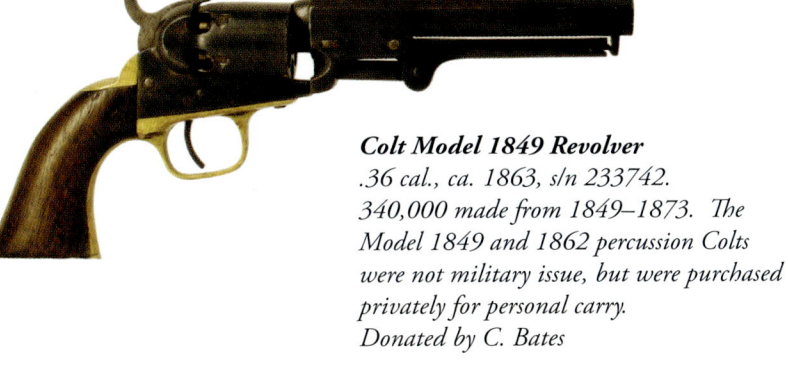

Colt Model 1849 Revolver
.36 cal., ca. 1863, s/n 233742.
340,000 made from 1849–1873. The
Model 1849 and 1862 percussion Colts
were not military issue, but were purchased
privately for personal carry.
Donated by C. Bates

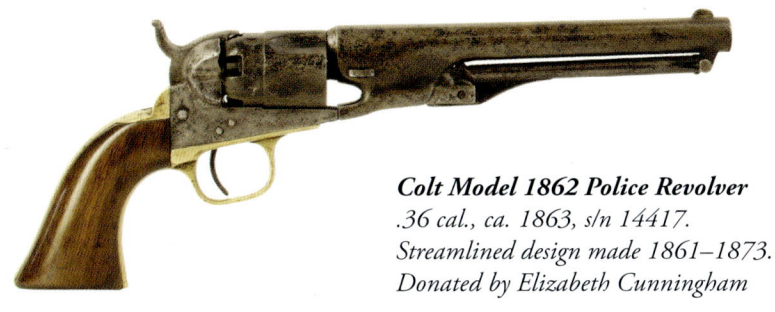

Colt Model 1862 Police Revolver
.36 cal., ca. 1863, s/n 14417.
Streamlined design made 1861–1873.
Donated by Elizabeth Cunningham

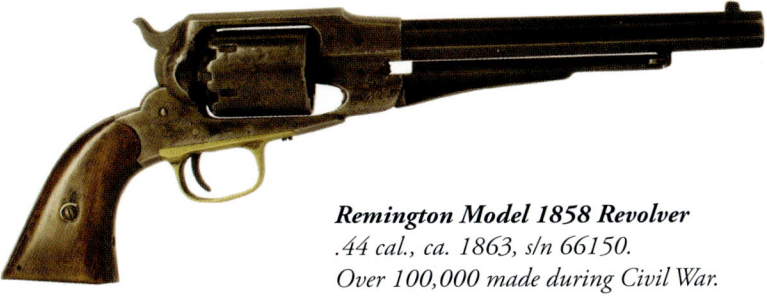

Remington Model 1858 Revolver
.44 cal., ca. 1863, s/n 66150.
Over 100,000 made during Civil War.

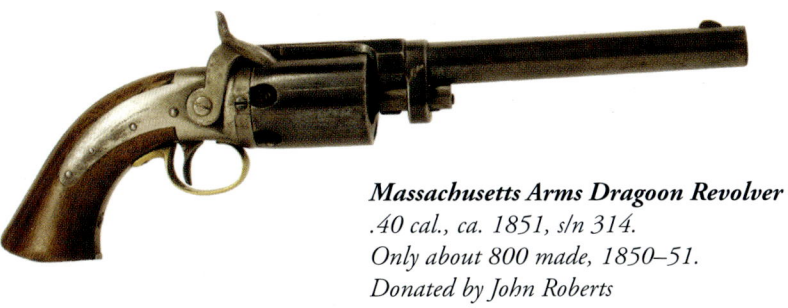

Massachusetts Arms Dragoon Revolver
.40 cal., ca. 1851, s/n 314.
Only about 800 made, 1850–51.
Donated by John Roberts

Savage Navy Model Revolver
.36 cal., ca. 1861.
About 20,000 made during the Civil War.

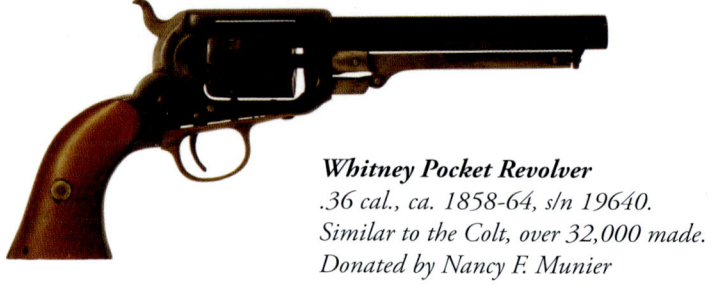

Whitney Pocket Revolver
.36 cal., ca. 1858-64, s/n 19640.
Similar to the Colt, over 32,000 made.
Donated by Nancy F. Munier

Smith & Wesson Model Two Revolver .
32 rimfire, ca. 1864, s/n 43453.
"Old Model Army." 77,000 made 1861 to 1874. The S&W tip-up spur-trigger revolvers were among the first to chamber self-contained metallic cartridges, offering a distinct advantage in loading and durability of ammunition over their contemporary cap and ball percussion revolvers. Like many of the other handguns shown here, there were not official military issue, but were purchased by soldiers of both sides for personal carry.
Donated by the family of Morgan Vance

Smith & Wesson Model One, 2nd Issue
.22 rimfire, ca. 1860s, s/n 53748.
Considered the first widely produced cartridge revolver.

LeFaucheaux Pinfire Revolver
9mm, ca. 1860-70.
Imported pinfires were carried by both sides. The pinfire system was an early type of self contained metallic cartridge, with an internal primer, and a firing pin built into the cartridge, protruding from the rim to be struck by the hammer.

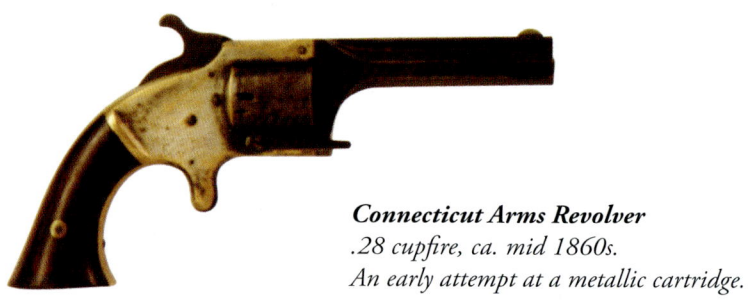

Connecticut Arms Revolver
.28 cupfire, ca. mid 1860s.
An early attempt at a metallic cartridge.

Confederate Kerr Revolver
.44 cal., ca. 1860s, s/n 2502.
With nearly all firearms manufacturers located in the North, the South was hard pressed to arm its troops. A few small Southern manufacturers produced a limited number of guns, but many Confederate weapons were imports, captured Union arms, or personal guns. This British-made sidehammer revolver was a popular southern import, and this example is CSA marked.
Donated by William T. Bundy

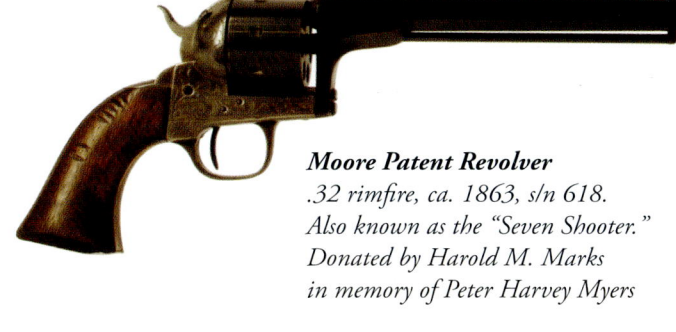

Moore Patent Revolver
.32 rimfire, ca. 1863, s/n 618.
Also known as the "Seven Shooter."
Donated by Harold M. Marks
in memory of Peter Harvey Myers

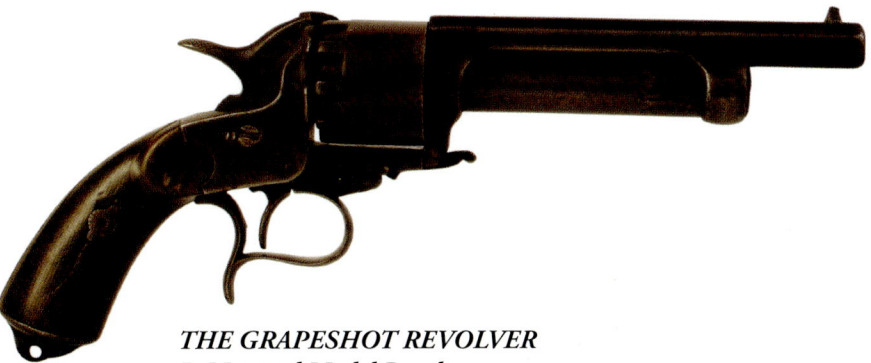

THE GRAPESHOT REVOLVER
LeMat 2nd Model Revolver
.42 cal. & 20 ga., ca. 1861, s/n 960.
Imported by the Confederacy from Europe, the LeMat features a nine shot cylinder which revolves around a second, lower, smoothbore barrel. This shotgun barrel is fired by moving the swiveling hammer nose. This formidable cavalry weapon was favored by CSA Generals Stonewall Jackson, J.E.B. Stuart, and P.G.T. Beauregard.
Donated by Estate of Robert E. Petersen.

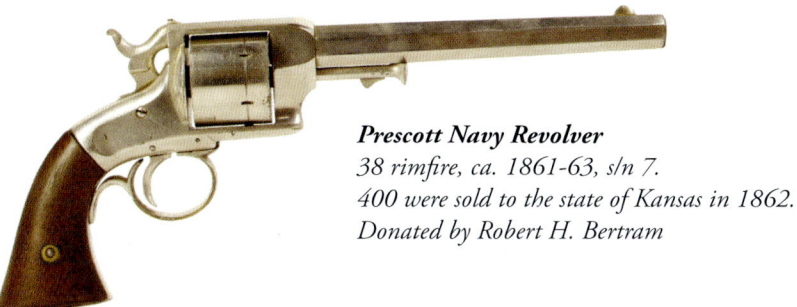

Prescott Navy Revolver
38 rimfire, ca. 1861-63, s/n 7.
400 were sold to the state of Kansas in 1862.
Donated by Robert H. Bertram

ANNIE OAKLEY (1860–1926)

Born Phoebe Ann Mosey, Annie Oakley became known to millions around the world as "Little Sure Shot" for her extraordinary marksmanship. She honed her shooting prowess from an early age when she began hunting to support her six siblings and widowed mother. A market hunter, she was able to earn enough money to pay off the mortgage on her family's house. She gained notoriety at the age of 15 when she won a shooting match against marksman Frank E. Butler, whom she would go on to marry.

As the world's preeminent trick shot artist, Oakley had a remarkable career with Buffalo Bill's Wild West Show from 1885 to 1901. Her stunts included using a firearm to split a playing card on edge from 30 paces, hit dimes tossed into the air, shoot cigarettes out of people's mouths, and snuff out candles. She quickly gained top billing for the show and drew sold out crowds to see her perform.

In an era when Buffalo Bill's name was more widely recognized around the world than that of George Washington, Annie Oakley may legitimately be considered America's first female superstar in the entertainment field.

During her career, Oakley taught thousands of women to shoot. She believed that all women should learn how to use firearms, not only because it was a form of physical and mental exercise, but also in order to defend themselves. In Annie's words: "I want to see women rise superior to that old-fashioned terror of firearms. I would like to see every woman know how to handle them as naturally as they know how to handle babies."

Smith & Wesson Model One Third Issue, *.22 Rimfire, ca. 1880, s/n 126236. Attributed to Annie Oakley. She gave it to a young boy with the admonition to practice. Donated by Welton M. Modisette.*

ANNIE OAKLEY

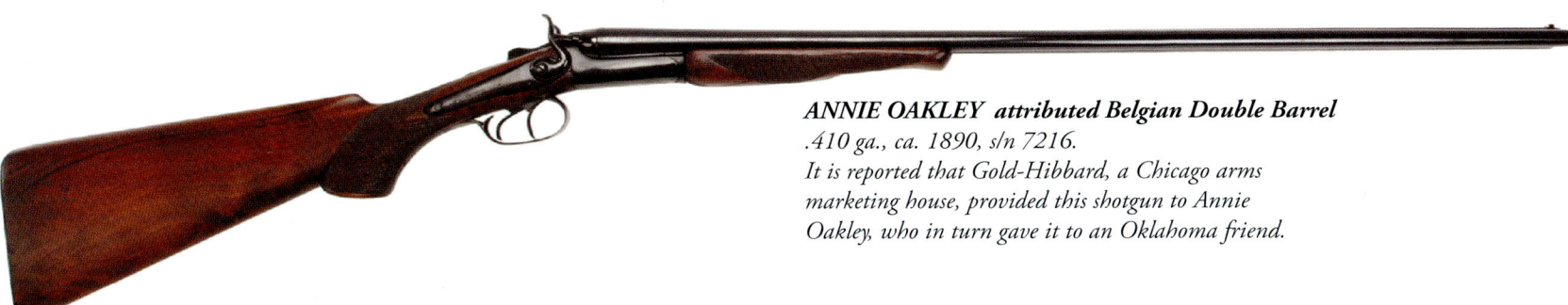

***ANNIE OAKLEY* attributed Belgian Double Barrel**
.410 ga., ca. 1890, s/n 7216.
It is reported that Gold-Hibbard, a Chicago arms marketing house, provided this shotgun to Annie Oakley, who in turn gave it to an Oklahoma friend.

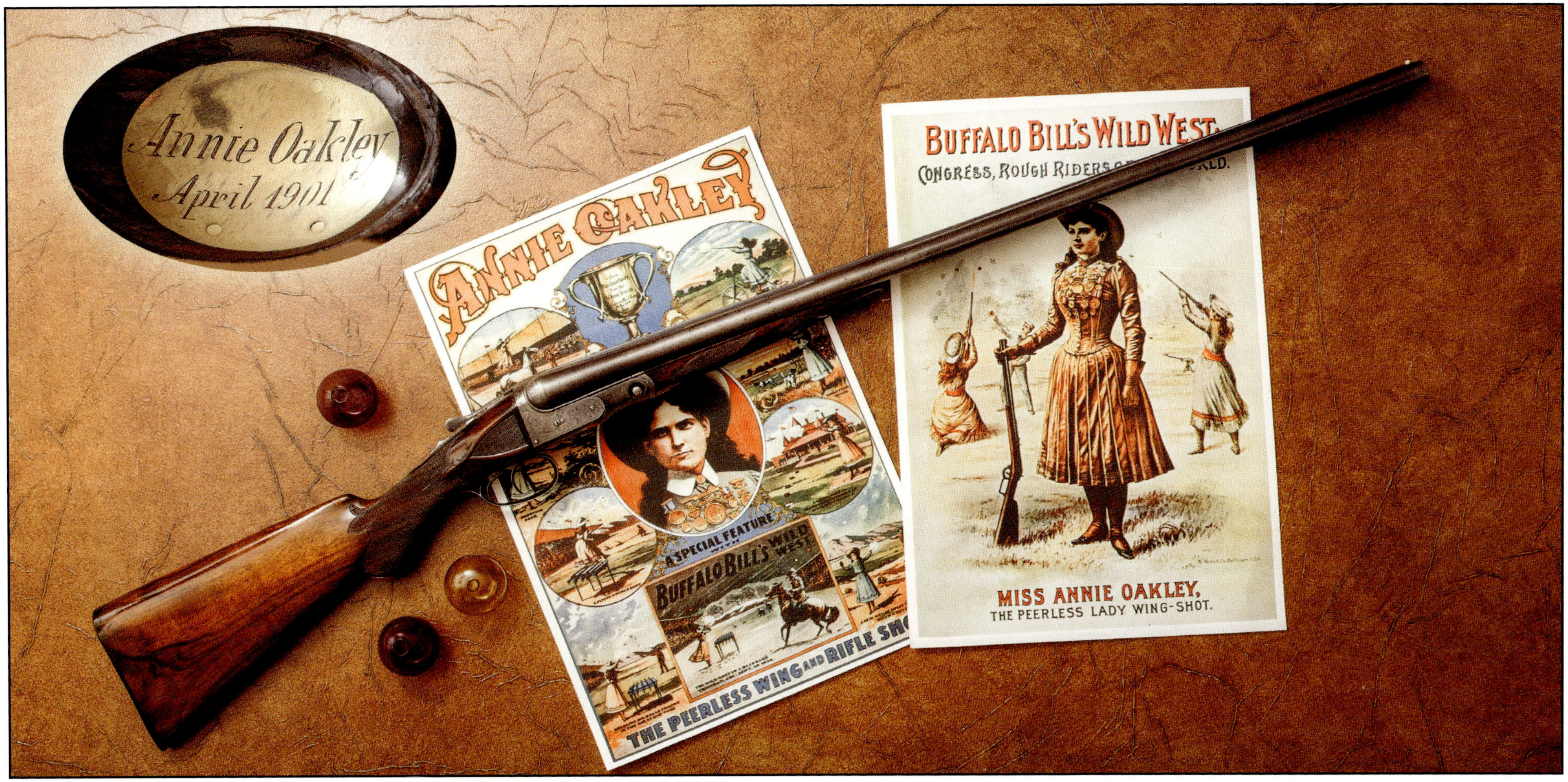

ANNIE OAKLEY's Parker Double Barrel *12 ga., ca. 1880, s/n 102516.*
This Parker shotgun was a gift from Frank Butler to his wife, Annie Oakley (1860-1926), and is well documented by the Parker Factory records.
Donated by the Estate of Robert E. Petersen

LAWMEN AND OUTLAWS

When the Civil War began in April of 1861, it brought with it a period of violence and turbulence our young nation had never before witnessed. Men were forced past their limits by the violence perpetrated during the years of brother-against-brother, neighbor-against-

neighbor savagery. When the war ended, there were bitter feelings on both sides that made it difficult for many of the soldiers to return to a normal life in the post war environment. Men reacted in a variety of ways. Many would respond to the lessons learned from the

JOHN WESLEY HARDIN
Colt 1877 Double Action Thunderer
.41 Colt, ca. 1890, s/n 73728

On May 6, 1895 Deputy Sheriff Will Ten Eyck of El Paso, TX arrested John Wesley Hardin (1853-1895) at the Gem Saloon for "unlawfully carrying a firearm." In his arrest report he noted the serial number. This rare occurrence establishes this gun as Hardin's. Engraved by Cuno Helfricht.

Loaned by Kurt House

JESSE JAMES
Smith & Wesson Schofield and Holster
.45 S&W, ca. 1875

Revolver and holster attributed to outlaw Jesse James.

Loaned by Jim and Eve Supica

BLACK JACK KETCHUM
Engraved Colt Single Action Army Revolver
.45 Colt, ca. 1882, mixed serial numbers

Tom "Black Jack" Ketchum was a notorious outlaw and train robber in the American Southwest, running with the likes of the Hole in the Wall Gang.

Donated by Ron Adolphi

LAWMEN AND OU

Perhaps no arms capture the public i and imagination like the sixguns of t especially those carried by the Lawme Outlaws of this iconic time and place are some of those revolvers.

HOW NOT TO ROB A TRAIN

Black Jack's last heist was a novel affair, and he came to a bad end.

In August 1899 after nearly a decade of banditry, Black Jack decided to rob a New Mexico train single handedly. He chose the exact same train his brother Sam had robbed the previous month and flagged it down at the exact same location. The conductor, likely having learned from the recent unpleasantness, shotgunned Black Jack off his horse and left him to lie beside the tracks. A posse came by to collect him the next day, and shipped him off to prison in Colorado where his wounded arm was amputated. He was returned to New Mexico Territory for trial, found guilty of "felonious assault upon a railway train," and sentenced to hang.

Some say he'd gained weight in prison. Others that the hangman simply miscalculated. Whatever the case, when the trap door in the scaffold opened, Black Jack's head was popped neatly from his body by the noose. The attendant photograph of the spectacle was a popular postcard for some time to follow. To add insult to grievous injury, capital punishment for "felonious assault upon a railway train" was later found to be unconstitutional.

CAPT. FRANK HAMER
Colt 1873 Single Action Army
.45 Colt, ca. 1898, s/n 180260

Texas Ranger Captain Frank Hamer (1884-1955) is best known for ending the criminal careers of Bonnie & Clyde in May, 1934. This gun was a gift from his brother, a fellow ranger, Harrison Hamer. Engraved by Cuno Helfricht.

Loaned by Kurt House

violent confrontations of war and become notorious outlaws while others would be celebrated as the lawmen who stood up to protect a fragile post-war peace.

The guns carried by these lawmen and outlaws in the Old West capture the public imagination and interest perhaps more than any other firearms. These are some of those revolvers.

Col. John Rankin's Smith & Wesson Russian
.44 Russian, ca. 1870s, s/n 39197

Inscribed "Col. John K. Rankin, Lawrence, Kansas" on the backstrap. Rankin was the only person to offer armed resistance to Quantrill's raid, engaging two of the guerillas in a pistol fight.

7th Calvary (Battle of Little Big Horn)

7th Calvary (Battle of Little Big Horn)

BAD BOB MELDRUM
Colt 1873 Single Action Army
.45 Colt, ca. 1904, s/n 252818

"Bad Bob" Meldrum (1866-?) often worked both sides of the law and was a known associate of Tom Horn. This gun was thought to have been presented to him by the Tomboy Gold Mining Co. while he was Town Marshal of Telluride, CO. His whereabouts after 1926 are unknown. Engraved by Cuno Helfricht.

Loaned by Kurt House

JESSE JAMES attributed Smith & Wesson Schofield and Holster, .45 S&W, ca. 1875, s/n 273.
Loaned by Jim Supica

JESSE JAMES was born the son of a Baptist minister / commercial hemp farmer on September 5 1847 in Clay County, MO.

At age 16, Jesse and his older brother Frank rode with Confederate guerillas under the command of Bloody Bill Anderson.

After the war, Frank and Jesse are believed to have committed the first known daylight bank robbery at Clay County Savings in Liberty, MO, on February 13, 1866.

For the next ten years, the James Gang became probably the most notorious outlaws in the country, robbing banks, trains, and stagecoaches. They attracted the attention of the Pinkerton Detective Agency, who staged a raid on the James farm in 1875. An incendiary device thrown into the homestead exploded, blowing the arm off Jesse's mother and killing his younger half brother. This event, along with admiring newspaper coverage of the gang's exploits, contributed to a growing public sympathy for the James brothers.

The glory years of the James gang ended in 1876 with their ill-fated raid on a bank in Northfield, MN. The citizenry shot the gang to ribbons, with only Frank and Jesse escaping. Attempts to form a new gang met with only moderate success.

Jesse was shot in the back of his head while straightening a picture on the wall by fellow gang member Bob Ford on April 3, 1882.

During the life of Jesse James, the feelings between Northern and Southern sympathizers was intense and many were reluctant to view James as an outlaw. Some thought of him more as a Robin Hood or as a soldier of the South.

JOHN WESLEY HARDIN's Colt 1877
Double Action Thunderer, .41 Colt, ca.
1890, s/n 73728.
Loaned by Kurt House

JOHN WESLEY HARDIN a.k.a. "Little Arkansas" was born in 1853 near Bonham, TX, the son of a Methodist preacher, and died August 19, 1895, at the hands of John Selman Sr. in El Paso, TX. He was 42 at the time of his death.

Trouble started early for Hardin. At age 13 he stabbed and nearly killed a classmate over a girl. Two years later, at the age of 15, he killed his first man, a former slave named Maje, over the outcome of a wrestling match. This was followed by the killing of 3 Union soldiers sent to arrest him.

Hardin was busy over the next 7 years claiming to have committed nearly 30 killings, but on August 24, 1877, the Texas Rangers caught up with him on a train in Florida. He was arrested and eventually tried and sentenced to Huntsville prison for 25 years.

He was released from prison on February 17, 1894. Having studied the law while in prison, he passed the Texas bar and set up shop as a lawyer in Gonzales, TX. His life changed little from before prison, and he met his end the afternoon of August 19 1895 when Constable John Selman Sr. shot him from behind in the Acme Saloon in El Paso, TX.

This gun has unusually excellent provenance as an outlaw's revolver. On May 6, 1895, Deputy Sheriff, Will Ten Eyck of El Paso TX, arrested John Wesley Hardin at the Gem Saloon for "unlawfully carrying a firearm." In his arrest report he noted the serial number of this gun, a rare occurrence in that era, establishing this gun as Hardin's.

It was shipped to El Paso dealer Ketelson & Degetau on December 30, 1889, and is engraved by Cuno Helfricht.

John Wesley Hardin

Frank Hamer

CAPT. FRANK HAMER's Colt 1873
Single Action Army, .45 Colt, ca. 1898, s/n
180260.
Loaned by Kurt House.

FRANCIS AUGUSTUS HAMER – a.k.a. Frank was born March 17, 1884 in the city of Fairview, Wilson County, TX, the son of a blacksmith. He joined the Texas Rangers in 1906, and died in 1955, six years after retiring from the Rangers.

Frank Hamer was a lawman through some of the worst years of the Great Depression. Jobs were scarce and living was hard. There were many who barely scratched out an honest living, but there were also those who followed an easier path, living outside of the law, robbing, and killing at will. It was a time that needed the likes of Texas Ranger Frank Hamer.

Though best remembered for ending the murderous careers of Bonnie and Clyde Barrow, and the following publicity and movie, Frank, in the true nature of the Texas Rangers, seldom talked about his career as a lawman. However Ranger Captain Bill McDonald was talking about men like Frank Hamer, when he said, "No man in the wrong can stand up against a fellow that's in the right and keeps on a-comin'." In life, Frank Hamer was a lawman who kept on a-comin'.

This gun is inscribed to his brother, a fellow Ranger, Harrison Hamer. It is New York style engraved.

BAD BOB MELDRUM's Colt 1873
Single Action Army, *.45 Colt, ca. 1904, s/n 252818. Silver-plated and engraved by Cuno Helfricht.*
Loaned by Kurt House.

ROBERT MELDRUM, a.k.a. Bad Man Bob, a.k.a. Hair Trigger Bob was born in 1866. His date of death is unknown. He simply disappeared in 1926, his fate remaining one of the great mysteries of the Old West.

Meldrum was born one year after the end of the Civil war, and lived during a time of western expansion; an era of conflict between cattle barons and small ranchers. He was a man of small stature, 5 feet 6 inches tall, and slight of build weighing barely 140 pounds, with dark hair and grey eyes, but tough as nails and lightening quick with his gun. He dealt with problems in a very direct way, but his mean streak was exhibited whenever things didn't go just his way. During his lifetime, he reportedly killed 14 men, at least two of whom were unarmed. Not a great deal is known about Meldrum. There are no books written about him, there was never a movie made about him, but without doubt he was a most interesting character of his time.

As a marshal in Wyoming and Colorado towns, he "had no reservations about shooting someone if he thought they needed it." In his 20s he worked with Tom Horn and is reputed to have been involved in some of the range war killings credited to Horn.

This Colt was presented to Robert "Bad Man Bob" Meldrum by the Tomboy Mining Company of Telluride, Colorado.

Bad Bob Meldrum

BAT MASTERSON

Masterson wore many hats during his lifetime: buffalo hunter, Indian fighter, civilian scout, gunfighter, lawman, and even newspaper columnist. In 1877, Bat settled in Dodge City, where he became Under-Sheriff and eventually Sheriff. By 1891, he had moved to Denver, where he took up journalism in the local paper. In 1902, Bat moved to New York City, serving as a Deputy U.S. Marshal. From 1909. until his death in 1921, he travelled the country reporting on boxing matches for New York's Morning Telegraph.

Bat Masterson

BAT MASTERSON'S
Colt Single Action Army
.45 Colt, ca. 1888, s/n 128770

"Send to my address C.O.D. one of your 45 caliber pistols nickel plated. Make the barrel a little longer than the ejector rod. Make it very easy on trigger and make front sight rather high and thick. Send as soon as possible."

- Letter from Masterson to Colt, ordering this Colt SAA.

Loaned by Dick Burdick

BASS REEVES

Bass Reeves was one of the most prolific lawmen of the Old West, and was the first African-American to be appointed as a U.S. Deputy Marshal west of the Mississippi.

Born into slavery in 1838, Reeves escaped from his owner during the Civil War and found refuge in Indian Territory (present day Oklahoma). He was taken in by Native Americans, from whom he learned the land, tracking skills and Indian languages, skills which later served him well. After the Civil War, Reeves moved to Van Buren, Arkansas, with his wife and children, where he was often recruited to help local Deputy Marshals track outlaws.

In 1875, he was officially commissioned as a Deputy U.S. Marshall under the "Hanging Judge" Isaac C. Parker. Reeves reportedly arrested more than 3,000 people during his 32 year career as a Deputy Marshal. His most difficult arrest was of his own son, Bennie, in 1902. Bennie was accused of murdering his wife when he found out she had an affair, and was found guilty of the crime.

Reeves transferred to the federal court in Paris, Texas, in 1893, and then to the Muskogee Federal Court in 1897. At age 69, he took a job with the Muskogee Police Department. He passed away 1910. His funeral was said to have been attended by hundreds of people, white, black and Native American.

DEPUTY U.S. MARSHAL BASS REEVES' Cold Single Action Arm Revolver. *.32 WCF, ca. 1895, s/n 161628. On loan from the U.S. Marshals Museum, Ft. Smith, Arkansas. Donated to them by Reeve's great-nephew, Judge Paul Brady.*

COL . JOHN RANKIN's S&W Russian Model, *.44 Cal S&W, ca. 1870, s/n 39197. Loaned by Jim Supica.*

COL. JOHN KNOX RANKIN – (Soldier/Statesman/Businessman) Born the son of the Reverend Robert Henderson on November 3, 1837, died October 29, 1913, at the hands of a man known as Howard Wynn, an employee of the Lawrence Paper Mill. Rankin was 75 years old at the time of his death.

On August 21, 1863, then Lt. John K. Rankin was on leave with his brother Capt. William A. Rankin in Lawrence, KS, while serving as a member of The Second Kansas Volunteer Infantry. It was that day that William Quantrill led 450 guerillas in a deadly raid on the town of Lawrence. As the Rankins turned a corner they came upon two raiders shooting at a man lying in his yard. The Rankin's drew their guns and rushed toward the two horsemen. Just then, four other raiders came up behind them and they all began shooting. It was not known how many shots were exchanged, but both Rankins emptied their revolvers. Lt. Rankin believed he wounded one of the raiders severely, as he saw him slump in his saddle.

John Rankin and his cousin were the only two men who stood up to the raiders that hot August morning. Lt. Rankin went on to exemplary service during the Civil War and a life of respect and service to his country. In his later years as a business man, he became half owner and manager of the Griffin Ice Company of Lawrence. It was there that a man known as Howard Wynn, who had been drinking heavily, became incensed, feeling he had been shorted on the weight of a block of ice. He attacked Col. Rankin, leading to the Col's death. The man who had faced down Quantrill's raiders and survived numerous battles during the Civil War, died over the weight of a block of ice.

Black Jack Ketchum's Engraved Colt Single Action Army Revolver
.45 Colt, ca. 1882, mixed serial numbers.
Donated by Ron Adolphi

TOM "BLACK JACK" KETCHUM was a notorious outlaw and train robber in the American Southwest, running with the likes of the Hole in the Wall Gang. Black Jack's last heist was a novel affair, and he came to a bad end.

In August 1899, after nearly a decade of banditry, Black Jack decided to rob a New Mexico train single-handedly. He chose the exact same train his brother Sam had robbed the previous month and flagged it down at the exact same location. The conductor, likely having learned from recent unpleasantness, shotgunned Black Jack off his horse and left him to lie beside the tracks. A posse came by to collect him the next day, and shipped him off to prison in Colorado where his wounded arm was amputated. He was returned to New Mexico Territory for trial, found guilty of "felonious assault upon a railway train," and sentenced to hang.

Some say he'd gained weight in prison. Others that the hangman simply miscalculated. Whatever the case, when the trap door in the scaffold opened, Black Jack's head was popped neatly from his body by the noose. The attendant photograph of the spectacle was a popular postcard for some time to follow. To add insult to grievous injury, capital punishment for "felonious assault upon a railway train" was later found to be unconstitutional.

Black Jack Ketchum

183

(Billy the Kid, inset)

PAT F. GARRETT

PAT GARRETT'S THUNDERER
Colt 1877 Double Action Revolver
.41 Colt, ca. 1902, s/n 138671
This gun was presented to Garrett by fellow Customs workers in 1902, and is so inscribed.
Loaned by Arnold Duke

PAT GARRETT

Born in Alabama in 1850 and raised in Louisiana, Garrett headed west in 1869 after both of his parents died. In 1876, he started buffalo hunting in Texas and then became a cowboy in New Mexico. Garrett became Sheriff of Lincoln County, New Mexico, in 1880 and immediately began his hunt of "Billy the Kid." He caught up with Billy in July 1881 and shot him twice, ending the career of one of the Wild West's most infamous outlaws. He moved to Texas and became a Lieutenant with the Texas Rangers in 1884, resigning his commission a year later. In 1901, he was appointed Collector of Customs in El Paso by President Theodore Roosevelt. Garrett was murdered in 1908, but it remains unclear to this day exactly who killed him.

ADJ. GEN. W. W. STERLING's
Colt 1873 Single Action Army
.45 Colt, ca. 1933, s/n 354870.

Owned by Adjutant General W. W. Sterling
and engraved "Sterling, Co. D." Sterling
enlisted as a Private in the Texas Rangers
and rose to Adjutant General, the only
Ranger to do so. Engraved by Wilbur Glahn.
Loaned by Kurt House

Texas Ranger Captains, ca. 1932.
Standing, left to right, Capt. J. A. Brooks,
Gen. W. W. Sterling, Capt. Frank Hamer,
and Capt. John R. Hughes. Seated is Capt.
Dan Roberts.

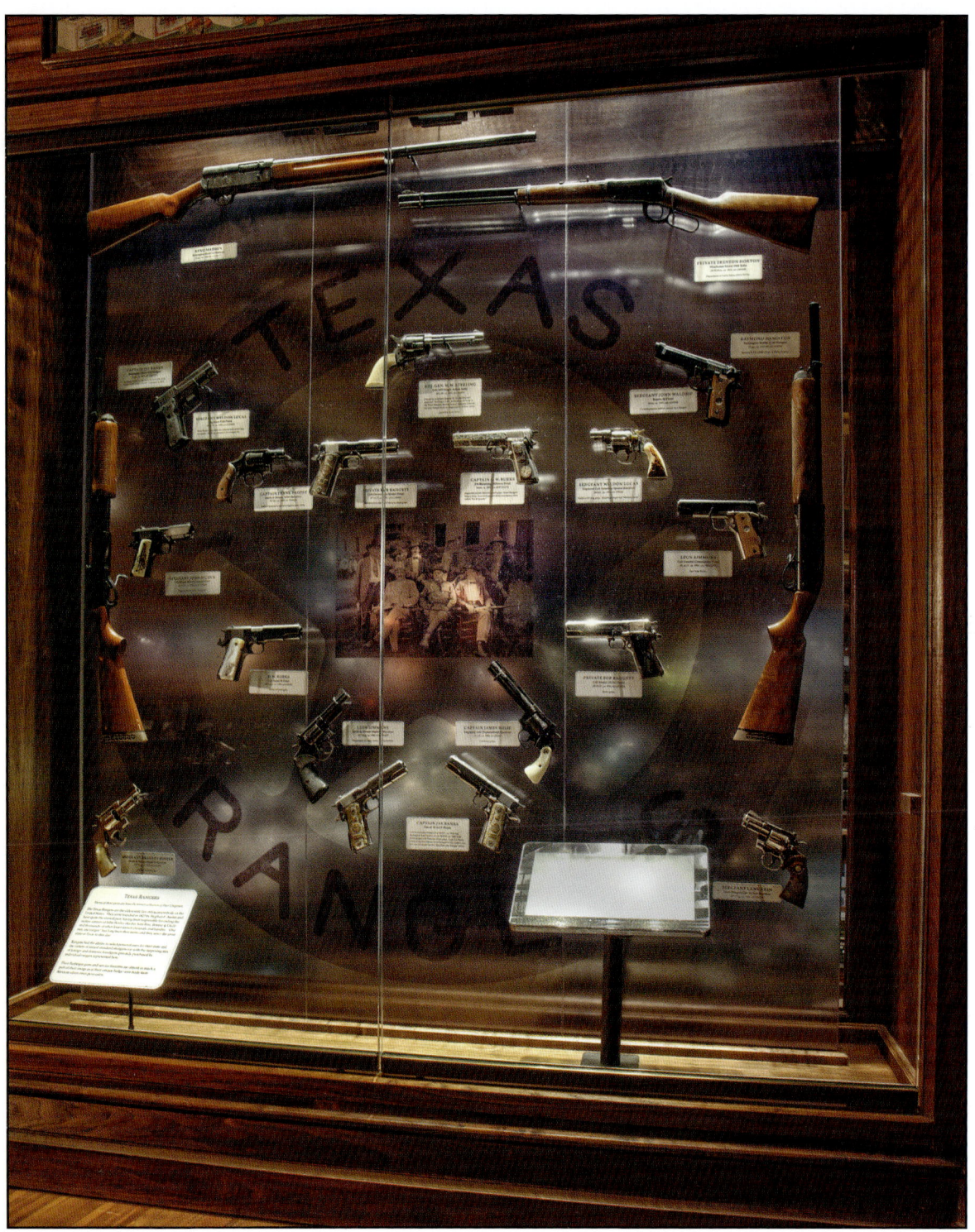

TEXAS RANGERS

Featuring Texas Ranger guns donated by Paul Chapman

In the summer of 1823, Stephen F. Austin, a former Missourian, was in the business of establishing colonies of American settlers in South Texas. The Mexican revolution had wrested Mexico from Spain. Austin was working with the current Mexican government, who agreed to honor his father's Spanish land grants for up to 300 American homesteaders. The land being settled was a no man's land occupied by hostile bandits and raiders. These outlaws and Indians, numbering in the thousands, were regularly raiding the Texican homesteads, killing and looting at will. Around August of 1823, Austin declared in writing that he would employ ten men to act as Rangers for the common defense of the homesteads. The wages to be paid would be fifteen dollars a month, payable in property. The Rangers were to furnish their own clothing, weapons, and horses. Austin provided food, ball, and powder. Each Ranger was armed with side-arms, musket, and a knife.

Firearms used by these earliest Rangers were muzzleloading flintlocks. Knives varied, with most being Bowie type knives with heavy and durable blades. Horses were of the utmost importance to the Rangers and at times the recruiting process centered as much on the horse as the man. As has continued to modern day Rangers, there were no uniforms and in the earliest days, no badge.

In 1874, fifty years after the first ten Rangers began patrolling the frontiers, the Texas Legislature created the Frontier Battalion, consisting of six companies of 75 Rangers each, under the command of Major John B. Jones, a veteran of the Civil War. By mid-summer, the Frontier Battalion had been deployed to the most remote frontiers of Texas. There had been more than 40 parties of Indians raiding the settlements. By September of 1875, no Indian raids were reported anywhere in the battalion's area of operations, a piece of Texas 100 miles wide stretching 400 miles from the Red River to the Rio Grande. The Rangers reported nineteen engagements and had pursued forty bands that they could not overtake. They fought their last Indian engagement six years later, in January 1881, in the mountains of West Texas. Their attention was then turned to feuds, barbed-wire fence cutters, killers, robbers, and lynch mobs.

In the late 19th and early 20th centuries, Rangers had a hand in bringing to justice (or the graveyard) outlaws such as John Wesley Hardin, Sam Bass, and Bonnie and Clyde, and in apprehending a would-be assassin at a summit meeting between American President William Howard Taft and Mexican President Porfirio Diaz.

The old-time Ranger tradition of being resolute in the face of overwhelming odds has given rise to what has become the unofficial Texas Ranger motto. The story goes that a Ranger was sent to quell a potential riot. Upon his arrival, a civic father supposedly asked where the rest of the Rangers were, and was given the laconic response "One riot… one Ranger."

Appealing as the story is, it probably didn't happen exactly that way. The quote may be based on a response attributed to Texas Ranger Captain Bill McDonald when he was sent to quash an illegal boxing match in 1896. Upon arrival, he was asked a similar question and allegedly replied, "Hell, ain't I enough? There's only one prizefight." The fight was moved to Mexico, where it was actually attended by several Rangers and other lawmen, more likely as enthusiastic spectators than in any official role.

The 20th century saw a new type of Ranger evolve. While they still had their Wild West, Frontier Battalion reputation, they were becoming the detectives that we know today. On Sept 26, 1905, a woman and her children were found murdered on a farm in Jackson County, TX. Local police officers made an arrest and the Rangers and state troops were called to protect the prisoner from lynching. When

the defendant was tried, the result was a hung jury, and another trial scheduled. At the request of the court, Ranger Captain McDonald reopened the investigation. He located key evidence in the form of three bloody fingerprints that had been found in the home of the victims. McDonald followed this evidence to another suspect and was able to convict the murderer, acquitting the original suspect.

In 1937, the Rangers were merged into the Texas Department of Public Safety.

The Texas Rangers' equipment has changed greatly since their early days. Rangers themselves have transformed from grizzled South Texas Indian fighters, who provided their own clothing, weapons and horses, to some of today's most modern and scientific criminal detectives. Their firearms improved with the times and the Colt .45 SAA became a mainstay sidearm until John Browning perfected his 1911. Shortly thereafter many Rangers adopted the Colt platform, first in .45 auto, then later in the Super .38 caliber.

The modern Ranger recruit is issued a laptop computer, a digital camera, and an audio recorder. Today, these are combined within their cell phones and evidence collection kits, along with more traditional crime fighting weapons that include the SIG SAUER 1911 TACOPs

pistol. The DPS SOG (Department of Public Safety, Special Operations Group) has authorized officers the additional option to carry a duty issued SIG SAUER P226 DAK in .357SIG or the .45 caliber Colt (1911 type semi-automatic). They are also issued an AR-type rifle in .223 cal., a 12 gauge tactical shotgun, gas mask, body armor, helmet and baton. For taking prisoners, they are issued hand cuffs and leg irons.

With all of the modern equipment available to today's Rangers, one tradition continues into the 21st century. They still don't wear official uniforms. The choice of

clothing is up to each Ranger, though white hats, Western style clothing, and boots are recognized as their unofficial "uniform."

Through most of the history of the Texas Rangers a wide variety of guns were employed. The simple rule was, if you could qualify with the gun, you could carry it. Some of these guns are called "barbecue guns," as the social life of most Rangers involved fellowship with his colleagues and their families at the back yard barbecue, where they carried these ornate, beautifully engraved and valuable guns for protection and show.

Texas Rangers gathered at El Paso to stop the illegal Maher–Fitzsimmons fight, 1896. At the front row from the left are Adj. General W Mabry, and Captains. J Hughes, J Brooks, Bill McDonald (author of the famous phrase "One Riot, One Ranger") and J Rogers.

Large frame double action revolvers by Colt and Smith & Wesson were widely favored by many Rangers throughout much of the 20th century. Early favorites in .45 Colt and .44 Special later gave way to .357 Magnums such as these.

Top - **SGT. BRADLEY FOSTER's S&W Model 27 Revolver,** *.357 Mag, ca. 1970, s/n S131497. Mother-of-pearl grips.*

Bottom - **SGT. LANE AKIN's Colt Python Revolver,** *.357 Mag, ca. 1969, s/n E18329.*

TEXAS RANGER CAPTAIN JAY BANKS

In August of 1987, when Captain Jay Banks died at the age of 75, friends and colleagues from Texas and all over the country were at his funeral. He had been one of the best known Texas Rangers in their history. He was the model for the Texas Ranger statue at Dallas Love Field, appeared on several television game shows of the era, and was featured on the cover of Time magazine with the caption, "One Riot, One Ranger." But it was in April of 1957, when he and fellow Rangers John Klevenhagen and Jim Ray fought a fierce gun battle, that Banks upheld the legendary and heroic saga of the Rangers by personally bringing an end to mad dog killers Gene Paul Norris and his partner Bill Humphrey.

Norris was a professional criminal and Oklahoma ex-con. He was suspected of over 40 murders and was on the FBI's Ten Most Wanted list. He was known as "the smiling killer." Humphrey, a.k.a. "Silent Bill," and Norris were planning the biggest bank robbery of their criminal careers. They plotted to rob the Carswell Air Force Base branch of the Fort Worth National Bank on the day the military payroll arrived.

Their plans were to take the bank's cashier and her minor son hostage, steal her car, use the post entry sticker on the car's windshield to gain access to the post, and then ambush the armored car guards when they showed up with the payroll. Once they had the money, they planned to return to the cashier's home, kill the woman and her son, collect their getaway car, and escape. It looked like a fool proof plan. However, they had the attention of the FBI and were being wire tapped. The FBI notified the Rangers.

Texas Ranger Jay Banks, who had just been promoted to Captain, realized that Norris would be casing the bank prior to the robbery and staked out the bank and the cashier's home. Sure enough, as Officer Banks was watching the bank branch, Norris and Humphrey appeared in their hot rod Chevrolet. The would-be bank robbers were on the alert for any signs of surveillance and spotted the stake out. The chase was on. Humphrey put the pedal to the floor and sped off, breaking through a road block and reaching speeds of nearly 120 miles per hour. With Humphrey at the wheel, Norris was shooting at the pursuing Banks.

In a chase akin to a modern action movie, the gun fight went on for over 20 miles, until Humphrey lost control of the hot rod Chevrolet and slid to a stop by a creek. Both robbers bailed out of the car shooting as they ran. Humphrey fell first, near the car. Norris appeared to be getting away when the sound of Captain Banks M3 Grease gun filled the air. When the autopsy was performed Norris, had over 25 bullet holes in his body.

"The smiling killer" had met his end. He had been ranked as one of Texas's worst criminals since Clyde Barrow. His murdering career was brought to an end on April 29, 1957, through the heroic efforts of Captain Jay Banks of the Texas Rangers.

GUNS OF TEXAS RANGER CAPTAIN JAY BANKS *Remington Model 870 Shotgun, 12 ga., ca. 1975, s/n V185178V. Inscribed "NEVER DRAWN IN ANGER NOR DROPPED THRU FEAR." Presented in 1979.* **Pair of Colt Government Model Pistols,** *.45 ACP, ca. 1950, s/n C226291 & ca. 1944, s/n 1403782. Ambidextrous safety and Mexican silver grips*

Donated by Paul Chapman

RANGER BRANTLEY FOSTER's FN/Browning High Power Pistol, *9mm, ca. 1985, s/n 245PT02732. Engraved nickel Mexican pearl grips. Some Rangers keep a fancy decorated gun for dress occasions, often called "Bar-B-Q guns."*

LEON SIMMONS' Colt Combat Commander Pistol *.45 ACP, ca. 1986, s/n 70BS64150. Two-tone finish.*

CLASSIC COLTS   The Ranger preference for Colts in .45 caliber continued well into the 20th century as 1911s in .45 ACP slowly gained favor over Single Action Armies in .45 Colt

PRIVATE BOB BADGETT's Colt Government Model Pistol, *.45 ACP, ca. 1935, s/n C128365. With ambidextrous safety and Mexican silver grips, and **Colt Model 1911A1 Pistol** .45 ACP, ca. 1944, s/n 1078652. With ebony grips.*

PRIVATE TRENTON HORTON's Winchester Model 1894 Rifle. *.30-30 Win. ca. 1952, s/n 1989886. Department of Public Safety (DPS# 25726).*

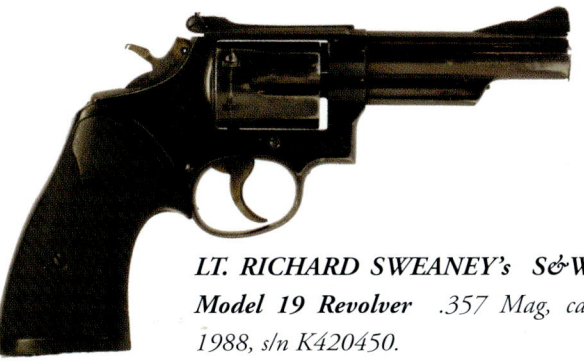

LT. RICHARD SWEANEY's S&W Model 19 Revolver .357 Mag, ca. 1988, s/n K420450. Department of Public Safety (DPS) #222028.

CAPTAIN FRANK PROPST's S&W M10-5 Revolver. .38 Special. ca. 1988, s/n D358256. The hammer has been bobbed to prevent snagging when drawn.

SERGEANT WELDON LUCAS's Engraved Colt Detective Special Revolver. .38 Special. ca. 1970, s/n 376141. Nickel with stag grips. Backstrap engraved "Weldon Lucas."

In recent decades, a variety of semi-auto pistols have gained favor with Texas Rangers. Top to bottom:
SGT. WELDON LUCAS' Sig Sauer P220 Pistol, .45 ACP, ca. 1990, s/n G225625
SGT. JOHN WALDRIP's Beretta 92 Pistol, 9mm, ca. 1985, s/n A00092I
SGT. JOHN AYCOCK's Colt Model 1991A1 Compact Pistol, .45 ACP, ca. 1999, s/n CPO9694.
Stag grip panels with Ranger seal

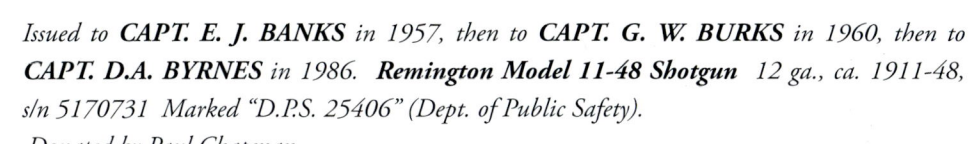

Issued to **CAPT. E. J. BANKS** in 1957, then to **CAPT. G. W. BURKS** in 1960, then to **CAPT. D.A. BYRNES** in 1986. **Remington Model 11-48 Shotgun** 12 ga., ca. 1911-48, s/n 5170731 Marked "D.P.S. 25406" (Dept. of Public Safety).
Donated by Paul Chapman

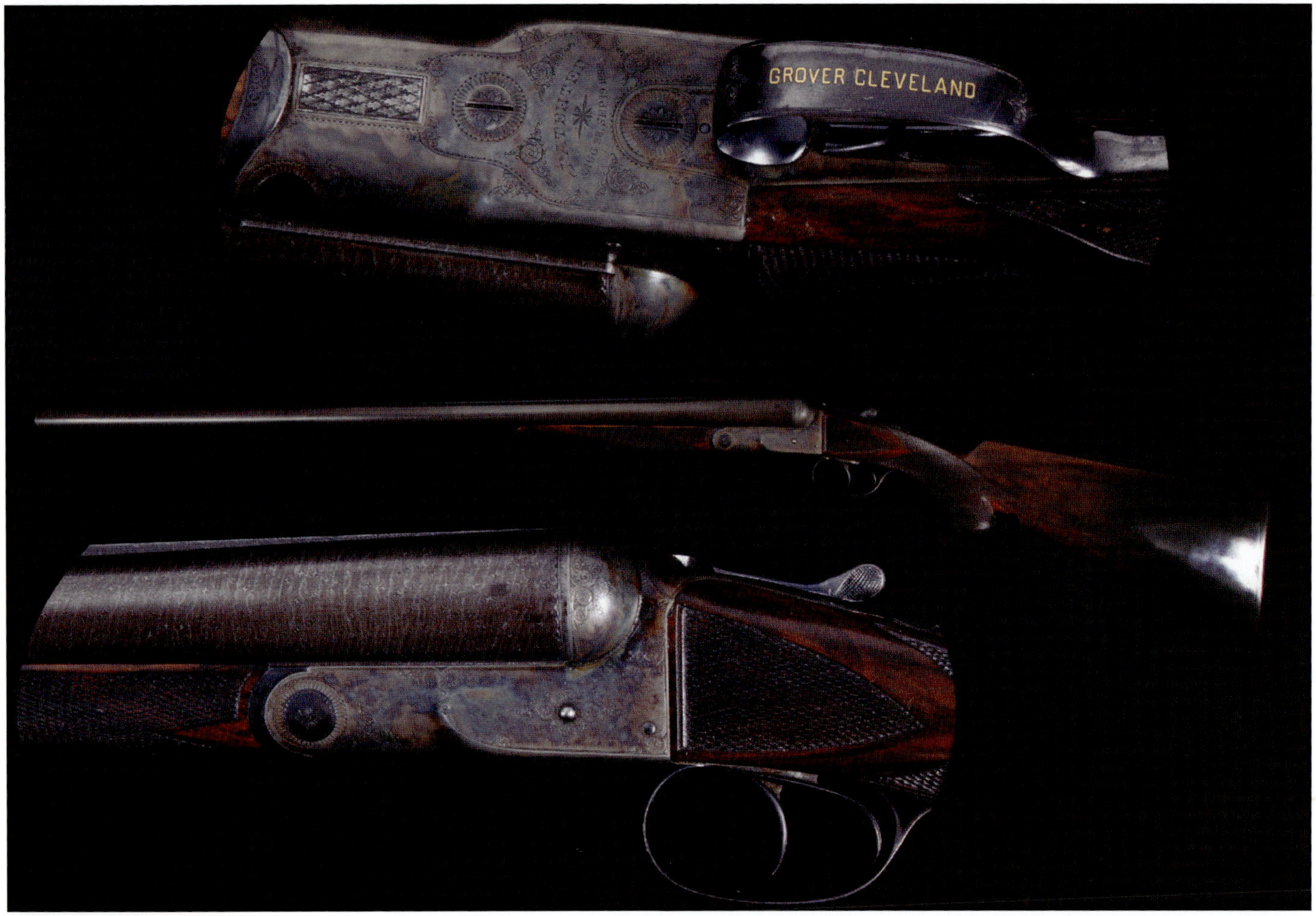

HISTORIC ARMS

At left:
***PRESIDENT GROVER CLEVELAND's
biggest Colt Shotgun ever. Colt Model
1883 side-by-side hammerless shotgun,***
*8 ga., ca. 1885, s/n 7624.
Although best known for revolvers in the late
19th century, Colt also produced double barrel
shotguns in 12 ga. and 10 ga. from 1878
to 1895. This is the only known example
chambered for the massive 8 gauge.
Donated by the Estate of Robert E. Petersen*

Opposite Page - ***PRESIDENT
DWIGHT D. EISENHOWER's
Winchester Model 21 shotgun,***
*20 ga., ca. 1950, s/n 25923.
President Dwight David Eisenhower
(1890-1969) was given this shotgun by
Robert Woodruff, CEO of Coca-Cola. It
bears an inscribed plaque that reads: "To a
straight shooter from a friend" along with
five gold stars inlaid on the triggerguard.
This shotgun was brought to the Museum by
a former U.S. Secret Service agent, whose
initial duty assignment with President
Eisenhower included firing this shotgun
during a bird hunt. His last official duty
was to honor the wishes of Mrs. Mamie
Eisenhower by delivering this shotgun to the
NRA as a donation.
Donated by General J. D. Eisenhower*

PRESIDENT GROVER CLEVELAND (1837 – 1908)

Born in New Jersey, Cleveland holds the distinction of being the only president to serve two non-consecutive terms and is the only president to be married in the White House.

Cleveland was old enough to serve in the Civil War and, under the Conscription Act of 1863, he would have had to serve or pay a substitute to serve for him. He chose the latter option, paid a Polish immigrant $150 to take his place, and continued his career as a lawyer.

Branching out from the law, Cleveland spent time as sheriff of Erie County, mayor of Buffalo, and governor of New York. Setting his sights on the highest office in the land, he ran for president in 1884.

When Cleveland began his first term as president in 1885, he moved into the White House as a bachelor. His wife, Frances Folsom, was 27 years younger than him when they wed in the Blue Room in 1886. John Philip Sousa and the U.S. Marine Band provided the music at the wedding.

He lost re-election in 1888, but ran again in 1892 and won. After his second term, he retired to New Jersey and served as a trustee at Princeton. In 1907, he fell ill and died of a heart attack in 1908 at the age of 71.

PRESIDENT DWIGHT D. EISENHOWER (1890 – 1969)

Born in Denison, TX, Eisenhower moved to Abilene, KS, when he was two. One of seven boys in the family, he developed an interest in history and the military at a young age.

Beginning with an appointment to West Point in 1911, Eisenhower set out on a prestigious military career. In World War I, he served under notable Generals John J. Pershing and Douglas MacArthur. He rose through the ranks and by World War II, he was a five-star general. Eisenhower served as the Supreme Commander of invading Allied forces in France on D-Day in 1944.

At the end of World War II, he assumed the role of Chief of Staff of the Army. After his military career, he served a brief tenure as president of Columbia University.

During the 1952 election, his simple "I Like Ike" slogan served him well. Eisenhower entered the White House in 1953 and served two terms; he was the first term-limited president under the 22nd Amendment. His tenure in office is most remembered for ending the Korean War and creating the Interstate Highway System. While in office, the last two states – Alaska and Hawaii – were admitted to the Union.

Upon retirement, he and his wife Mamie moved to a working farm near Gettysburg, PA. In 1967, they deeded their farm to the National Park Service; it is now open to visitors. Eisenhower died in 1969 at the age of 78 and was buried in Abilene, KS.

SERIAL NUMBER ONE GUNS

In addition to guns owned and used by famous and infamous individuals, "Historic Firearms" include milestones in firearms manufacturing history. Each of the guns in this section has a serial number of "1."

In most cases, this will indicate that it is the first gun of a particular model to be produced. Other times, it may indicate a prototype or be a "batch number," or the significance may be unclear.

Prior to the early 1800s, most guns were not serially numbered. Colt was one of the first large makers to assign a unique number to each individual gun, starting with 1 on the first gun of a particular model produced and going up from there. Smith and Wesson, Winchester, and others adopted a similar system. Some manufacturers, such as Remington, would "batch number" some of their models during the mid to late 19th century, starting with "1" and going through "999" or "9999" and then starting over.

By the early 20th century, the practice of serially numbering firearms had been widely adopted by most major manufacturers. However, it was still common to not number less expensive models, notably low grade shotguns and .22 rifles. From the mid-19th century through today, some makers also used "assembly numbers." These numbers would be marked on most major parts of the gun to help keep hand-fitted pieces together through assembly. Sometimes the serial number would also serve as an assembly number, but sometimes a totally different unrelated number was used.

The Gun Control Act of 1968 required that each individual gun of a particular model have its own unique serial number. Since that time, each firearm produced has had such a designation. Sometimes a manufacturer will start a model with a number other than "1." Prototype or pre-production samples may have serial numbers that are different from production model serial numbering, and sometimes custom serial numbers are available for VIP customers.

Loaned by Jim Supica

Colt 1851 Navy Model .40 Caliber Prototype Serial Number 1, *ca. 1850s.*

In the 1850s, Colt attempted to develop a model with more power than their handy holster size .36 caliber Model 1851 Navy that was also smaller than their massive .44 caliber Dragoon. Before settling on the rebated cylinder Model 1860 Army, they experimented with a .40 caliber revolver on the 1851 Navy frame. This is s/n 1 of four produced.

Sharps U.S. Model 1870, Serial Number 1 *.50-70, ca. 1870.*
After the Civil War, the U.S. military assembled a small number of these as they searched for a metallic cartridge, breech-loading rifle to replace the muzzle-loaders of the 1860's. This Second Type Sharps rifle is #1 of 300 made. Eventually the military settled on the trapdoor action.

Porter Turret Rifle 3rd Model, Serial Number 1 *.50 cal. perc, ca. 1850s.*
This alternate approach to developing a multi-shot revolving firearm used chambers arranged like the spokes of a wheel. It's likely that the potential for chain fires with some of the chambers aiming at the shooter was partially responsible for its failure to gain popularity.

SERIAL NUMBER ONE GUNS

EARLY REPEATING HANDGUNS

Colt's revolver system was not the only early successful repeating handgun. Throughout the 1830s and into the 1840s, the pepperbox, which featured a rotating cluster of barrels, was more popular than the revolver. Others used double barrels for a quick second shot.

Upper right to lower left:

Manhattan Pepperbox Pistol, Serial Number 1, *.28 cal., ca. 1850s.*
It is believed that each configuration of this pepperbox had its own serial number range, which would make this the first of the six-shot 4.5" barreled model.

British Pepperbox, Serial Number 1, *.36 cal., ca. 1830s-50s.*
As with many British pepperboxes, maker and significance of the serial number are unknown.

Allen & Thurber Double Barrel Single Trigger Pistol, Serial Number 1, *.34 cal., ca. 1850s.*
When both hammers are cocked, the first pull of the trigger fires the right barrel and the second pull fires the left.

SINGLE SHOT DERRINGERS

Compact single shot pistols were popular as concealed carry for personal defense or casual plinking guns in the mid 19th century. Top to bottom:

Frank Wesson Model 1859 Pistol, Serial Number 1, *.30 rimfire, ca. 1859.*
Unusual toggle-switch barrel opening mechanism.

Allen & Wheelock Center Hammer Pistol Serial Number 1, *.32 rimfire, ca. Early 1860s.*
No-lip variation with extractor. This model may have been batch numbered.

Brown Southerner, Serial Number 1, *.41 rimfire, ca. 1869.*
Previously made by Merrimack Arms Co., this is the first one made by Brown Manufacturing.

S&W New Model Number Three .38 Winchester Serial Number 1 *.38-40 (.38 WCF), ca. 1900.*
The S&W New Model No. 3 is sometimes considered the most advanced revolver design of the 19th century Most were chambered for .44
Russian. This variation in .38 Winchester was introduced as its own model with a separate serial number range. With only 74 produced, this is
one of the rarest S&W models.

Pieper Style Prototype Revolving Rifle Serial Number 1 *7.65 mm, ca. 1896.*
This unmarked gun is believed to be a possible tool room prototype
for the Pieper carbine, some of which were used by the Mexican mounted police, the "Rurales."

Smith and Wesson Schofield, Serial Number 1 *.45 S&W, ca. 1875.*
The Schofield was designed for the U.S. Army and was used during the Indian Wars. This is the first one made. After it was de-accessioned by the Army, the barrel was shortened, the gun was nickel plated, and it was one of the Schofields purchased by Wells Fargo & Co.'s Express service to arm their messengers.

POCKET REVOLVERS

Compact spur-trigger single-action rimfire revolvers enjoyed wide acceptance as concealable defensive handguns in the mid-1800s.

Top to bottom:

Allen & Wheelock Sidehammer, Serial Number 1, *.32 rimfire, ca. early 1860s.*
Third Model long-cylinder variation. It isn't known whether these were serial or batch numbered.

Marlin No. 32 Standard, Serial Number 1, *.32 rf, ca. 1876.*
Believed to be the first production gun of this model. Factory engraved with original simulated ivory grips.

Remington Iroquois, Serial Number 1, *.22 rimfire, ca. 1878-88.*
Fluted cylinder variation of this 7-shot spur trigger revolver. References vary as to whether this model was serial or batch numbered, leaving the significance of this #1 unknown.

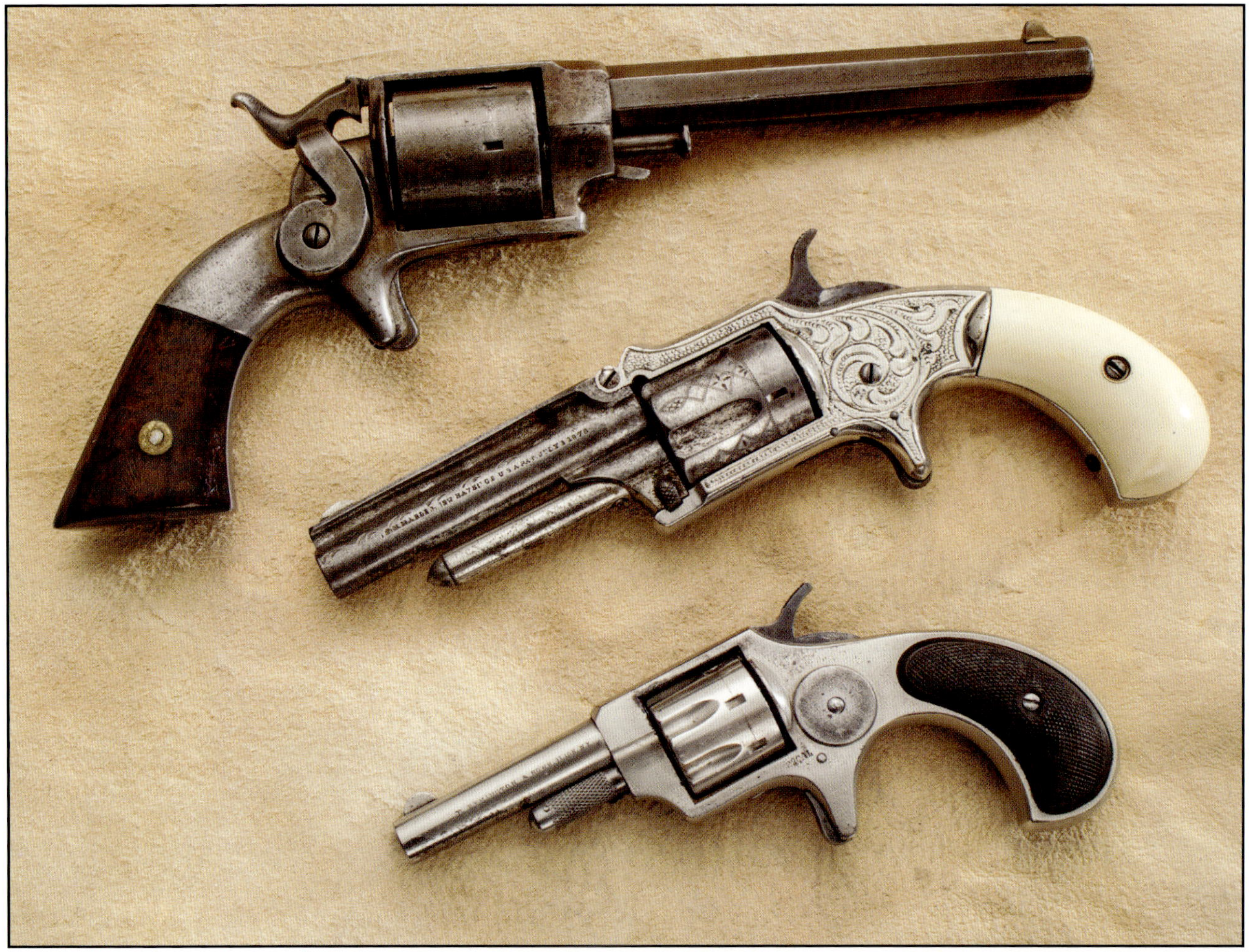

Baby Hammerless Model 1910, Serial Number 1, *.32 S&W, ca. 1910s.*
Folding trigger revolver manufactured by R.F. Sedgely, with previous similar models by Columbian Firearms and Kolb. Smaller .22's were much more common than the larger .32's.

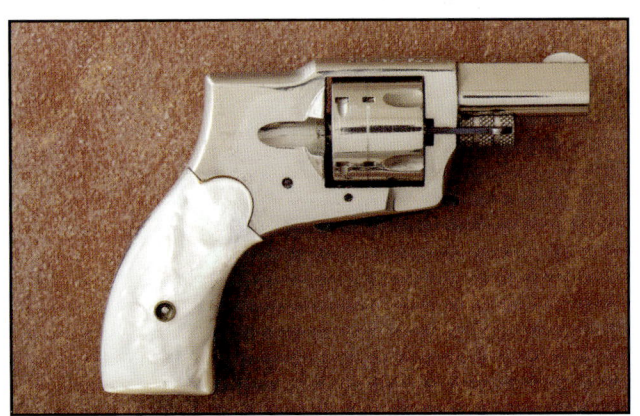

E. A. Prescott Navy Model Revolver, Serial Number 1 *.38 rimfire, ca. 1862. Most of these were issued to Kansas militia in the Civil War. This one was rode hard and put away wet.*

BULLDOG REVOLVERS

From the 1870s through the early 20th century, these revolvers offered a step up from most rimfires in a still compact package. The Bulldog designation was widely used by both American and European makers. It generally refers to a compact double action solid frame revolver with a fairly large caliber compared to the size of the gun.

Top to bottom:

Westley Richards RIC Revolver, Serial Number 1, *.450 cf., ca. 1870s.*
"Royal Irish Constabulary" pattern revolver; maker & significance of serial number unknown. British proofed.

Bulldog Revolver, Serial Number 1, *.450 cf., ca. 1870s.*
"British Bulldog" Webley pattern revolver; significance of the serial number is unknown. British proofed.

Charter Arms Undercover, Serial Number 1, *.38 Spec, ca. 1965.*
The compact revolver remained popular throughout the 20th century and into the 21st. This is the first of this five shot lightweight revolver, and the first individual gun ever produced by the Charter Arms company. Engraved by Colt master engraver Al Herbert.

Rossi Triple-Lock, Serial Number PMD 1, *.44 Magnum, ca. 1972.*
Prototype for a large frame Rossi revolver, this is one of only two ever made. Based on a 1908 S&W design, this model has a third locking lug joining the crane to the frame, resulting in the only .44 Magnum Triple-Lock pattern gun known.

PROTOTYPE SUB-COMPACT PISTOLS

The movement to semi-auto pistols for defensive police and civilian concealed carry led to the development of smaller, lighter guns.

Top - **Firearms International D9 Prototype Serial Number 1**, *9mm, ca. 1976. One of only two made. Also considered for production by Iver Johnson, this could have been the earliest ultra-compact 9mm semi-auto.*

Bottom - **Iver Johnson Pony Prototype, Serial Number 001,** *.380 acp, ca. 1978. Although never mass produced by Iver Johnson, limited numbers of similar models were offered by Colt, Star, FI, and Garcia.*

SMITH & WESSON PISTOLS

The late 20th century saw the introduction of numerous new models of semi-auto pistols by the famed revolver manufacturer.

Left - **S&W Sigma SW40F Serial Number SGM0001,** *.40 S&W, ca. 1994.* *First gun of the first production run of the S&W Sigma. This polymer framed semi-auto was designed to compete with the Glock.*

Right - **S&W Model 3914 Serial Number TDF0001,** *9mm, ca. 1989. Believed to be the first production Model 3914 compact pistol.*

Marlin Model 37 Rifle, Serial Number 1 *.22 S, L, LR, ca. 1922.*
Pump action rifle.

Winchester / Cooey
Model 70 Experimental
Serial Number EXP. 1
.30-60, ca. 1960s.
Made in Winchester's New Haven model shop as a prototype, this was intended for the Canadian & European markets.

Marlin Model 100SB Smoothbore Rifle, Serial Number 1, *.22 rf shot, ca. 1940.*
Designed to shoot .22 shot cartridges for close range pest control, or to shoot miniature clay targets.

COMPETITION FIREARMS

GUNS OF CHAMPIONS

Target practice and target competition doubtless began with the earliest development of firearms. When the modern Olympics were reinstituted in 1896, shooting was incorporated into the games and two American brothers brought home the first Gold medals for the United States. Today, shooting sports rank third in the number of medals the United States has won in the Olympics.

Competitive shooting takes a number of forms, from tack-driving precision bench rest, through fast-moving tactical scenario oriented practical shooting, to the challenging moving targets of clay bird shotgunning, or even the just-plain-fun of cowboy action shooting. The NRA's National Matches, held every year at Camp Perry, OH since 1907, offer civilians and military alike the chance to compete in a wide range of disciplines with an even wider age range.

Shown here are guns that have been used to set records and win championships at the highest level of shooting excellence. Some of these firearms may look futuristic to the non-competitor, but you can bet that each feature has a specific task that helps give our world class athletes the edge in competition.

At the center of the case is an Olympic Gold medal and the .22 pistol that won the prestigious award in Rome at the 1960 Olympic Games, exemplifying the challenge and reward to be found in American competitive shooting sports.

OLYMPIC GOLD
Lt. Col. William McMillan's High Standard Olympic Pistol, .22 Short, ca. 1960, s/n 785158.

McMillan's Gold Medal in the 1960 Olympics was the only handgun medal won by the USA.

Donated by the Estate of Lt. Col. William McMillan USMC

COMPETITION FIREARMS

JIM CARMICHEL's Remington Model 700 Rifle,
.308 Win., ca. 1980, s/n A6264757.
Used by writer and NRA Board member Jim Carmichel in competition, where he would tell
others that the duct tape was the only thing holding the gun together.
Donated by Jim Carmichel

S/SGT FRANKLIN TOSSAS' PERFECT SCORE Presentation M1 Garand Rifle,
.30-06, ca. 1960, s/n 478949.
Presented to S/Sgt Tossas who fired the first perfect score in USAF competition, using a
Winchester Model 70.
Donated by Kenneth Brodeur

THURMAN RANDLE's Remington Model 37 Rifle *.22 LR, ca. 1938, s/n 2744.*
NRA President Thurman Randle used this at Camp Perry matches.
Donated by John R. Wark

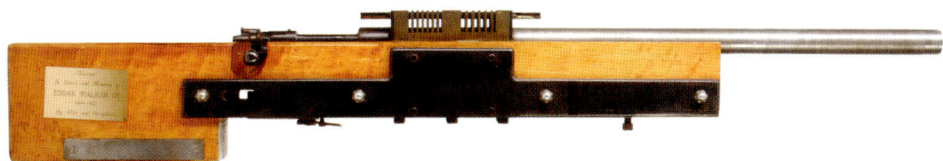

EDGAR WALKER's Benchrest Rifle,
.22 wildcat, ca. 1965, s/n 87141. Walker set many national records with this Mauser action gun. Donated by Arletta Walker

JIM CARMICHEL's
Jarrett/Remington XP-100 Rail Gun
.22 wildcat, ca. 1980, s/n 854. Built for solid accuracy platform. Donated by Jim Carmichel

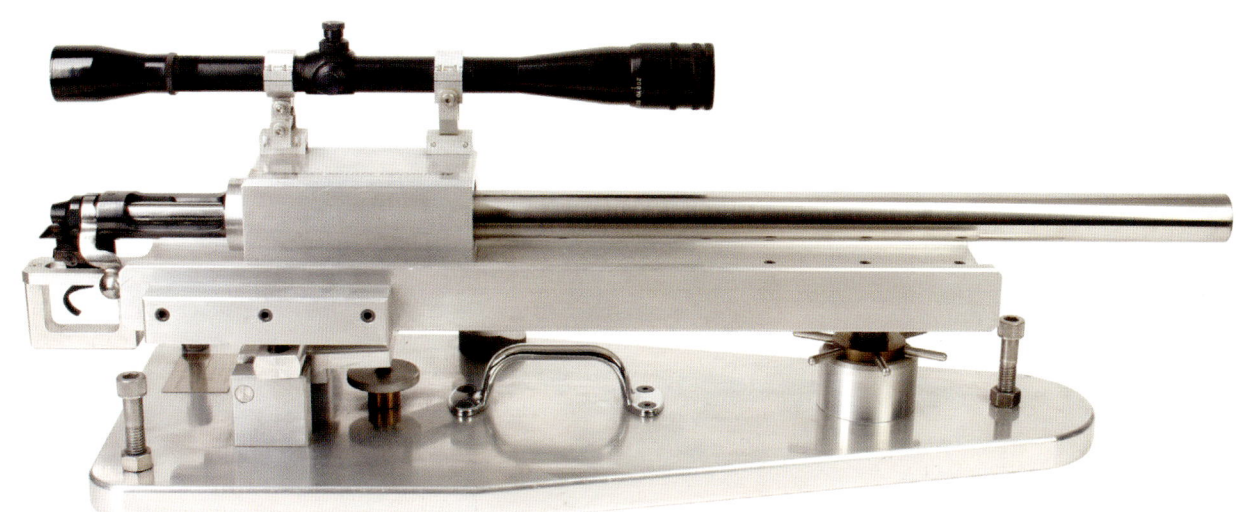

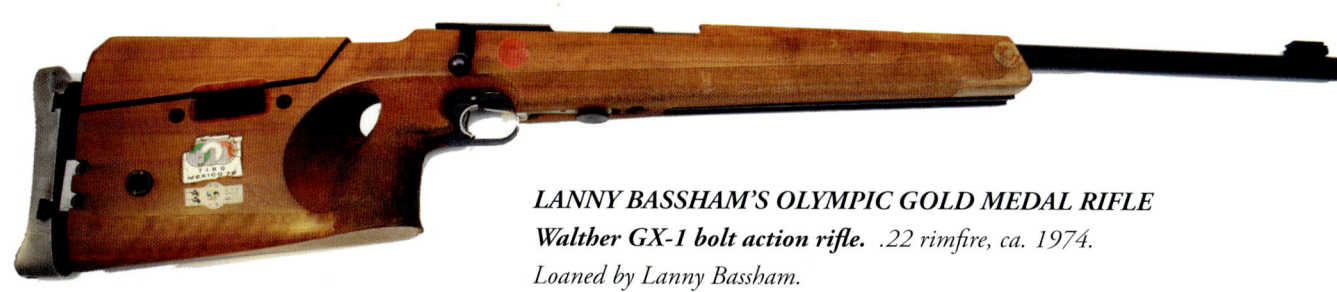

LANNY BASSHAM'S OLYMPIC GOLD MEDAL RIFLE
Walther GX-1 bolt action rifle. *.22 rimfire, ca. 1974. Loaned by Lanny Bassham.*

United States shooter Lanny Bassham won the gold medal in smallbore three position at the 1976 Summer Olympics in Montreal using this rifle. After winning silver at the 1972 Olympics, he sought a design that would suit him better. Bassham dropped the butt plate, angled the pistol grip so the wrist doesn't break when shooting while standing, offset the rail for his offhand rest, lowered the barrel below the edges of the stock, raised his sight bases, and angled the forend up. Although the engineers at Walther disagreed with some aspects of the design, they created this stock to his specifications. His fellow competitors called it "the oar," but beauty is as beauty does, and it served to bring home the gold. Lanny Bassham is pictured at left on the day he brought the rifle to the Museum for display. Bassham's 35 medals in international rifle competition currently sit him at third all-time among US shooters. He set four world records along the way.

U.S. SPRINGFIELD MODEL 1903 RIFLE
Collection donated by Joseph LoRubbio

As the Colonel of the 1st US Volunteer Cavalry in Cuba in 1898, Theodore Roosevelt noticed that the Mauser rifles used by the Spanish had quite the advantage over the black powder U.S. trapdoor rifles, and even the newly adopted smokeless powder Krags used by his own Rough Riders. As President in 1901, he oversaw the adoption of the 1903 Springfield rifle as the standard service rifle of the United States Army.

Initial production was for a new military cartridge, the .30-03, but in a few years an improved cartridge, the .30-06, was adopted. Modeled in part after the world renowned Mauser '98 twin lug bolt action, the 1903 Springfield became the standard US service rifle from 1903 - 1936 and remained active in one variation or another until the end of the Vietnam War in 1975.

Shortly after the adoption of the '03, a new National Guard rifle range opened on the shores of Lake Erie in 1907. Camp Perry is the largest shooting range in the world, and home to the NRA & CMP National Matches each summer, which is considered to be the World Series of shooting.

The Model 1903 rifle dominated the prestigious Service Rifle component of the National Matches for over a half century, and has been used to set numerous long range rifle records. The Farr rifle and the Hession rifle in the front of this case are remarkable examples of this heritage.

A CHAMPION'S RIFLE
TO DEFEND A BRITISH HOME
U.S. Model 1903 Springfield .30-06,
ca. 1905-06, s/n 264631.

In the early decades of the 20th century, Maj. John Hession was one of the world's greatest long range shooters. The brass plaque on the butt of this rifle lists some of his wins and records set. However, in the early years of WWII, a plea came from England to Americans to lend private firearms to help defend British homes from an anticipated German invasion. Maj. Hession added another plaque reading "For obvious reasons, the return of this rifle after Germany is defeated would be deeply appreciated," and sent his prized '03 across the Atlantic. *Donated by Mrs. John W. Hession*

GEORGE FARR'S WALK-ON WINNER
U.S. Model 1903 Springfield Rifle
.30-06, ca. 1921, s/n 1216470.

It was George Farr's first time at the Camp Perry National Matches. On the last relay of September 9, 1921, the 62-year-old Washington state resident was issued a rifle from an armory rack and made history. Using the iron sights on a Springfield M1903 he had never fired before, along with a crude spotting scope, Farr shot an incredible string of 71 consecutive bull's-eyes at his 1000-yard target, using government issue, tin-plated .30-'06 ammunition. Only fading twilight prevented further shooting. Farr's world record feat quickly attracted the attention of his fellow shooters on the line, who pooled their dollars to make a presentation of the rifle. *Donated by Dr. William Farr*

NRA Test U.S. Model 1903 Springfield
.30-06, ca. 1934, s/n 1483770.
Used for NRA testing & evaluation; fitted with a Lyman 48 rear sight.
Donated by James W. Davis

U.S. Model 1903 Springfield Rifle *.30-06 s/n 255129.*

Gen. Julian Hatcher's U.S. 1903 Mark I *.30-06, ca. 1919-20, s/n 1164966.*
The Mark I has an ejection port added for installation of the Pedersen device.
Donated by General Julian Hatcher

U.S. Model 1903 Remington Rifle *.30-06, s/n 3032644.*

U.S. Model 1903A3 Remington Rifle *.30-06, s/n 3451407.*
Aperture rear sight. 1943 barrel.

U.S. Springfield Model 1903 Rifle

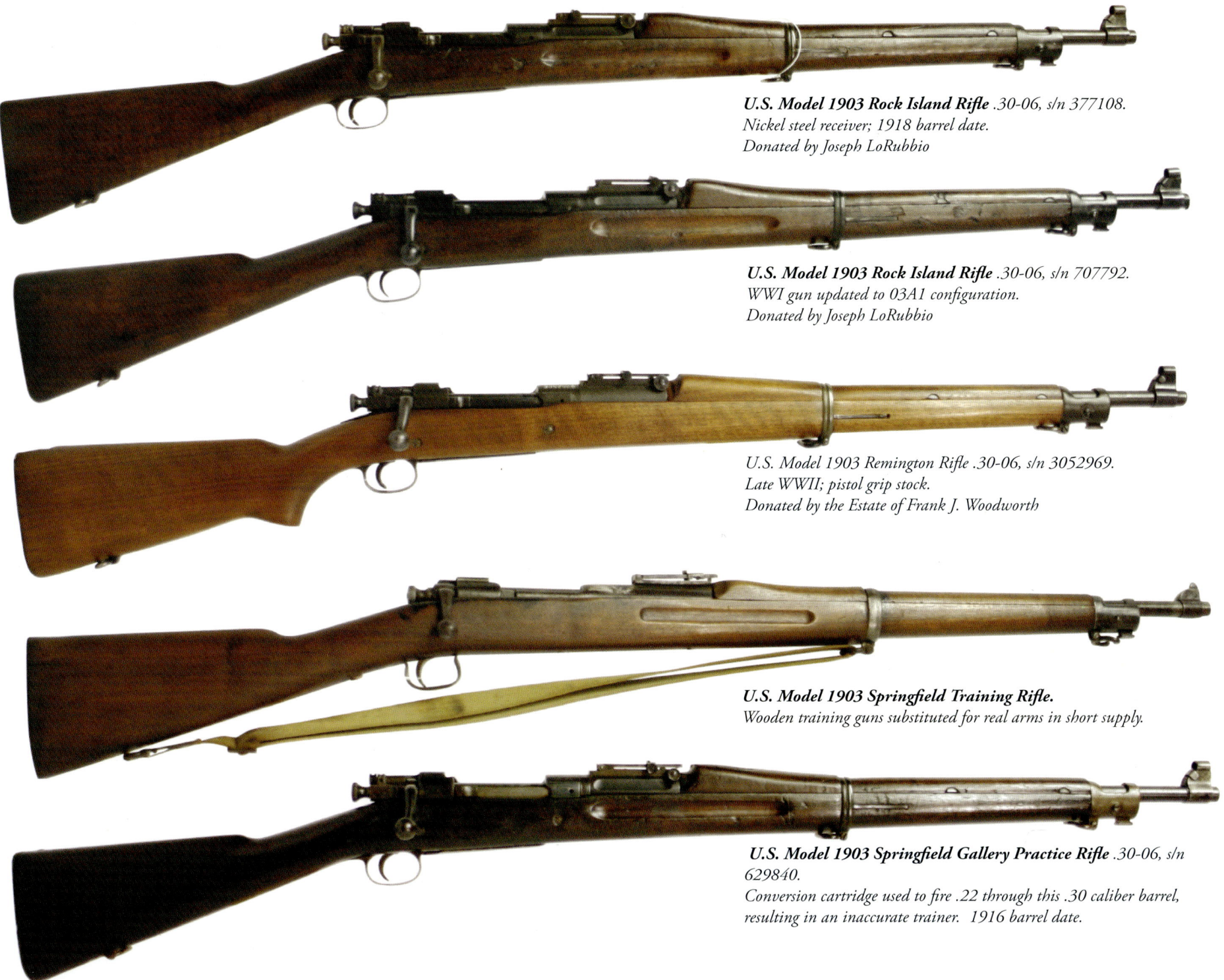

U.S. Model 1903 Rock Island Rifle *.30-06, s/n 377108.*
Nickel steel receiver; 1918 barrel date.
Donated by Joseph LoRubbio

U.S. Model 1903 Rock Island Rifle *.30-06, s/n 707792.*
WWI gun updated to 03A1 configuration.
Donated by Joseph LoRubbio

U.S. Model 1903 Remington Rifle .30-06, s/n 3052969.
Late WWII; pistol grip stock.
Donated by the Estate of Frank J. Woodworth

U.S. Model 1903 Springfield Training Rifle.
Wooden training guns substituted for real arms in short supply.

U.S. Model 1903 Springfield Gallery Practice Rifle *.30-06, s/n 629840.*
Conversion cartridge used to fire .22 through this .30 caliber barrel, resulting in an inaccurate trainer. 1916 barrel date.

U.S. Model 1903 National Match Rifle
.30-06, ca. 1921-28, s/n 1256466.
Accurized for competition shooting.
Donated by Frank Bulawa

U.S. Model 1922 Springfield Rifle
.22 LR, ca. 1933, s/n 2335.
Adapted to rimfire ammunition for practice.

U.S. Model M2 Springfield Third Type
.22 LR, ca. 1933, s/n 12415.
Popular for both military and civilian matches.

U.S. 1903 Springfield Gallery Practice Rifle
.22 LR, ca. 1907-18, s/n 586834.
Rimfire variations are used as low-recoil trainers that retain the weight and feel of the issue arm.

Sporterized Model 1903 Springfield Rifle
.30-06, ca. 1924-33, s/n 1408436.
Many returning G.I.s and hunters favored a military action modified to a sporter.
Donated by Richard W. Taylor

BARRACKS RACK

This inter-war barracks rack was designed to securely hold the standard issue U.S. military arms of that era — the 1903 rifle and 1911 pistol.

Shooting Jacket

ELEGANT ARMS

The origin of decorated arms is lost in the mists of prehistory. The role of humans' earliest weapons in providing food and insuring survival made them some of the earliest and most important tools. The impulse to decorate and personalize them must have accounted for some of humankind's first artistic endeavors.

As societies and technology evolved, the bond between art and arms logically continued. Whether king or tribal chieftain, weaponry represented the means to acquiring and holding political power, and the enhancement of these to suit the status of the owner was a given. By the time the first firearms were developed, the tradition of decorating arms had long been established and continued through the centuries to today.

The decoration of metal by carving designs and images is an exacting art; mastered by relatively few, and only after years of practice. The engraver must have an artist's eye for layout, design, composition and form, and then the ability to manifest his vision. He must combine the skills of the graphic artist and the sculptor on a very small and unforgiving steel canvas.

Embellished guns fit-for-a-king are on exhibit in the NRA National Sporting Arms Museum as shown by the royal guns earlier in this book and the exceptional Fatou fowler leading off this section. Other exhibits show elegant cased handguns and fine multi-barrel sporting long guns.

The demand for ornate firearms blossomed in the 19th century, as represented in the "Engraved Guns of the Old West" exhibit featuring work by master engravers such as Cuno Helfricht, L.D. Nimschke, and Gustave Young. Early auto-pistols were subject to similar decoration, amply illustrated in the "Savage Pistols" display.

Today, the popularity of decorated firearms may be greater than ever. Elegant arms shown here range from fine British "best guns" such as the Holland and Holland double rifles and exceptional custom guns of the Pachmayr Collection, to mass produced commemorative firearms that make "the Joy of Collecting" accessible to all gun enthusiasts.

NAPOLEON BONAPARTE   (1769–1821)

Napoleon Bonaparte is one of the most recognizable and studied military leaders in French history. A skilled tactician, he led successful campaigns during the French Revolution, declaring himself emperor of the French people in 1804.

During the Napoleonic Wars, his military prowess led to a streak of victories and broadened French influence. By 1812, he had extended the French empire to most of continental Europe. In order to maintain the French sphere of influence in these newly loyal territories, Napoleon formed extensive alliances and promoted friends and family members to rule other European countries as French vassal states.

A series of decisive military defeats led to Napoleon's downfall, including a failed invasion of Russia in 1812. His heavily battered army was unable to prevent an invasion of France in 1813. With his country overrun and his military defeated, Napoleon was forced to abdicate as emperor and go into exile in Elba, an island off the coast of northern Italy. In a last ditch effort to regain power, he escaped Elba in 1815, briefly returned to power, but was defeated at the Battle of Waterloo in June of that year. Napoleon never regained power. He spent the final six years of his life in British confinement on the island of Saint Helena off the west coast of Africa.

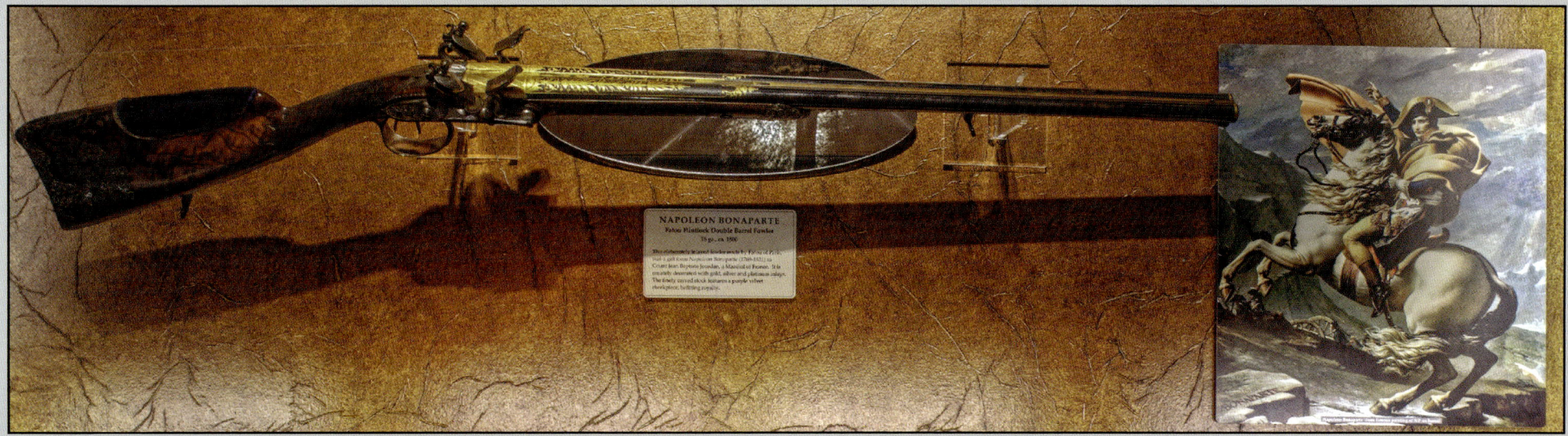

NAPOLEON BONAPARTE
Fatou Flintlock Double Barrel Fowler *16 ga., ca. 1800.*
This elaborately inlaid fowler, made by Fatou of Paris, was a gift from Napoleon Bonaparte (1769-1821) to Count Jean Baptiste Jourdan, a Marshal of France. It is ornately decorated with gold, silver, and platinum inlays. The finely carved stock features a purple velvet cheekpiece, befitting royalty.

217

ELEGANT ARMS

FINE BRITISH CASED HANDGUNS
Donated by Dr. Harold Cottle

The second half of the 19th century is seen as the Golden Age of firearms , both in terms of mechanical evolution and embellishment. Firearms came to represent wealth and station in life. No gentleman of the age was without a brace of cased pistols, a silk topper, and a walking stick. The English excelled at the fine art of manufacturing, embellishing, engraving, and casing firearms for the discriminating buyer.

This collection of English cased guns includes both the percussion and early cartridge sidearm, including pinfire (PF), rimfire (RF), and centerfire (CF) ignition. There are British made guns, along with American and Continental specimens. Marking on guns and labels in cases may identify the manufacturer or the distributor of the arms.

The typical British casing includes compartments for accessories and ammunition. This was especially important with percussion handguns, where the accoutrements might include cleaning rod, screwdrivers, powder flask, bullet mold, cap box, patch box, spare nipples with nipple wrench, and even a spare cylinder to permit a quick reload.

Moore's Patent Revolver
.32 teat-fire, ca. 1864-70, s/n 18617.

Belgian Pepperbox
7.5mm RF, ca. 1870-90.

Allport S&W Model One Type
.22 RF, ca. 1889-95, s/n 806.

J. D. Dougall Galland Type,
.45 CF, ca. 1850–91, s/n 574.

Deane, Adams & Deane Revolver
.45 cal. ca. 1850–72.
Donated by J.H. DeFrees

London Marked Revolver
.38 RF, ca. 1857–67, s/n 40439.

Mortimer
Webley's Patent Revolver
.45 CF, ca. 1862–1900, s/n 879.

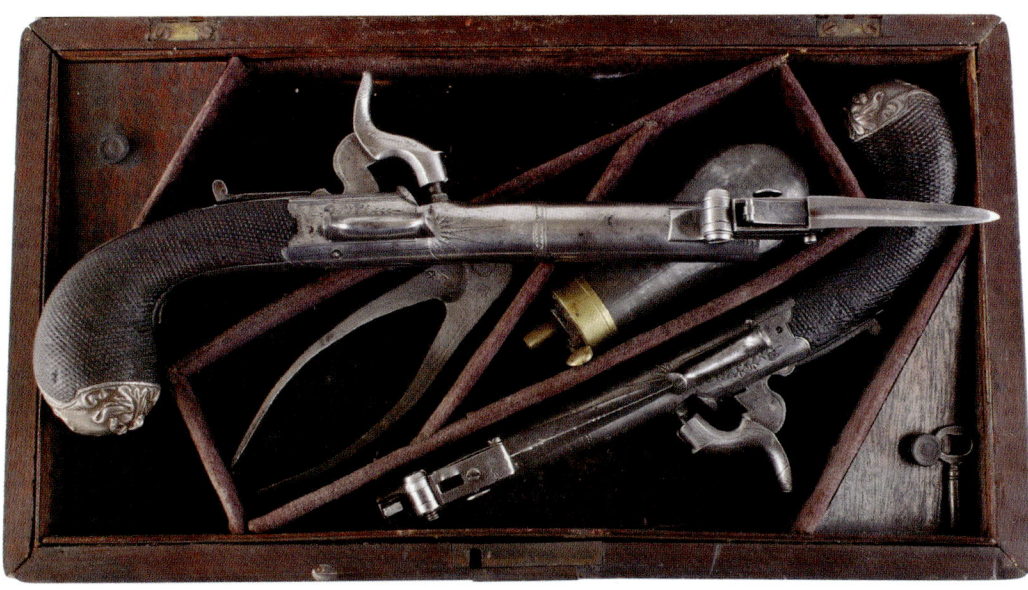

Simmons Bayonet Pistols
.49 cal., ca. 1830-40.

Tranter Revolver,
.45 cal. ca. 1850-72, s/n 2718T.

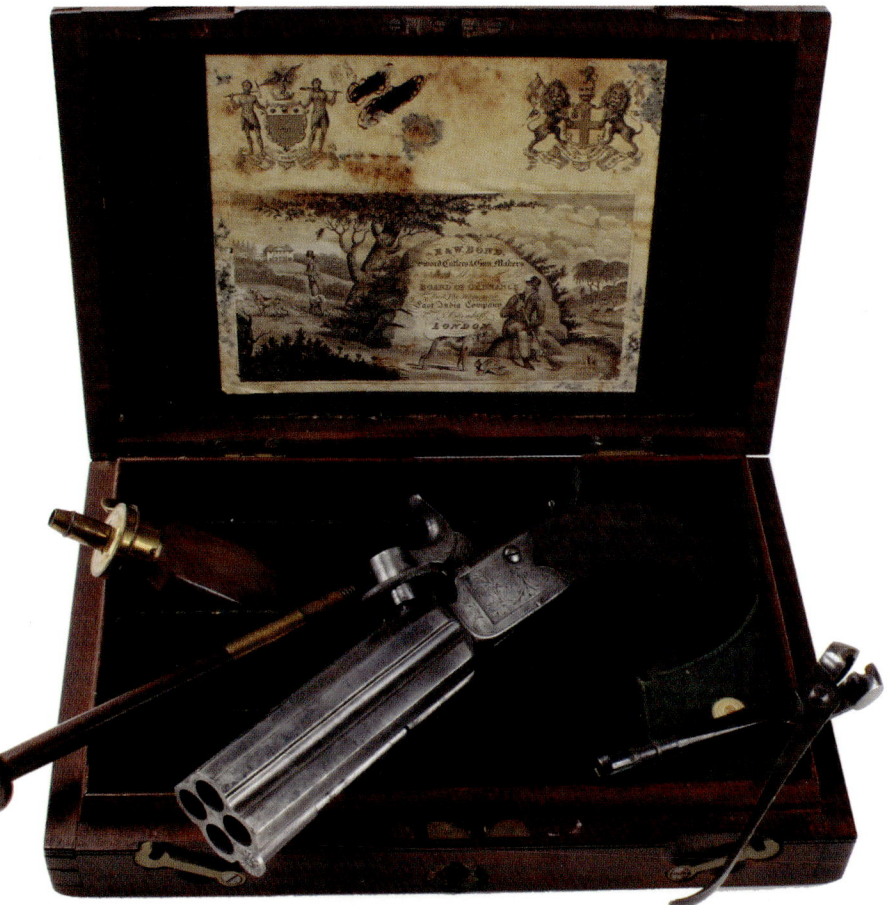

E&W Bond 4-Shot Pepperbox
.52 cal., ca. 1836-45.

221

Charles Ingram Adams Revolver
.45 cal. ca. 1842–75, s/n 60470P.

Tranter's Patent Revolver, .22 RF, ca. 1868–76, s/n 33105.

John Blanch & Son Revolver. .30 RF, ca. 1848–99.

J. Robinson Richmond Revolver, .38 CF, ca. 1870–83, s/n 172.

Tranter Spur Trigger Revolver, 8mm PF, ca. 1852–72, s/n 8821.

Belgian Pinfire Revolver, 9mm PF, ca. 1860–80, s/n 258724.

ENGRAVED GUNS OF THE OLD WEST

The Colt Single Action Army, or "Peacemaker," may be the most recognized handgun in the world, thanks to decades of exposure in movies and television. While the sturdy reliable Colt was certainly popular, it was far from the only big revolver of the post-Civil War, pre-20th century West. The Smith & Wesson Model Three topbreak revolvers (American, Russian Schofield, New Mod. #3, and Double Action models) were produced in greater numbers than the Colt large frame cartridge revolvers during this era. Remington handguns were also widely popular, and the unusual but exceptionally well-made twist-open Merwin Hulbert had its advocates.

This era was also a golden age of firearms engraving. Fancy scroll decoration and deluxe pearl and ivory grips could be ordered direct from the factory or added elsewhere, most notably in New York. The resulting shootable works of art were treasured possessions of wealthy and prominent individuals for special gifts or personal enjoyment. The engraving was all done by hand.

Some of the most gifted and famous engravers of this era include L.D. Nimschke, Cuno Helfricht, and Gustave Young.

Only a very small percentage of firearms from this era were engraved. Today, they are eagerly sought by collectors, historians, Old West aficionados, and art lovers.

DELUXE COLTS FOR COLORADO AND NEW MEXICO LAWMEN

These exceptional Colt Single Action Army revolvers were factory engraved and shipped west, for special presentations.

*Left - **Lower to Hernage Presentation Colt SAA,***
.44-40 Colt, ca. 1888, s/n 53075.
J.P. Lower owned and operated Sportsman's Depot in Denver, the largest Colt retailer in the region. He ordered this exquisite gun for his business associate and part time Deputy Sheriff, Henry J. Hernage. Engraved by Cuno Helfricht.

*Right - **One-of-a-kind Colt Single Action Army Sheriff's Model,***
.45 Colt, ca. 1897, s/n 172734.
Special order short barrel SAA's made without ejector rods are called "Sheriffs Models" or "Storekeeper Models." This is the only known silver-plated, factory engraved 3 1/2" Sheriff's Model ever made. Shipped to Deputy Sheriff Johnie Johnson of Grant County, New Mexico. Engraved by Cuno Helfricht.

Both loaned by Kurt House

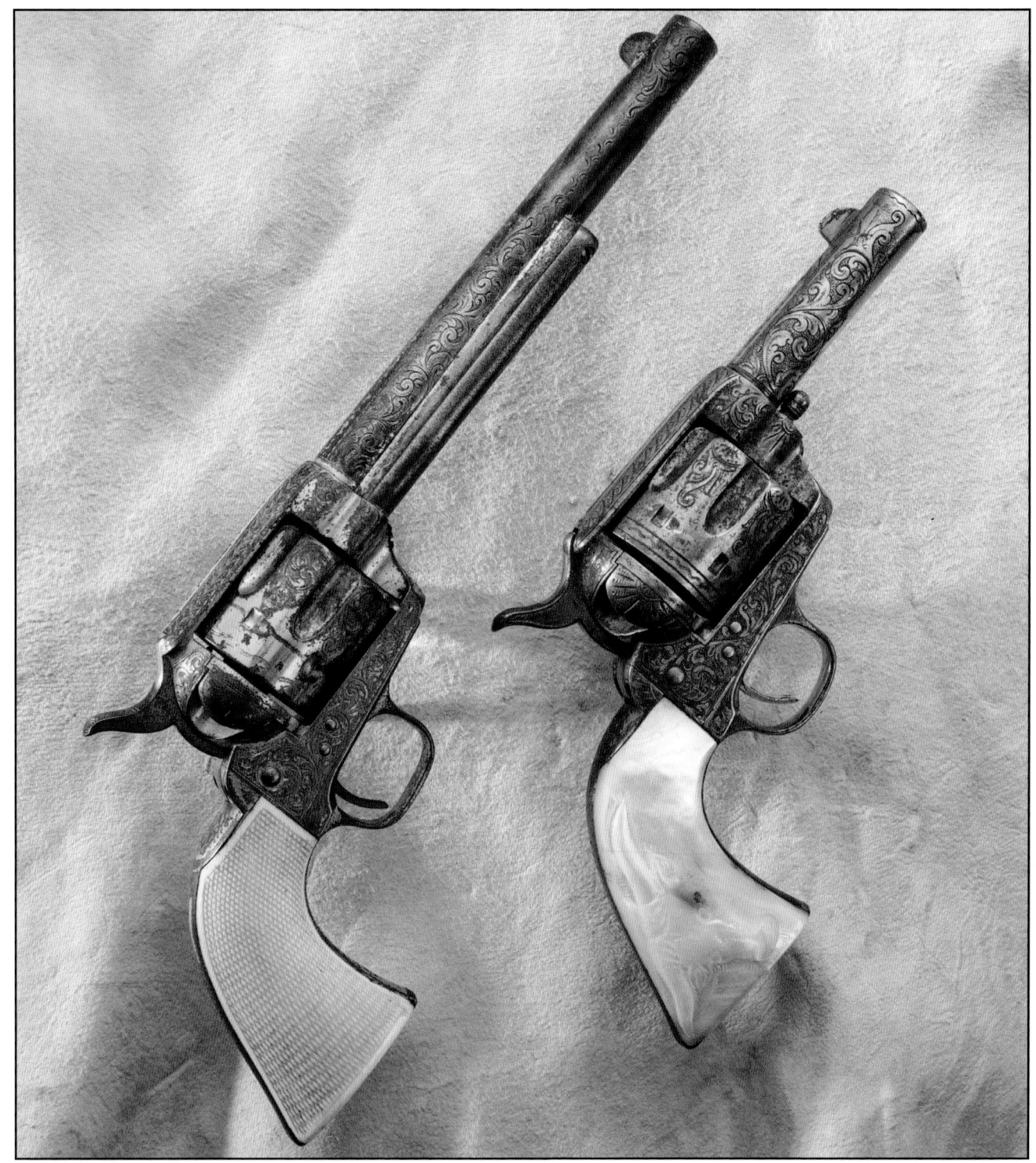

Lenders for this exhibit:
* *Colts - Kurt House*
* *Remingtons - Remington Arms Company*
* *Smith & Wessons - Jim Supica*

Gold inlaid Colt 1873 Single Action Army .44 Russian, ca. 1903, s/n 242701.
This revolver is one of only a dozen known to have been inlaid in gold during the pre-war era.
Engraved by Cuno Helfricht and shipped to a shop in Birmingham, AL.
Loaned by Kurt House

PRESENTATION THUNDERERS

The Colt Model 1877 Double Action revolver was the first double action revolver produced by Colt. It was nicknamed the "Lightning" in .38 Colt caliber and the "Thunderer" in .41 Colt. A few were made in .32 caliber, nicknamed the "Rainmaker.

These two were factory engraved as special pieces for prominent individuals.

Gov. Hawley's Colt 1877 Double Action Thunderer,
.41 Colt, ca. 1879, s/n 15321. This engraved Colt was presented to Joseph R. Hawley (1826-1905) during his tenure as Governor of Connecticut. His Lt. Governor was Oliver Winchester. Engraved by Cuno Helfricht.

Presentation Colt 1877 Thunderer,
.41 Colt, ca. 1879, s/n 19784. This gold washed cylinder double action has grips inscribed with the name "M. Strauss." Engraved by Cuno Helfricht.

Both loaned by Kurt House

ELEGANT ARMS

COLT'S BIG DOUBLE ACTION REVOLVER

A year after the mid-sized Model 1877 Double Action revolver, Colt introduced a full-sized Model 1878 Double Action Revolver. It was capable of handling the same powerful cartridges in .45 Colt class as the Single Action Army. *Loaned by Kurt House*

Top - **Colt Model 1878 Frontier Six Shooter,**
.44-40 Colt, ca. 1893, s/n 32746.
Only 250 1878's were factory engraved, this one by Cuno Helfricht.

Bottom - **Colt 1878 Double Action Sheriff's Model,**
.45 Colt, ca. 1891, s/n 27554.
New York, Nimschke style engraving. Very few engraved short barrel Sheriff's Model 1878s exist.

Merwin Hulbert Open Top Revolver, .44 CF, ca. 1870s-80s, s/n 6206.

MERWIN HULBERTS. The unusual twist-open Merwin Hulbert revolver was a strong competitor to Colt, S&W and Remington in the mid 1870s through 1880s. A button on the bottom of the frame is pushed to allow the barrel & cylinder to be rotated 90 degrees and pulled forward together. Partial opening allows only fired cases to be selectively extracted with loaded rounds remaining in the cylinder. Some have argued that it is the finest machined revolver of the era. The factory engraving, as shown here, was in a unique and somewhat primitive "punch-dot" style, sometimes with panel scenes. While not as elaborate as the carved engraving on its competitors, it is colorful and eye-catching.

Large frame .44 caliber Merwin Hulberts can be found in a variety of configurations, including Open Top or Topstrap, single or double action, and square butt "Frontier Army" Models or birdshead butt "Pocket Army" models. They were also offered in smaller framed .38 and .32 centerfire caliber models. *Loaned by Larry Jones*

ELEGANT ARMS

FACTORY ENGRAVED REMINGTONS   *Loaned by Remington Arms Co.*

DERRINGERS. The Remington Double Derringer is probably the best known of derringer type handguns. They were manufactured from the late 1860s through the mid 1930s, with copies still manufactured today. They live in the popular imagination as the quintessential "riverboat gambler's" hideout piece.   However Remington and other manufacturers offered a range of single and multiple barrel vest pocket pistols. *Loaned by Remington Arms Co. Top to bottom:*

* ***Remington Double Derringer,*** *.41 rimfire, ca. 1866-1935, s/n 2899. Factory engraved and gold plated.*

* ***Remington Vest Pocket Pistol,*** *.41 rimfire, ca. 1865-88, s/n 2415. Aka "Saw Handle Derringer."*

* ***Remington-Elliott Single Shot Derringer,*** *.41 rimfire, ca. 1867-88, s/n 6755. Factory pearl grips.*

REVOLVERS. Remington revolvers enjoyed significant popularity in the Old West. Frank James surrendered his pair of 1875s to Gov. Crittenden when he abandoned the outlaw trail, and reportedly endorsed them as "the hardest and surest shooting pistol made." While some claim the Remington single actions are copies of the Colt design, a quick look at the earlier percussion revolvers by each company suggests that it's more likely that Colt borrowed from the sturdy solid frame Remington pattern. *Loaned by Remington Arms Co.*

Top:

Remington Model 1875 Revolver, *.44 CF, ca. 1875-89, s/n 772.*

*Bottom:

Remington Model 1890 Revolver, *.44-40 Win. ca. 1891-95, s/n 83.*

Smith & Wesson New Model Number Three
.44 Russian, ca. 1893, s/n 27917.
Rare panel scene factory engraving by Gustave Young. Used by S&W in international expositions and later presented to world champion revolver shooter Oscar Olson.

Smith & Wesson Revolving Rifle,
.320 Rev. Rif. ca. 1884, s/n 516.
Factory engraved by the Young family. Essentially a long barreled New Mod. No. 3 with a detachable shoulder stock. This is one of only two known factory engraved revolving rifles.

SMITH & WESSON DOUBLE ACTION REVOLVERS

Beginning in the early 1880s and through the early 20th century, S&W offered three sizes of topbreak double action revolvers. The small frame was a five shot .32, the medium a five shot .38, and the large frames, shown here, usually .44 caliber sixshooters.

Below - **Smith & Wesson .44 Double Action,**
.44 Russian, ca. 1885, s/n 13192.
Tight English scroll style engraving by L. D. Nimschke.
Inscribed "V. L. Emerson."

Right & Center - **Smith & Wesson .44 Double Action**,
.44 Russian, ca. 1881, s/n 590.
Nimschke-style scroll engraved with gold wash contrasting parts.

SMITH & WESSON MODEL THREE SINGLE ACTION REVOLVERS

The S&W Model 3 large frame sixshooter was offered in several different models. Introduced in 1870, it was the first widely popular American large frame metallic cartridge revolver. It took the Colt SAA until the dawn of the 20th century to catch up with S&W Model 3 production, but with much of the S&W production going to foreign military orders, the big Colt was likely more often seen in the Old West. The topbreak S&W was much quicker to reload, but the sturdy Colt had a reputation for reliability under harsh conditions.

Top to bottom:

Smith & Wesson American Model, *.44 rimfire, ca. 1870s, s/n 30509. New York style scroll engraving with carved ivory grips.*
Smith & Wesson Russian Model, *.44 Russian, ca. 1870s, s/n 32906. Gold plated and scroll engraved with eagle motif.*
Smith & Wesson Schofield, *.45 S&W, ca. 1870s, s/n 8275. New York style scroll engraved.*

MULTI-BARREL AND SINGLE SHOT LONG GUNS

Not all hunting arms rely on repeating actions, as beautifully illustrated by these guns from the last half of the 19th and first half of the 20th centuries. Most shooters are familiar with double barrel shotguns, but the available options don't stop there. Combination guns feature a smoothbore barrel for shot and a rifled barrel for bullets. When in side by side configuration, these are sometimes called cape guns.

Combination guns may have more than two barrels. A three barreled gun is called a drilling and usually consists of two shotgun barrels of the same gauge plus a rifle barrel. Four barrel guns are called vierlings. Combination guns are more popular in Europe, where mixed-bag hunting for multiple types of game is more popular than in the U.S. Often, these European sporting arms feature intricate engraving on the metal and ornate carving decoration of the stock.

Burgsmueller Drilling
16x16 ga. & 9mm, ca. 1876–1900.
Donated by J.H. DeFrees

Bernard Damas Fin Shotgun. *14 ga. PF, ca. 1850–80, s/n 5697.*
Donated by John R. Moos

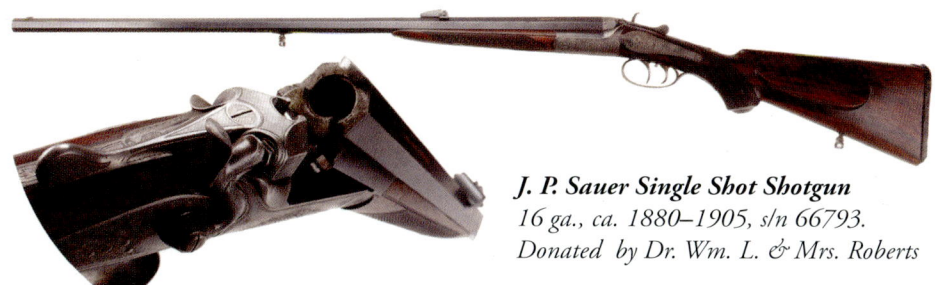

J. P. Sauer Single Shot Shotgun
16 ga., ca. 1880–1905, s/n 66793.
Donated by Dr. Wm. L. & Mrs. Roberts

German A. Frohn Falling Block Rifle,
7.65mm, ca. 1865–1910, s/n 621921.
Donated by Frank Bulawa

I Wunderlich Percussion Shotgun,
20 ga., ca. 1850-75.
Donated by Raymond E. Dirkin

Austrian Cape Gun
16 ga. & 6.5mm, ca. 1880-1905, s/n 1676.

Carl Zimmerman Drilling
12x12 ga. & 9.3mm.
Donated by Hugh W. Roll

Emil Kerner Drilling
16x16 ga. & 9mm, ca. 1900–23.
Donated by Mrs. Donald Lewin

French Darne Sliding Breech Shotgun
12 ga., ca. 1900–60, s/n 18196.
Donated by Mrs. V. R. Mueller

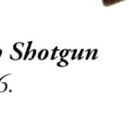

YACHTING ELEGANCE

The arms of two famous yachts, along with other examples of late 19th and early 20th century elegant arms.

Yachting Guns of Yesteryear

ARMS CHEST OF THE YACHT UNITED STATES

Henrietta Howland Robinson (1834–1916) was once the richest woman in the country and known as the "Wicked Witch of Wall Street." She was also one of the most notorious misers ever known. Her son, Edward Howland Robinson "Ned" Green (1868–1936), lost one of his legs as a result of her penurious ways of seeking treatment for him after an accident. Promising his mother that he would not marry until he was 40, he found other outlets upon which to spend his inheritance. He owned one of the world's largest private yachts, the SS United States, and stocked it full of custom firearms, an unrivaled coin collection, illegal liquor, and women of negotiable virtue. The firearms in this sea chest were from Colonel Green's SS United States and were made by Colt and Winchester with special order maple stocks and gold plated frames. They include:

Four Colt Pre-Woodsman .22 semi-auto pistols.

Three Winchester 1890 .22 pump rifles.

Two Winchester 1894 lever action rifles.

One Winchester 1895 lever action rifle.

Donated by Eldon Owen

Yacht United States, sunk at anchor

Pideault et Cadier Perrin Revolver,
12 mm Perrin, ca. 1860s, s/n 20.
Rococo engraving.
Donated by General Julian Hatcher

S&W Triple Lock Revolver,
.44 Special, ca. 1907-15, s/n 3543.
The S&W .44 Hand Ejector was nicknamed the "Triple Lock" for the three locking points joining the closed cylinder to the frame. It was the first large frame swing-out cylinder "N-frame" introduced by S&W; a frame size that was eventually used for the .44 Magnum Model 29. This rare target model is factory engraved and silver-plated.

Caldwell H. Colt's Colt 1878 Double Action Revolvers,
.45 Colt, ca. 1884/1887, s/n 13616 & 19410.
This exquisite factory engraved pair of revolvers were once the property of Caldwell Colt (1853 - 1894), a son of Colonel Samuel Colt. He was Commodore of the Larchmont, NY Yacht Club and his yacht, The Dauntless, was home to these revolvers during his lifetime. Engraved by Cuno Helfricht. Both guns have pearl grips decorated with yacht flags.
Loaned by Kurt House

ELEGANT ARMS

SAVAGE PISTOLS

While most shooters today know Savage Arms as manufacturers of sporting long guns, in the early 20th century they produced very popular .32 and .380 semi-auto pistols. They were marketed directly at the personal defense, with advertising such as "It Banishes Fear!," "A Match for any Burglar," and "This Gun Gives Her Nerve,"marketing to women purchasers.

Extraordinary M1907 Cased Pair
.32 ACP, ca. 1911, s/n 35594 & 35269
Factory engraved cased pair, pearl grips, one blue and one gold, one of two such sets purchased by P. J. Noel. Finest cased pair known.

Gold Engraved Savage M1907
.32 ACP, ca. 1912, s/n 72400
Unusual engraving in the style of William Gough.

Engraved Savage M1907
.32 ACP, ca. 1913, s/n 86158
Pearl grips inscribed with DGJ monogram.

Gold Damascene Savage M1907
.32 ACP, ca. 1913, s/n 81731

SAVAGE PISTOL FINISHES AND GRIPS
s/n 29848, 14237, 46675, 73678 & 1357
While most Savage pistols were blue with hard rubber grips, a number of finish and grip options were available on special order. Rare options shown here include two tone "pinto" finish, nickel, and silver plate, along with very rare examples of "Tuxedo grips" - a striking combination of pearl and hard rubber.
Savage Collection Loaned by Bailey and Tia Brower

**Savage Model
on Factory Exhibi**
.45 ACP, ca. 19
The Savage .45 ACP
"runner-up" in the U.
Trials of 1911. The 20
the trials were sold to
hand carved wood sl
Savage for their public
Donated by Baily a

242

SAVAGE PISTOLS

The wood carving in the center of the exhibit is an exhibit piece by the Savage company and holds a very rare .45 ACP Model 1907 - the pistol that was the runner up to the Colt 1911 in the U.S. military trials for the adoption of a new service sidearm. The guns in this exhibit are unique examples from the collection of Bailey Brower, author of the definitive work on the subject, *"Savage Pistols."*

Guns in this exhibit loaned by Bailey and Taz Brower

Within the exhibit image, the following labels appear:

Bailey Brower's Savage M1915
.380 ACP, ca. 1915-16, s/n 10580B

Custom engraved with gold inlay and Princeton medallion ivory grips.

SAVAGE PISTOLS

Loaned by Bailey and Taz Brower

Although known today primarily for their sporting long guns, Savage Arms Company of Utica, NY made some of the most popular "pocket pistols" of the early 20th century. In total, over 265,000 Savage Models 1907, 1915 and 1917 we made between 1907 and 1926. Most chambered the .32 ACP round, but they were also offered in .380 ACP. Colorful Savage advertising of the era offered "Ten Shots Quick", and promised "It Banishes Fear."

These exceptional specimens have special engraving, finish, and/or custom grips. They are from the collection of the author of the definitive work on the subject, *Savage Pistols*, Bailey Brower, Jr.

Knights of Pythias M1917
.32 ACP, ca. 1921, s/n 245653

Factory engraved, gold-plated and cased for presentation to William Ladew of the Knights of Pythias by Utica NY Mayor J.K. O'Connor. Arguably the finest pistol ever made by Savage.

Brig. Gen. Maus' Savage M1907
.32 ACP, ca. 1911, s/n 33179

Factory A engraved and inscribed to Medal of Honor recipient Brigadier General Marion P. Maus, leader of Apache Scouts in the Indian Wars.

Engraved Savage M1915
.380 ACP, ca. 1915-16, s/n 10632B

Rarest model, factory B engraved, with custom exposed cocking handle on this "hammerless" pistol.

Engraved Savage M1907
.32 ACP, ca. 1909-10, s/n 90566

Factory C engraved, with early fragile thin pearl grips with SAC medallion.

243

ENGRAVED SAVAGE PISTOLS
Loaned by Bailey and Taz Brower. Left to right:

Gold Engraved Savage M1907,
*.32 ACP, ca. 1912, s/n 72400.
Unusual engraving in the style of William Gough.*

Gold Damascene Savage M1907,
*.32 ACP, ca. 1913, s/n 81731.
Pearl grips.*

Engraved Savage M1907,
*.32 ACP, ca. 1913, s/n 8615B.
Pearl grips inscribed with DGJ monogram.*

SAVAGE PISTOL FINISHES AND GRIPS *s/n 2984B, 14237, 46875, 7387B & 81357.*
While most Savage pistols were blue with hard rubber grips, a number of finish and grip options were available on special order. Rare options shown here include two-tone "pinto" finish, nickel and silver plate, along with very rare examples of "Tuxedo grips" - a striking combination of pearl and hard rubber. Loaned by Bailey and Taz Brower

BRIG. GEN. MARION P. MAUS (1850–1930)

Born in 1850 in Maryland, Maus graduated from West Point in 1874. He served in three major conflicts during his military career – the American Indian Wars, the Spanish-American War, and the Philippine Insurrection. As an Army Scout in 1877, he assisted in the pursuit and capture of the legendary Chief Joseph.

In 1885 he was engaged as the commander of a contingent of Apache scouts as part of a force dispatched to Mexico to capture Geronimo. While he and the combined force of U.S. Cavalry troopers and Apache scouts were trailing Geronimo in the Sierra Madre Mountains of Mexico, they were ambushed by the Indian Chief and his warriors in a narrow canyon pass.

Maus and his men took cover behind boulders, but one trooper was hit before he could take cover and was lying exposed to the enemy fire. Maus ran to drag him to the safety of the rocks but when he cleared cover, several Apaches appeared and rushed him. Maus shot and killed them all, then dragged the wounded soldier to cover. As he rejoined the action, he saw Geronimo taking cover behind a rock with his head exposed. Maus, an expert marksman, fired a shot that grazed the rock near Geronimo's head, temporarily blinding him and leading to the cessation of the attack.

After this incident, Geronimo sent a letter to Maus' Commanding General. It said, "Maus was the bravest man I have ever seen." He also said that if Maus hadn't killed several of his best warriors and almost killed Geronimo himself, the patrol would have been wiped out.

For his actions in this engagement, Maus was awarded the Congressional Medal of Honor for bravery.

Maus rose to the rank of Brigadier General in 1906. That same year, while stationed in California, he helped maintain order in San Francisco after the huge earthquake in April. He retired in 1913 and died in 1930 at the age of 79. Maus is buried with his wife in Arlington National Cemetery.

Extraordinary M1907 Cased Pair, *.32 ACP, ca. 1911, s/n 35194 & 35269.*
Factory engraved cased pair, pearl grips, one blue and one gold; one of two such sets purchased by P. J. Noel, and the finest cased pair known.
Loaned by Bailey and Taz Brower

Medal of Honor Recipient
Brig. Gen. Maus' Savage M1907,
.32 ACP, ca. 1911, s/n 33179.
Factory engraved and inscribed to Medal of Honor recipient Brigadier General Marion P. Maus, leader of Apache Scouts in the Indian Wars.
Loaned by Bailey and Taz Brower.

FINE CUSTOM GUNS

Ever since the first wheel locks were built over 600 years ago, arms makers have embellished them and fashioned them into works of fine art. The engraver's art on gun steel exemplifies how finely intricate craftsmanship can transform a stock firearm into a museum worthy object d'art.

FINE CUSTOM GUNS

Dubiel Classic Sporter Rifles *ca. 1975–90*
These were Texas made, in limited numbers as fine custom-grade sporting rifles.
Donated by Dr. John Tyson
Shown immediately below, top to bottom:
    .243 Win. ca. 1975-90, s/nT-111-S.
    .270 Win. s/n T-145-M.
    7mm Rem. Mag. s/n D-028-M.
    One of fewer than 100 made with a left-handed action.

Mosaic stock Winchester Model 70 Rifle *.222 Rem, ca. 1950, s/n 146048.*
The stock is made from 100 individual pieces of wood.
Donated by John Leland Abright

MAG-NA-PORT BIG FIVE
Ruger Super Blackhawk Revolvers
.44 Magnum, ca. 1983.
Each of these custom revolvers features the Mag-na-port recoil reduction system. They represent the African Big Five game animals - Elephant, Rhino, Cape Buffalo, Lion, and Leopard. Each is custom cased. S/n's 83-73414, 84-64829, 83-19042, 84-18429, 84-92958.
Donated by Dr. Charles B. Covert

Star Model 1920 Pistol *7.65mm, ca. 1940–50, s/n 74093.*
Gold damascene.
Donated by Herb Allee

Mauser HSc Pistol *7.65mm, ca. 1950, s/n 831728.*
Celtic knot engraving by Ralph Bone.
Donated by John Ying

Engraved Remington #4 Rifle
.22 LR, ca. 1920-30.
Engraved by Ralph Bone.
Donated by John Ying

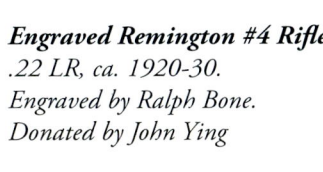

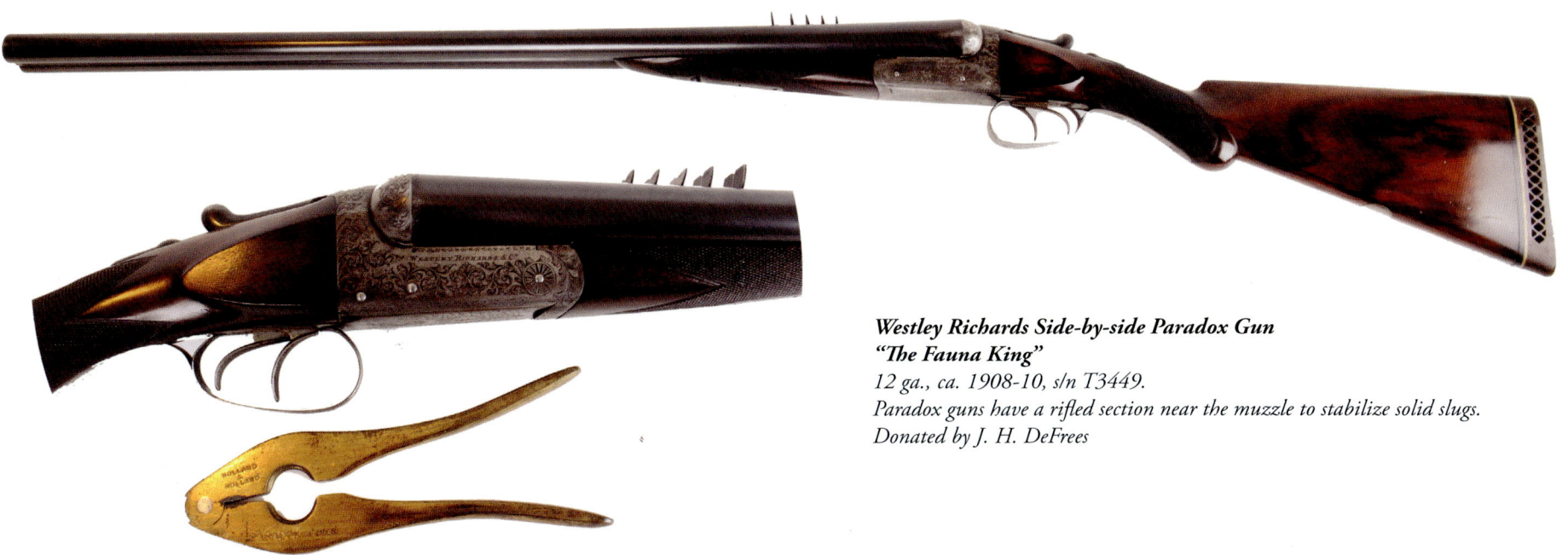

Westley Richards Side-by-side Paradox Gun
"The Fauna King"
12 ga., ca. 1908-10, s/n T3449.
Paradox guns have a rifled section near the muzzle to stabilize solid slugs.
Donated by J. H. DeFrees

Smith & Wesson .22/32 Revolver
.22 LR, ca. 1915–35, s/n 245281.
Engraved by Ralph Bone. Donated by John Ying

Smith & Wesson Model 15 Revolver
38 Special, ca. 1986–91, s/n K107663.
Engraved by Ray Viramontez.

James Purdey & Sons
Side by Side Shotgun
10 ga., ca. 1907, s/n 19036.
Donated by P. C. Dorsey

Roy Vail Hammerless Side
by Side Shotgun *12 ga., ca.*
1960–65, s/n 94753.
Hand-built custom shotgun.
Donated by Roy Vail

HOLLAND AND HOLLAND DOUBLE RIFLES

These two rifles by Holland and Holland are among the finest and most powerful sporting firearms in existence. They are chambered for the .600 and .700 Nitro Express cartridges, suitable for the largest dangerous game of Africa.

NITRO EXPRESS CARTRIDGES

The following information gives some perspective on the power of these cartridges compared to conventional ammunition with the muzzle energy of each round expressed in "foot-pounds," derived from the weight of the bullet and the muzzle velocity. The figures given are generalizations; various loadings will differ a bit.

.22 Long Rifle - 150 ft./lbs.
9mm pistol - 400 ft./lbs.
.44 Mag., revolver - 1,000 ft./lbs.
.223 Rem. - 1,325 ft./lbs.
.30-06 - 2,800 ft./lbs.
.458 Win. Mag. - 4,700 ft./lbs.
.600 Nitro Express - 7,600 ft./lbs.
.700 Nitro Express - 8,900 ft./lbs.

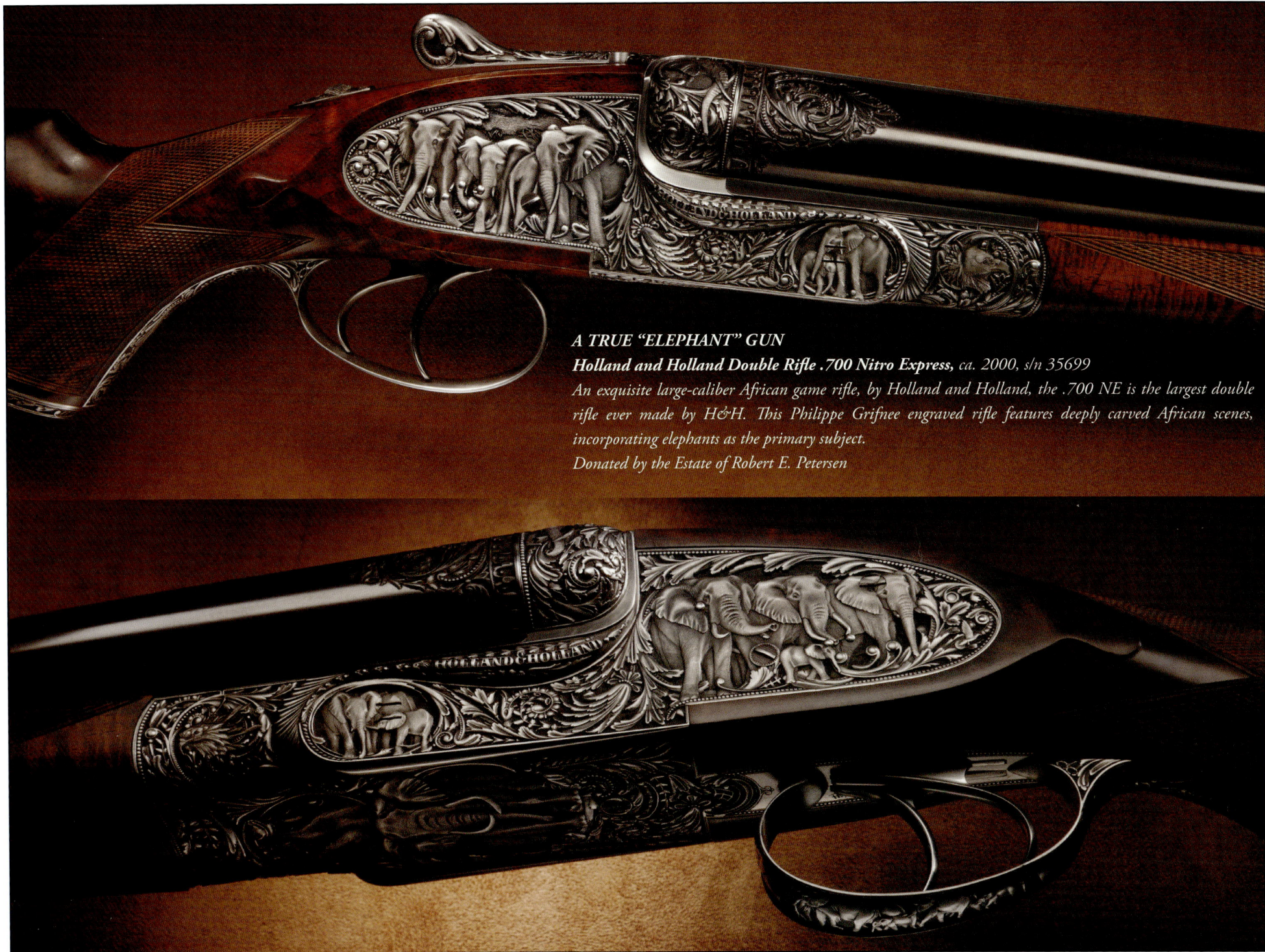

A TRUE "ELEPHANT" GUN

Holland and Holland Double Rifle .700 Nitro Express, *ca. 2000, s/n 35699*

An exquisite large-caliber African game rifle, by Holland and Holland, the .700 NE is the largest double rifle ever made by H&H. This Philippe Grifnee engraved rifle features deeply carved African scenes, incorporating elephants as the primary subject.

Donated by the Estate of Robert E. Petersen

FOR AFRICAN BIG GAME

Holland and Holland Double Rifle .600 Nitro Express, ca. 2000, s/n 35602.

This rifle, with a deep relief full coverage engraving by Philippe Grifnee, represents the finest rhino hunting gun ever made by the venerable firm of Holland and Holland. Various species of rhino are featured, with Indian rhino on triggerguard, Sumatran and Javan rhinos on top, black rhino on right frame, and white rhino on left and bottom of the frame. It is fitted in a rare two tiered alligator covered case by Vince Rickard.

Donated by the Estate of Robert E. Petersen

FRANK PACHMAYR (1906–1997)

Born into a Los Angeles gunmaking family, Frank Pachmayr began working as an apprentice to his father August. He started his own business during the Great Depression. In those lean times, the shop survived by repairing police duty sidearms and buying unredeemed pawnstore guns, refinishing them and then offering them as "like new" pieces for bargain hunters. Pachmayr's patenting of a revolver grip adapter in 1931 and "Whiteline" rubber shotgun recoil pads in 1932 also helped to put his small shop on the map.

By the end of WWII, Pachmayr's manufacturing operation had spread over an eight-block area of downtown Los Angeles and the boom was on. Fulfilling orders from returning soldiers and sailors for custom rifles and shotguns soon became Frank Pachmayr's new full-time business. Creating accurized .45 pistols for competitive shooters was a sideline that brought the target business to his door. Elaborately embellished Winchester and Parker shotguns were among the more popular Pachmayr offerings to celebrity Hollywood gun owners.

Building his own lumber mill to produce the high-grade walnut needed for his custom arms, Pachmayr was to become a national figure for custom arms production and also managed to assemble one of the nation's finest personal arms collections. In 2013, a special selection of the arms from this collection was loaned by the Frank and Nanita Pachmayr Foundation to the NRA National Sporting Arms Museum at Bass Pro Shops in Springfield, MO.

Von Lemerke & Detmold Shotgun, *28 ga., s/n 259746. Von Lemerke & Detmold was a New York City retailer of fine European sporting goods.*

***Charles Daly
Diamond Quality
Shotgun,***
12 ga., s/n 1071.

EXCEPTIONAL CUSTOM SHOTGUNS
*Typical of the Pachmayr Foundation
collection, left to right.*

Winchester Model 21 Shotgun, *12 ga., s/n 22723.*

Charles Daly Diamond Grade Side by Side Shotgun, *12 ga.,
s/n 1825.*

Parker Brothers Side by Side Shotgun, *12 ga., s/n 147917.*

Mannlicher Schoenauer Bolt-Action Rifle
8mm, s/n 23125.

Charles Daly
Diamond Grade Shotgun
12 ga., s/n 1192.

French Freres
Side by Side Shotgun,
16 ga., s/n 1378.

W.W. Greener Side by Side Shotgun, 20 ga., s/n 66175.

**James Purdey
Side by Side Shotgun**
12 ga., s/n 26217.

THE PACHMAYR COLLECTION

Pachmayr was one of the first American gunsmiths to offer a custom takedown conversion of the Model 1903 Springfield rifle.

Left - **DWM Berlin Takedown Sporter Rifle,** *6.5mm, s/n 6878*

Right - **Pachmayr Takedown M1903 Springfield Rifle,** *6mm, s/n 278635*

Frank Pachmayr

Kreighoff Sporting Bolt-Action Rifle
6.5mm, s/n 10118.

Katsenes Side by Side Shotgun
12 ga., s/n 5763.

Von Lemerke & Detmold Shotgun
12 ga., s/n 254828.

Parker "Pachmayr Invincible" Shotgun *28 ga., s/n 236956.*

Pachmayr, emulating the finest grade Parker shotguns, offered upgraded Parkers with his own engraving and special accents, including horn trigger guards. This example is one of only a few ever made of the highest Invincible grade.

Westley Richards Side by Side Shotgun
20 ga., s/n T7239.

FAMILY TRADITION

Emile Pachmayr Side by Side Shotgun

16 ga., s/n 2112.

This custom shotgun was done by Emile Pachmayr, Frank Pachmayr's grandfather.

Frank Pachmayr

Colt/Pachmayr Combat Special Pistol
.45 ACP, s/n 70BS80327.

Frank Pachmayr's enhancements of 1911 pattern pistols are legendary, and greatly influenced the resurgence of this American classic in the last half of the 20th century.

Piotti Side by Side Shotgun

12 ga., s/n 8079.

Winchester Model 21 Shotgun

12 ga., s/n 8603.

Parker Brothers Side by Side Shotgun
12 ga., s/n 222605.

Winchester Model 21 Shotgun, *12 ga., s/n 27273.*   ***Parker Brothers Side by Side Shotgun,*** *20 ga., s/n 215548.*

Remington Model 31F Shotgun
20 ga., s/n 557230.

Griffin & Howe Side by Side Shotgun
28 ga., s/n 555.

German Side by Side Shotgun

12 ga., s/n 2500.

Heym Side by Side Shotgun

16 ga., s/n 26193.

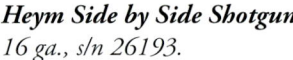

J.P. Sauer & Sohn Side by Side shotgun,
12 ga., s/n 126027.

J.P. Sauer & Sohn Side by Side Shotgun
16 ga., s/n 126016.

THE JOY OF COLLECTING

Commemorative firearms occupy a special niche in the collecting field. All major manufacturers, and even many smaller ones, have created commemorative firearms to honor everything from Statehood Centennials to Eagle Scouts. While some gun collectors seek out historical firearms or old production models in pristine condition, still others enjoy guns that express both their love of firearms and an event, person, or subject that are significant to them.

Zane Grey Marlin Model 336 Carbine,
.30-30 Win. ca. 1971, s/n ZG01949. 7,871 produced.
Donated by Joseph Kerensky, Jr.

Legendary Frontiersman Winchester Model 1894,
.38-55 Win. ca. 1979, s/n LF03990. 19,999 produced.
Donated by the Estate of Bertha A. Baier

NRA Centennial Winchester Model 1894 Musket,
.30-30 Win. ca. 1971, s/n NRA35255. 47,380 produced.

Cheyenne Commemorative Winchester Model 1894,
.30-30 Win. ca. 1977, s/n CH06708. 13,000 produced.
Bequest of the Estate of David C. Ritchie.

Savage 75th Anniversary Model 1895,
.308 Win. ca. 1970, s/n 1871AS. 9,999 produced.
Donated by Savage Arms Co.

WWII Pacific Theatre Colt Model 1911A1,
.45 ACP, ca. 1970, s/n 1911ETO. 9,960 produced.
Donated by Colt

Texas Wagon Train
Smith & Wesson Model 544,
.44-40 Win. ca. 1986, s/n TWT0070.
7,800 produced.
Donated by Gregory McGraw

THE THURSTON ARMS COLLECTION

The firearms in this section are from the remarkable collection of Doc J. Thurston Jr., and Doc J. Thurston III. Father and son shared a passion for firearms history and a love of hunting.

The Thurston Collection includes arms of all types from all eras, ranging from ancient arms to exquisite custom guns from recent decades. It includes a special focus on guns of the Civil War and Old West and firearms oddities. In accordance with Doc, III's wishes, the collection will be displayed in a permanent Thurston Collection Gallery in an NRA Museum.

Shown here are examples of their personalized highest grade hunting arms.

Father and son doubles:

Top:

Holland & Holland Royal Ejector Consecutive Pair of Double Barrel Rifles

.375 Flanged Magnum, s/n 32127 & 32128, ca. 1929, Both ornately engraved.

Bottom:

Holland & Holland Royal DeLuxe Consecutive Pair of Shotguns

12 ga., s/n 40981 & 40982, ca. 1989, The highest grade offered by this prestigious British maker, these are engraved by P. Coggan, and feature hand detachable sidelocks.

Each pair of guns has mongrams inlaid in the stocks, one reading "D.J. Thurston Jnr." and the other "D.J. Thurston III."

CHAMPLIN FIREARMS INC.
PRESENTS
GARY SWANSON'S
NORTH FORK RAMS
CALIBER .270 WIN.

BILL RINEE	RIFLEMAKER	MARVIN HUEY	CASEMAKER
DOUG HILL	RIFLEMAKER	WILLIAM CROWLEY	TOOLMAKER
DAN GOODWIN	ENGRAVER	JACK WALDEN	KNIFEMAKER
MAURICE OTTMAR	STOCKMAKER	W. A. PIERCE	SCRIMSHANDER

FINE CUSTOM RIFLES

Champlin North Fork Rams Rifle
270 Win., s/n FNAWS1984, ca. 1984, The case marked "Champlin Firearms Inc., presents Gary Swanson's North Fork Rams." Outstanding custom gun by the best craftsmen with their names listed in the lid. Thurston Collection

Lawson Browning Midas Grade Rifle
.375 H&H Mag., s/n 8X45021, ca. 1968. This began as a Midas Grade Browning, customized by noted custom gunmaker Harry Lawson. "Doc Thurston" is inscribed on the barrel, and light handling marks suggest he likely used this rifle in Africa. Thurston collection

A PAIR OF PARADOXES

A paradox gun is a double barrel firearm with barrels that are smoothbore for most of their length, with only the last few inches of the barrel rifled. This is intended to allow the shooter to fire traditional shotshells or special solid slug paradox bullets, suitable for heavy game. The bit of rifling in the end of the barrel increases the accuracy of the heavy projectiles.

Top:

Cased Holland & Holland Royal Paradox Ejector Gun, two barrel set

12 bore, s/n 15887, ca. 1911

Cased two barrel set, hammerless. One set shotgun barrels; one set paradox barrels. Barrels are made in H&H Paris shop in France by Jean Breuiel in St. Etienne, numbered to gun. Thurston Collection.

Bottom:

Holland & Holland Paradox Gun

8 bore, s/n 11941, ca. 1890

Massive hammer eight bore gun, suitable for the heaviest African game. Thurston Collection.

European Snaphaunce Pistol

.46 cal., ca. 1720s
Finely chiseled steel mounts. The snaphaunce is an early form of flint ignition. It differs from the better-known, later flintlock design in that the striking plate for the flint does not double as a pan cover. Thurston Collection

Italian Flintlock Pistol

.58 cal., ca. 1750s
Ornately decorated and marked "Lazarino Comminazzo." The traditional flintlock action introduced the frizzen - a striking plate that also served as a pan cover to protect the priming powder charge. Thurston Collection

Pair of Remington Rolling Block Pistols

.50 Centerfire, ca. 1872-1888, Model 1871 Army, fully engraved and gold washed with ivory stocks. Thurston Collection

Pinfire Blunderbuss Flare Pistol

75mm pinfire, ca. early 20th century

The sea chest is marked "Master Antone Mandley, New Bedford," and also contains a brass telescope, pocket watch with whale fob, horn folding knife, and beadwork of sailing ship. Mandley was a whaling master from the 1890s-1920s., Thurston Collection

Manton Dangerous Game Rifle

One inch bore, mid-19th century

Appropriate for the heaviest game, the tiger decoration suggests this percussion rifle was made for hunting in India., Thurston Collection

SEARCH FOR A REPEATING RIFLE...

While the revolver mechanism provided an effective design for a repeating handgun, it had significant problems when applied to a long gun. In the 19th century several inventors came up with ingenious, if often flawed, attempts to develop a multi-shot long arm.

Top:
Gasser Style Revolving Rifle
8mm, s/n 57518, ca. late 19th century, High quality engraving with gold line inlay., Thurston Collection

Middle:
Cochran Underhammer Revolving Turret Rifle
.38 cal., ca. 1830s
At the same time Samuel Colt was experimenting with a repeating revolver with parallel chambers, Cochran and others were working on repeaters with a horizontal disk cylinder with the chambers splayed like spokes of a wheel. This could result in catastrophic accidents if the firearm "chain-fired" multiple chambers simultaneously. This one is marked Harrington and finely finished in the style of New York percussion rifles. Most known Cochrans have a full disc magazine. This half disc model is exceptionally rare. Thurston Collection

Bottom:
LeMat Pinfire Shotgun-Rifle Carbine
12mm & 28 ga. pinfire cartidges, ca. 1860s
The 9-shot revolver cylinder rotates around a smoothboore shotgun barrel., Thurston Collection

Octagon Barrel Colt Buntline Special

.45 Colt, s/n 28825, ca. 1876

This is the only known octagon barrel Colt Single Action Army. Author R. L. Wilson has called it "The rarest of all Colt single action revolvers." Special order SAAs with extra long barrels and detachable stocks were originally called "buggy rifles" by Colt. They have become widely known as "Buntline Specials" due to mythology created in early old west novels. The original barrel was cut to a shorter, handier length during the period of use. The current replacement barrel was made ca. 1960, Thurston Collection

Four Shot Double Barrel Shotgun

ca. 1850s

This percussion shotgun uses two superposed charges in each barrel to create four shot capacity.; a hazardous proposition by today's standards. Marked Dewalle Freres Brevette A Liege. Thurston Collection

15-Shot Hall Revolving Rifle

.38 cal., ca. 1850s

Very few examples of this percussion rifle exist, made by Alexander Hall of New York. Revolving percussion rifles presented a significant hazard to the shooter if multiple chambers fired simultaneously by accident. Thurston Collection

... A SOLUTION IS FOUND

By the 1860s, the tubular magazine lever action rifle had emerged as a solution that avoided the hazards of revolving and superposed long guns.

Rare Iron Frame Henry Rifle

.44 rimfire, s/n 176, ca. 1860

The Henry lever action was one of the first widely successful repeaters. This was made in the first year of production with an iron frame instead of the later brass., Thurston Collection

Officers Model Springfield Trapdoor
.45-80, ca. 1875-1885
Made by the government's Springfield Armory for private sale to military officers as hunting rifles based on the standard issue military rifle action. Thurston Collection

Early American Combination Gun
.44 & .45, cal. ca. 1830s
Made in the style of the American Long Rifle or "Kentucky Rifle", one barrel is rifled and the other smoothbore for shot. Double barrel Kentukies are scarce, and combination rifle/shotguns such as this one are quite rare. Thurston Collection.

Clark Gable Presentation Flintlock

.50 cal., ca. 1810s

This French Empire Period jaeger style flintlock rifle, fit for a king, dates from the early 19th century. In the mid-20th century it was inscribed as a special gift to Hollywood royalty "To the King (from) Duke, Ward, Jack and Spig on the buttplate. It is believed to be a presentation to Clark Gable from John Wayne and three studio executives in 1938. Thurston Collection

Kruschev Presentation Tula Arms Shotgun

12 ga, s/n 8101, ca. 1957

Soviet Premier Nikita Kruschev presented this Russian made full sidelock shotgun to Arthur Fleming, Sec. of Health, Education, and Welfare under President Eisenhower., Thurston Collection

SHANE (1953)
Jack Palance as Jack Wilson
Colt Single Action Army
.44-40 WCF, ca. 1884, s/n 110108.
Loaned by Al Frisch; Hollywood Guns &
Props

HOLLYWOOD GUNS

Small screen, silver screen, or footlights of Broadway, many saw and fell in love with their first firearm while it was in the hands of an actor. Watching the likes of the Duke or Matthew Quigley moviegoers not only gained an admiration for firearms, but also learned about the cowboy code, right and wrong, and the dire consequences for actions outside the law. The nation's Saturday morning heroes always wore white hats and carried a Peacemaker.

But what about those Peacemakers? Where did they come from? And all those flintlocks in *Northwest Passage* (1940)—how did they all fire so flawlessly? Did Raymond Massey really have a rare and valuable original Colt Paterson in *Reap the Wild Wind* (1942)? Oh, and by the way, how is it that John Wayne's Single Action Army used in *The Searchers* (1956) is at the Cowboy Hall of Fame, but there is an identical one in the NRA National Sporting Arms Museum with the same provenance? What gives?

It's called Hollywood Magic, my friend, and there isn't really much to it besides a few slight-of-hand illusions and some creative armorers.

From the earliest silent films such as *Birth of a Nation* (1915), studios rented real, working firearms from various gun wranglers located around the Los Angeles area. They worked them hard, abused them, and sent them back for a cleaning until they were needed for the next project. Sometimes the same gun was rented over and over again to numerous productions and could have been used by more than one famous actor in multiple award-winning films.

Sometimes, as in the case of Raymond Massey's Paterson, the revolver came from the private gun collection of renowned director Cecil B. DeMille, who was famous for loaning some of his rare and unique firearms to productions, just to change things up a bit. It was, however, standard practice to have three identical firearms for each principal actor. That way, if any problems or failures occurred, there was always an heir and a spare available to go into immediate action. It also explains how multiple guns can be attributed to the same movie and actor.

Those flawless flintlocks were actually blank-firing Model 1873 Trapdoor Springfield's with a bit of an exterior face-lift to make them look authentic. Hollywood bought tens of thousands of them from government surplus dealers almost 100 years ago, and they are still in use today in a variety of "looks close enough" roles.

The NRA Museum's collection of firearms from Hollywood reflects a deep admiration and appreciation for the films and shows that intrigued many and captured numerous imaginations for so many countless hours spent in a movie house or on living room couches.

TRUE GRIT *(1969)* & ***ROOSTER COGBURN***
(1975). Winchester Model 1892, .44-40 WCF, ca.
1892, s/n 7015.
Loaned by Al Frisch; Hollywood Guns & Props.

JOHN WAYNE's Colt Single Action Army,
.44-40 WCF, ca. 1901, s/n 207059.
The Duke's signature sidearm, 4-5/8" barrel with
imitation-ivory celluloid finger groove grips.
Loaned by Chris Hearn

THE WHITE BUFFALO *(1977),*
Charles Bronson as Wild Bill Hickock.
Colt Single Action Army. .44-40 WCF, ca.
1901, s/n 213295.
Loaned by Chris Hearn.

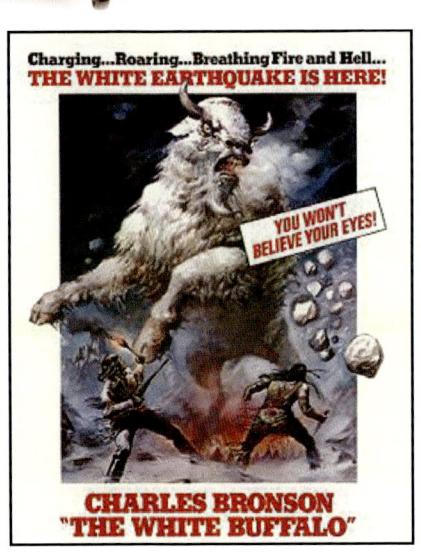

THE WILD BUNCH *(1969)*
William Holden as Pike Bishop
Colt Single Action Army. .44-40 WCF, ca.
1919, s/n 337237
Loaned by Chris Hearn

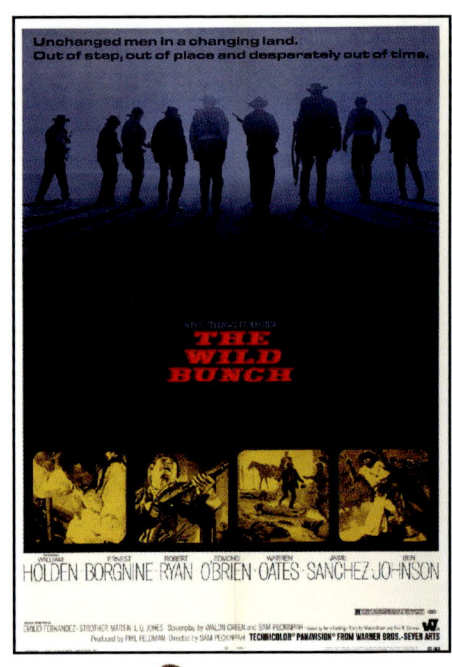

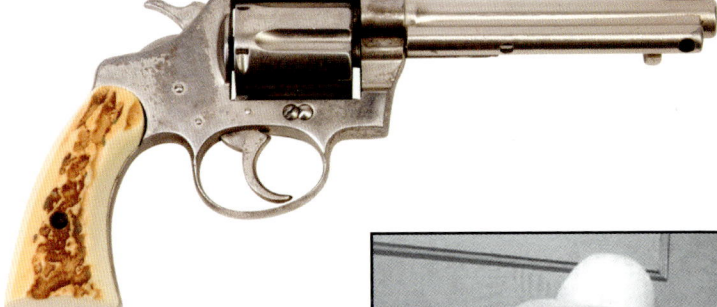

ANNIE OAKLEY
(1954-1957, ABC TV).
Gail Davis as Annie
Colt Police Positive .38 Special, ca.
1931, s/n 343673.
Loaned by Al Frisch; Hollywood Guns
& Props

Gene Autry & Gail Davis

THE LONG RIDERS *(1980)*
Robert Carradine as Bob Younger
Colt 1878 DA Frontier Sixshooter
.44-40 WCF, ca. 1894, s/n 33904.
Carradine starred with his brothers David
and Keith in this film. Their father, John
Carradine starred with John Wayne in
Stagecoach (1939)
Loaned by Al Frisch; Hollywood Guns &
Props

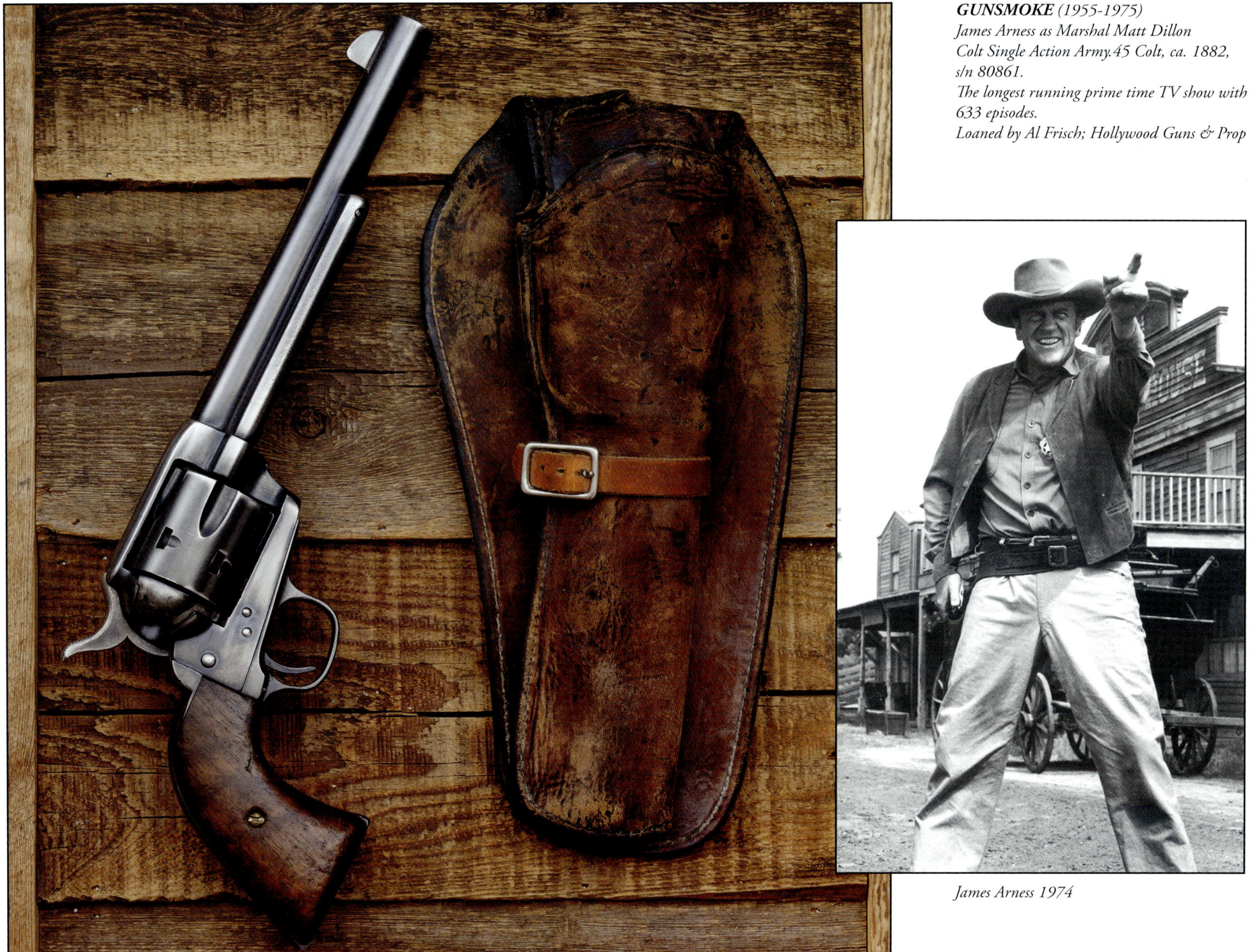

GUNSMOKE *(1955-1975)*
James Arness as Marshal Matt Dillon
Colt Single Action Army.45 Colt, ca. 1882,
s/n 80861.
The longest running prime time TV show with
633 episodes.
Loaned by Al Frisch; Hollywood Guns & Prop

James Arness 1974

SILVERADO *(1985)*
Kevin Kline as Paden
Webley Revolver
.476 Webley, ca. 1882, s/n 4853.
Loaned by Al Frisch; Hollywood Guns & Props

MAVERICK *(1984)*
Great Western Double Derringer
.38 Special, ca. 1959, s/n 2532.
Used by Mel Gibson as Bret Maverick in Maverick (1994).
Loaned by Al Frisch; Hollywood Guns & Props

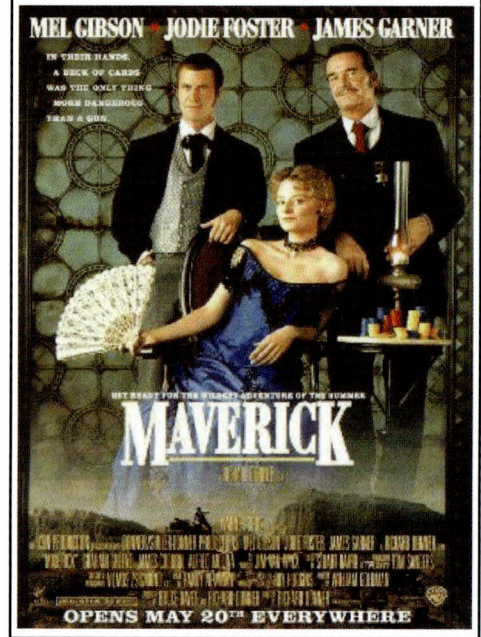

MAVERICK *(1976)*
James Garner as Marshall Zane Cooper
Navy Arms / Uberti Model 1875 (Replica)
.44 cal., ca. 1976, s/n 4352.
Loaned by Al Frisch; Hollywood Guns & Props

EL DORADO (1966)
Robert Mitchum as Sheriff J. P. Harrah
Winchester Model 1892
.44-40 WCF, ca. 1892, s/n 7017.
Loaned by Al Frisch; Hollywood Guns & Props

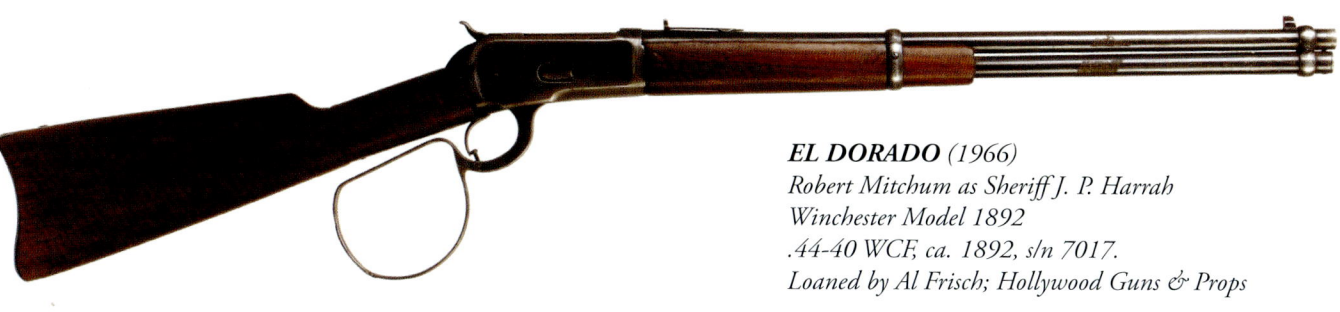

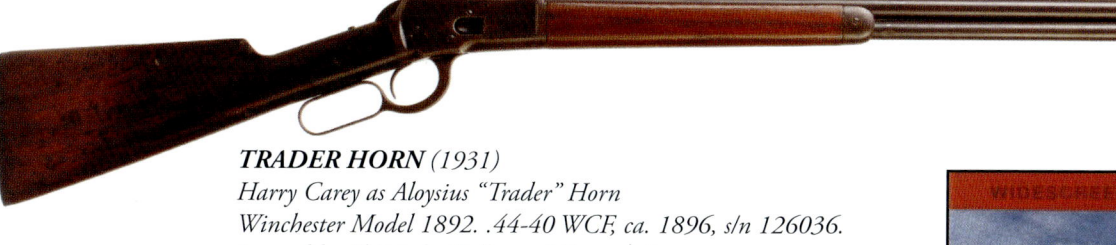

TRADER HORN (1931)
Harry Carey as Aloysius "Trader" Horn
Winchester Model 1892. .44-40 WCF, ca. 1896, s/n 126036.
Loaned by Al Frisch; Hollywood Guns & Props

NEVADA SMITH (1966)
Steve McQueen as Nevada Smith
P. Weiss combination gun 12 ga./.45 cal., ca. 1848, s/n 318. McQueen was
featured on the movie poster holding this rifle across his shoulders.

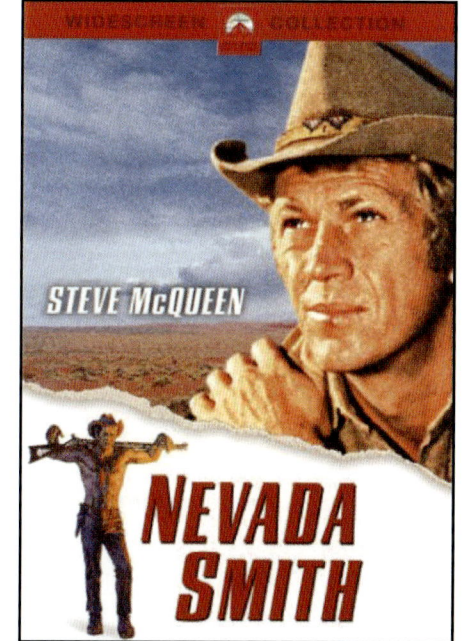

293

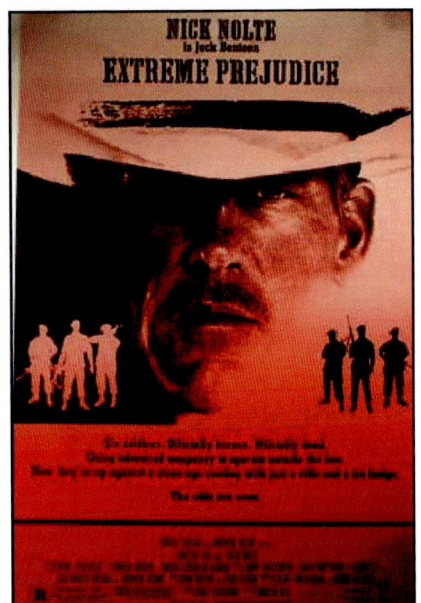

EXTREME PREJUDICE (1987)
Nick Nolte as Jack Benteen
Winchester Model 1892
.44-40 WCF, ca. 1892, s/n 6013.
Loaned by Al Frisch; Hollywood Guns & Props

AMBUSH AT CIMARRON PASS (1958)
Clint Eastwood
Winchester Model 1892
.44-40 WCF, ca. 1913, s/n 722216.
The Model 1892 was used in countless movies and TV shows with the
forend wood removed to simulate the earlier Henry rifle.
Loaned by Al Frisch; Hollywood Guns & Props

SHE WORE A YELLOW RIBBON (1949)
Springfield Model 1873
.45-70, ca. 1890, s/n 460484.
Used in John Ford's western Cavalry Trilogy's Rio Grande (1950), She Wore a
Yellow Ribbon (1949), & Fort Apache (1948).
Loaned by Al Frisch; Hollywood Guns & Props

Facing page

TRUE GRIT (1969)
Kim Darby as Mattie Ross- and -
The Outlaw Josey Wales (1976)
Clint Eastwood as Josey Wales
Uberti Model 1847 Walker Reproduction
.44 cal., ca. 1962, s/n 715.

HOLLYWOOD GUNS

ONE-EYED JACKS (1961)
Springfield Model 1873 .45-70, ca. 1889, s/n 391724.
Also used in *The Charge of the Light Brigade* (1936).
Loaned by Al Frisch; Hollywood Guns & Props

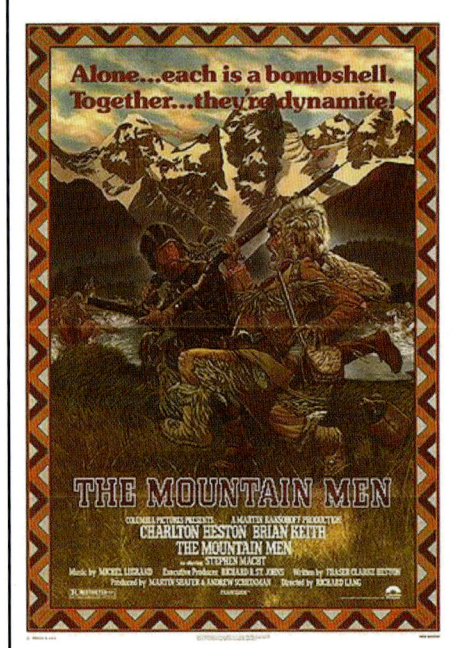

THE MOUNTAIN MEN (1982)
Charlton Heston as Bill Tyler
Upper gun - Long Rifle Reproduction .50 cal. flintlock, ca. 1978
Lower gun - Hawken Rifle Reproduction .45 cal. percussion, ca. 1978
Loaned by Al Frisch; Hollywood Guns & Props

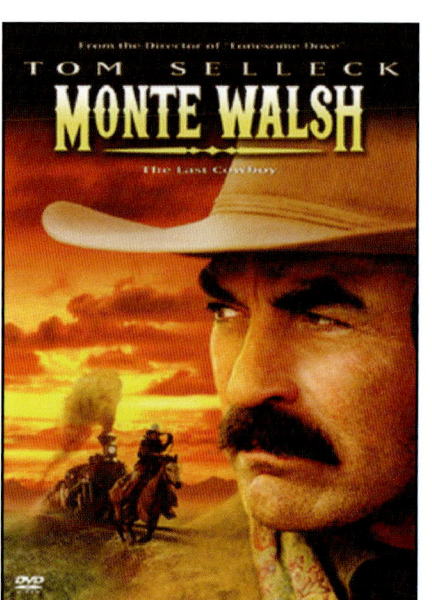

MONTE WALSH (2002)
George Eads as Frank "Shorty" Austin
Winchester Model 1887
12 ga., ca. 1898, s/n 63343.

Donated by Tom Selleck

TOM SELLECK (b. 1945)

Tom Selleck is a native of Detroit, MI, and is an NRA Life member, hunter, and firearms collector. He began an acting career in the late 1960s and hit stardom with his wildly acclaimed series *Magnum P.I.* which ran from 1980 – 1988. Currently he plays NYC Police Commissioner Frank Reagan in CBS's hit series *Blue Bloods* which premiered in 2010.

When not involved in a television series, Tom has starred in numerous western themed movies including *Quigley Down Under* (1990) and numerous adaptations of Louis L'Amor and Elmore Leonard stories. Tom has shown a personal and professional interest in recreating chapters of the American west in straightforward and honest depictions.

Much like the fervor created by Dirty Harry's Model 29 S&W magnum, Tom's Quigley character has given rise to annual Quigley shoots and a minimum 3 year waiting list for a near copy of his famous sporting rifle. These firearms were not only used by Tom during his film career but generously donated by him to the National Firearms Museum.

Tom is an inductee of the National Cowboy Hall of Fame and Western Heritage Museum's Hall of Great Western Performers. He has been honored with an Emmy as well as a Golden Globe award and continues to serve on the Board of Directors of the NRA.

MONTE WALSH *(2002)*
George Eads as Frank "Shorty" Austin
Colt 1873 Single Action Army
.44-40 WCF, ca. 1890, s/n 132052.

Donated by Tom Selleck

QUIGLEY DOWN UNDER (1990)
Tom Selleck as Matthew Quigley
Shiloh Sharps No. 3 Rifle
.45-110 CF, ca 1989, s/n 8899. Donated by Tom Selleck

INDEX

INDEX

INDEX

INDEX